OECD Rural Studies

Rural Well-being

GEOGRAPHY OF OPPORTUNITIES

This document, as well as any data and map included herein, are without prejudice to the status of or sovereignty over any territory, to the delimitation of international frontiers and boundaries and to the name of any territory, city or area.

The statistical data for Israel are supplied by and under the responsibility of the relevant Israeli authorities. The use of such data by the OECD is without prejudice to the status of the Golan Heights, East Jerusalem and Israeli settlements in the West Bank under the terms of international law.

Note by Turkey
The information in this document with reference to "Cyprus" relates to the southern part of the Island. There is no single authority representing both Turkish and Greek Cypriot people on the Island. Turkey recognises the Turkish Republic of Northern Cyprus (TRNC). Until a lasting and equitable solution is found within the context of the United Nations, Turkey shall preserve its position concerning the "Cyprus issue".

Note by all the European Union Member States of the OECD and the European Union
The Republic of Cyprus is recognised by all members of the United Nations with the exception of Turkey. The information in this document relates to the area under the effective control of the Government of the Republic of Cyprus.

Please cite this publication as:
OECD (2020), *Rural Well-being: Geography of Opportunities*, OECD Rural Studies, OECD Publishing, Paris, *https://doi.org/10.1787/d25cef80-en*.

ISBN 978-92-64-42430-2 (print)
ISBN 978-92-64-84916-7 (pdf)
ISBN 978-92-64-75417-1 (HTML)
ISBN 978-92-64-46803-0 (epub)

OECD Rural Studies
ISSN 2707-3416 (print)
ISSN 2707-3424 (online)

Revised version, October 2020
Details of revisions available at: *https://www.oecd.org//about/publishing/Corrigendum-Rural-well-being.pdf*

Foreword

Across the OECD, rural regions make up approximately 80% of all territory and are home to approximately 30% of the population. These lands, and the people that live on them, are the source of almost all the food, fresh water, energy, lumber, metals, minerals and other resources that make our way of life possible. They are also where we find unspoilt natural beauty, wildlife and Indigenous cultures whose intrinsic value is increasingly recognised, as is the duty to protect them. Rural places are, in short, vital to the prosperity and well-being of all people.

Yet, for many of the people, firms and communities in rural places, prosperity has felt distant. Over the past decades, OECD countries and regions have faced structural transformations affecting their development trajectories and whose benefits have disproportionately flowed to metropolitan regions. Globalisation, digitalisation, demographic and climate change, and the shocks of the global financial crisis and the current COVID-19 crisis are deeply shaping the economic landscape of rural communities. Today, more than ever, the distance between winners and losers feels ever widening and, in 24 out of 28 OECD countries (for which data are available), regional inequality in gross domestic product (GDP) per capita has increased since the 2008 financial crisis, with rural regions falling behind, particularly those far away from large cities.

Tackling the particular challenges and leveraging opportunities that are present in rural places requires a change in rural development policy. First developed over 40 years ago, the OECD's framework for rural development has helped guide member countries' efforts to increase prosperity and improve the well-being of rural people. It has continued to evolve throughout that period, keeping pace with changing times and reflecting the organisation's latest thinking.

Rural Well-being: Geography of Opportunities is the latest iteration of the OECD's framework for rural development, leveraging improved data and evidence-based analysis and, for the first time, broadening the scope of analysis from a purely economic one to encompass the environmental and social dimensions of well-being. The new approach places the well-being of citizens at the forefront of its objective and recognises the diversity of rural places thanks to a deeper understanding of their diverse and complex socio-economic systems and their connection to cities. The new framework's subtitle, *Geography of Opportunities*, reflects its central finding that while rural places are not without their challenges, they are also unquestionably places of opportunity, particularly with accelerated digitalisation. With well-designed rural policies to leverage local assets and executed in co-ordination across levels of government and between the government, the private sector and civil society, the Rural Well-being Policy Framework shows how rural development policy can deliver rural places that are more prosperous, connected and inclusive, and that offer greater well-being than ever before.

Acknowledgements

This report was produced in the OECD Centre for Entrepreneurship, SMEs, Regions and Cities (CFE), led by Lamia Kamal-Chaoui, Director, as part of the programme of work of the Regional Development Policy Committee (RDPC). The report was undertaken in close collaboration with country delegates to the OECD Working Party on Rural Policy (WPRUR).

The OECD team elaborating and drafting the report included Ana Moreno Monroy (Chapter 2), Andres Sanabria (Chapters 3, 4 and 5) and Lisanne Raderschall (Chapter 3), with input from, Arno Engel, Gareth Hitchings and Michelle Marshallian, under the supervision of Jose Enrique Garcilazo, Head of the Regional and Rural Policy Unit in the Regional Development and Tourism Division, led by Alain Dupeyras. Peter Wostner (Chair of WPRUR) and Joaquim Oliveira-Martins (OECD) provided scientific guidance on the manuscript. Tamara Krawchenko, Anne Kuhnen, Chris McDonald, Fernando Riaza, Laura Springare and Giulia Tosetti from the OECD provided valuable input to the report.

Special thanks for conveying valuable comments on various drafts of the report to Mark Cropper, Lewis Dijkstra and Zelie Peppiette (European Commission), Judith Winternitz (Australia), Hanna Dóra Hólm (Iceland), Saskia Franssen (Netherlands), Timothy Wojan (United States), Juuso Hieta (Finland) and Paolo Veneri (OECD). Eric Gonnard and Milenko Fadic (OECD) provided valuable statistical support. The OECD is also grateful for comments and guidance received from the delegates to the OECD RDPC and the Working Party on Rural Policy throughout the project.

Pilar Phillip (OECD) co-ordinated the production process of the report and Francois Iglesias (OECD) contributed to the formatting. Eleonore Morena and Andrew Brenner provided editorial assistance and Jeanette Duboys (OECD) prepared the manuscript for publication.

Table of contents

FIGURES

TABLES

BOXES

Follow OECD Publications on:

 http://twitter.com/OECD_Pubs

 http://www.facebook.com/OECDPublications

http://www.linkedin.com/groups/OECD-Publications-4645871

 http://www.youtube.com/oecdilibrary

 http://www.oecd.org/oecddirect/

This book has...

StatLinks

A service that delivers Excel® files from the printed page!

Look for the *StatLinks* at the bottom of the tables or graphs in this book. To download the matching Excel® spreadsheet, just type the link into your Internet browser, starting with the *https://doi.org* prefix, or click on the link from the e-book edition.

Executive summary

Rural Well-being: Geography of Opportunities presents the latest iteration of the OECD's policy framework on rural development. This newly updated framework reflects several important changes in rural development in recent years and takes advantage of the organisation's latest evidence-based analysis to improve understanding of the diverse and complex socio-economic systems that exist in rural places along with their connection to cities.

The analysis finds that rural places are facing stronger demographic pressures, with many countries experiencing population decline in rural regions. Rural regions also face challenges raised by an ageing population, with higher elderly dependency ratios than metropolitan regions in almost all OECD countries. The analysis also finds that the "penalty of distance" in rural economies can be quite substantial, despite the fact that most of the OECD's rural population lives within reach of cities. In 2017, GDP per capita in rural regions was 13 percentage points (p.p.) below the average, 16 p.p. lower in labour productivity levels and 8 p.p. lower in employment rates. Rural regions, especially those far from cities, have felt the effects of the 2008 global financial crisis more strongly, leaving many of them in a vulnerable position.

Looking forward, the new framework comes at a time when the shock of COVID-19 is still developing, while the impacts of the megatrends of globalisation, digitalisation, climate change and demographic change continue to shape the economic landscape of rural economies and expose the inadequacy of traditional place-insensitive policy solutions. At a time when the distance between "winners" and "losers" feels wider than ever, *Rural Well-being* offers governments timely policy advice to mitigate the challenges presented by these trends. Yet, as the subtitle *Geography of Opportunities* suggests, the framework is predominantly focused on the untapped potential of rural places and how to capitalise on the opportunities that change will bring, while remaining centred on the well-being of citizens.

Table 1. Challenges and opportunities by type of rural

Type of region	Challenges	Opportunities
Rural inside a functional urban area (FUA)	• loss of control over the future • activities concentrate in the urban core • managing land value pressures • matching of skills	• more stable future • potential to capture urban benefits while avoiding the drawbacks
Rural outside, but in close proximity to a FUA	• conflicts between new residents and locals • avoiding sprawl • competition for land and landscape preservation	• potential to attract high-income households seeking a better quality of life • relatively easy access to advanced services and urban culture • good access to transport
Rural remote	• highly specialised economies subject to booms and busts • limited connectivity and large distances between settlements • high per capita costs of services	• absolute advantage in production of natural resource-based outputs • attractive for firms that need access to an urban area, but not on a daily basis • can offer unique environments that can be attractive to firms and individuals

The new framework extends and refines the OECD's earlier work, replacing the urban-rural dichotomy with a continuum recognising three distinct types of rural places, each with stark structural differences, challenges and opportunities (Table 1): i) rural inside FUAs; ii) rural close to cities; and, iii) remote rural. Understanding each of the three types of rural leads to the possibility for shared action and more effectively targeted policy responses.

Rural Well-being also broadens the scope of analysis. Looking beyond the usual economic factors such as productivity and income, it encompasses the environmental and social dimensions of well-being to deliver a more holistic, people-centred approach of rural development.

Recognising that effective rural policies necessitate strong engagement of the private sector and civil society, as well as effective multi-level governance mechanisms to support collaboration between all levels of government, the new framework provides tools on how to better engage with relevant stakeholders, promote rural-urban partnerships and embrace multi-level governance. Recognising that rural people and businesses know their own needs best, the new framework suggests the use of new technologies to facilitate participation, and underlines the need for meaningful engagement. Furthermore, it acknowledges urban areas as key partners in increasing rural well-being and highlights ways for effective partnership and collaboration between policy makers from different levels of government.

Finally, *Rural Well-being* stresses the importance of designing rural policies through a place-based approach. This is a step beyond "rural proofing" (i.e. the application of a rural lens to adapt sectoral or national policies to rural places) that recognises the inefficiency of non-coordinated policy-making. Instead, policy design must be conducted with specific places in mind, considering the assets and leading industries for each, limits to labour mobility, and linkages to cities that make each place unique.

In sum, *Rural Well-being* shifts from a one-dimensional to a multi-dimensional view of rural policies with:

- **Three types of rural** – rural inside FUAs, rural close to cities, and remote rural, along with the interactions between rural places and cities.
- **Three objectives** – economic, social and environmental objectives and their interdependence
- **Three different stakeholders** – the government, the private sector and civil society.

The resulting framework (Table 2) is people-centred, placing the well-being of citizens at the forefront, while providing a greater understanding of rural regions and their diverse and complex socio-economic systems.

Table 2. Rural Well-being: Geography of opportunities

	Rural Well-being: Geography of opportunities
Objectives	Well-being considering multiple dimensions of: i) the economy, ii) society and iii) the environment
Policy focus	Low-density economies differentiated by type of rural area
Tools	Integrated rural development approach – spectrum of support to public sector, firms and civil society
Key actors & stakeholders	Involvement of: i) public sector – multi-level governance, ii) private sector – for-profit firms and social enterprise, and iii) civil society – non-governmental organisations and civil society
Policy approach	Integrated approach with multiple policy domains
Rural definition	Three types of rural: i) within a functional urban area, ii) close to a functional urban area, and iii) far from a functional urban area

1 Assessment and recommendations

Introduction

For more than 40 years, the OECD's policy framework on rural development has helped guide member countries' efforts to increase prosperity and improve the living standards of their citizens in rural places. This policy framework has provided a lens through which to evaluate effective policies and has played a key role in reshaping rural policies. It has also been regularly updated to reflect changing times, follow the organisation's latest thinking and include the latest evidence-based analysis.

Rural Well-being: Geography of Opportunities presents the latest iteration on this policy framework, reflecting several important changes in rural development in recent years. Fully taking into account the variety of situations characterising rural communities, the new policy framework leverages improved data and analysis while broadening the scope from the economic dimension to encompass also the environmental and social dimensions of well-being. The new approach places the well-being of citizens at the forefront of its objective and recognises the diversity of rural places thanks to a deeper understanding of their diverse and complex socio-economic systems and their connection to cities. The framework also looks to the future and unfolding megatrends such as globalisation, digitalisation, climate change and demographic change. It reflects on how these trends will impact rural economies and reviews policy options to mitigate the challenges and capitalise on opportunities as well as to develop resilience against emerging crises. Finally, recognising the strong interdependencies between different stakeholders and the need for partnerships between government, the private sector and civil society to successfully implement policies, the Rural Well-being Policy Framework focuses on governance mechanisms, including the OECD Principles on Rural Policy.

This updated Rural Well-being Policy Framework comes at a time when the unfolding impact of megatrends, coupled with the shocks of the global financial crisis and COVID-19, are shaping the economic landscape of rural economies and are exposing the inadequacy of traditional place-insensitive policy solutions. Today more than ever, the distance between "winners" and "losers" feels ever-widening and growing segments of the population feel they belong to "places that don't matter", in some cases fuelling populist and anti-establishment sentiments. With rural development policy being a growing priority for OECD governments, *Rural Well-being: Geography of Opportunities* offers timely guidance focused on the well-being of citizens and the untapped potential and opportunities of rural places.

A people-centred rural development framework can harness rural opportunities

The Rural Well-being Policy Framework extends and refines the OECD's earlier work, taking advantage of new analysis to reflect a greater degree of the diversity that exists in rural places for policy purposes. In place of an urban-rural dichotomy, the Rural Well-being Policy Framework identifies three types of rural from a rural-urban continuum: i) rural inside functional urban areas (FUAs); ii) rural close to cities; and iii) remote rural. The framework identifies the interactions between the three types of rural places and cities, each with stark structural differences, and distinct challenges and opportunities (Table 1.1). Understanding each of the three types of rural leads to the possibility of shared action and more effectively targeted policy responses.

The new framework broadens the scope of analysis. Looking beyond the usual economic factors such as productivity and income, it encompasses a multi-dimensional approach to regional inequalities and the environmental and social dimensions of well-being to deliver a more holistic, people-centred understanding of rural development.

Table 1.1. Challenges and opportunities by type of rural

Type of region	Challenges	Opportunities
Rural inside an FUA	• loss of control over the future • activities concentrate in the urban core • managing land value pressures • matching of skills	• more stable future • potential to capture urban benefits while avoiding the drawbacks
Rural outside but in close proximity to an FUA	• conflicts between new residents and locals • avoiding sprawl • competition for land and landscape preservation	• potential to attract high-income households seeking a better quality of life • relatively easy access to advanced services and urban culture • good access to transport
Rural remote	• highly specialised economies subject to booms and busts • limited connectivity and large distances between settlements • high per capita costs of services	• absolute advantage in production of natural resource-based outputs • attractive for firms that need access to an urban area but not on a daily basis • can offer unique environments that can be attractive to firms and individuals

The new framework also recognises that effective rural policies involve the engagement of a broad array of actors and multi-level governance mechanisms. A pooling of resources and capabilities across entities creates the ability to collectively accomplish what no individual actor can achieve independently. This demands the collaboration and engagement of governments at multiple levels, involvement of the private sector and civil society. To that end, the new framework provides tools for governments on how to better engage with relevant stakeholders, promote rural-urban partnerships and embrace multi-level governance. It recognises that rural people and businesses know their own needs best, suggests the use of new technologies to facilitate participation and underlines the need for meaningful engagement. Furthermore, it acknowledges urban areas as key partners in increasing rural well-being and highlights ways for effective partnership and collaboration between policy makers from different levels of government.

Lastly, the framework stresses the importance of designing rural policies through a place-based approach. This is a step beyond "rural proofing" (i.e. the application of a rural lens to help adapt sectoral or national policies to rural places) that recognises the inefficiency of non-coordinated policy making. Instead, policy design must be conducted with specific places in mind, considering the assets and leading industries for each, limits to labour mobility and linkages to cities that make each place unique.

In sum, rural well-being shifts from a one-dimensional to a multi-dimensional view of rural policies with:

- **Three types of rural** – rural inside FUAs, rural close to cities and remote rural, along with the interactions between rural places and cities.
- **Three objectives** – economic, social and environmental objectives and their interdependence.
- **Three different stakeholders** – the government, the private sector and civil society.

The resulting framework is people-centred, placing the well-being of citizens at the forefront while providing a greater understanding of rural regions and their diverse and complex socio-economic systems (Table 1.2).

The Rural Well-being Policy Framework is also oriented towards the future, particularly the unfolding megatrends of globalisation, digitalisation, climate change and demographic change. It reflects how these trends will affect different rural communities in different ways and, while it considers policy options to mitigate the challenges presented by these trends, it focuses mostly only how to capitalise on the opportunities they present across several strategic domains important to the future well-being of people living in rural places.

Table 1.2. *Rural Well-being: Geography of Opportunities*

Objectives	Well-being considering multiple dimensions of: i) the economy; ii) society; and iii) the environment
Policy focus	Low-density economies differentiated by the type of rural area
Tools	Integrated rural development approach – spectrum of support to the public sector, firms and civil society
Key actors and stakeholders	Involvement of: i) public sector – multi-level governance; ii) private sector – for-profit firms and social enterprise; and iii) civil society – non-governmental organisations (NGOs) and civil society
Policy approach	Integrated approach with multiple policy domains
Rural definition	Three types of rural: i) within an FUA; ii) close to an FUA: and iii) far from an FUA

A changing socio-economic landscape shapes opportunities and challenges for rural regions

A new internationally comparable territorial definition at the regional scale defining metropolitan and non-metropolitan regions integrates the fact that rural regions are diverse and have distinct policy needs. The new framework identifies three types of rural (e.g. non-metropolitan) regions: i) regions near a large city; ii) regions with or near a small/medium city; and iii) remote regions. Around 30% of the OECD population lives in rural regions and a clear message emerges from the distribution of people across these different types of rural region: the majority of rural populations have strong interactions with cities, as three-quarters of rural inhabitants live in regions closely connected to cities. Remote regions represent on average only a small share (8%) of the total OECD population but, in 7 OECD countries, they are home to more than 20% of the national population (e.g. mostly large, sparsely populated countries).

While important, many countries are facing population decline in rural regions. Metropolitan regions have been growing annually twice as fast as rural regions in the past two decades. As a result, in the period 2001-19, half of OECD countries with remote regions (13 out of 28) and 25% of countries with regions near a small/medium city experienced a population decline in those types of regions, as opposed to regions near a large city.

In addition to population decline, rural regions also face challenges raised by an ageing population. Elderly dependency ratios are higher in rural regions than in metropolitan regions in almost all OECD countries. This gap reaches 9 percentage points (p.p.) in 7 OECD countries. Amongst rural regions, the ones near a large city have the highest elderly dependency ratios (33%), followed by remote regions (31%) and regions with or near a small/medium city (31%). Between 2003 and 2019, remote regions experienced the largest increases in elderly dependency.

Although most of the OECD's rural population lives within reach of cities, the "penalty of distance" in rural economies can be quite substantial. The economic performance in rural regions in terms of gross domestic product (GDP) per capita, productivity and employment rates on average is below that of metropolitan regions. In 2017, GDP per capita in rural regions was 13 p.p. below the average, 16 p.p. lower in labour productivity levels and 8 p.p. in employment rates. Amongst rural regions, the gap was the highest in regions near a small/medium city.

Recent economic shocks triggered by the global financial crisis in 2008 and the current COVID-19 pandemic have changed the economic landscape of rural economies. Rural regions, especially those far from cities, felt more strongly the effects of the 2008 global financial crisis, leaving many of them in a vulnerable position to face the economic recession caused by COVID-19.

Prior to the global financial crisis, rural remote regions were actually growing faster than other regions. This economic convergence process stopped and reverted in the post-crisis period. After the 2008 crisis, the regions near a city grew faster than other rural regions. Therefore, large cities and their surrounding regions have weathered the effects of the crisis better than other regions.

This drag in performance of regions far from cities coincided with an increase in regional inequality in almost all OECD countries. In 24 out of 28 OECD countries, regional inequality in GDP per capita increased in the post-crisis period compared to the pre-crisis period. This trend resulted from the faster rise of GDP per capita levels in top regions. Greece was the only country in which lagging regions converged with the top region (Attica) between 2017 and 2000 but this was due to the very weak performance of the latter.

Economic shocks have occurred amid large structural transformations affecting the development trajectories of all regions. Globalisation and the offshoring of manufacturing jobs to emerging economies with cheaper labour costs have gradually decoupled the production of tradeable goods away from central locations. This process has accelerated the rise of the service economy as the most important sector across OECD countries. Typically, the service sector now represents 80% of total value-added in OECD countries.

Rural economies in OECD countries have not escaped these trends and have seen their economic base shift from traditional activities towards activities connected to global value chains (GVCs) and the service sector. The service sector has increased its importance not only in cities but also in rural regions. In 2017, the share of employment in services in remote regions was 71%, only 4 p.p. below the share in metropolitan regions (75%). Nevertheless, many rural regions, especially those far from cities, are over-specialised in traditional primary activities (e.g. resource extraction). In contrast, top rural regions are specialised in high-value-added services.

A more integrated and globalised economy enables productivity gains. These gains, however, appear to generate more jobs in rural regions close to large cities. In the majority of rural regions (57% for remote, 51% for near a small city and 68% for near a large city), productivity gains also generated employment gains. However, in some rural regions, productivity gains were concomitant with labour shedding. In fact, rural regions near small/medium cities were the only regions that had a negative contribution to employment growth (-0.9%) in the decade following the global financial crisis, while regions close to large cities and remote regions had small but positive contributions (1.7% and 7%). The bulk of employment growth, 92%, occurred in metropolitan regions during this period.

In addition to the current trends shaping the performance of rural regions and well-being of citizens, a number of structural transformations, including the three megatrends (digitalisation, demographic and environmental change), are also creating opportunities and challenges in rural regions (Table 1.3).

Table 1.3. Structural transformations are creating new opportunities for rural regions

Structural transformations	Implications for rural policy	Opportunities for rural regions
Global shifts in production and rise of the service industry	Increased competition from emerging economies calls for a shift to policies that promote differentiation and niche markets instead of low-cost manufacturing. GVCs need to be considered in policy making.	Access to the world as a market. Openness to foreign investment and promoting linkages between local start-ups and small- and medium-sized enterprises (SMEs) and multinational enterprises (MNEs) may strengthen the performance and growth of high-value-added tradeable activities. Exporting technical services and expertise to emerging markets may become a key growth driver for rural economies.
Well-being as a priority	Citizens demand good living standards and reduction of inequalities; this requires integrated and holistic policy responses.	A differentiated concept of well-being provides an improved understanding of rural assets, such as better personal security and natural environment, more social capital and greater food security.
Rural-urban linkages	Globalisation increases inter-relations between rural and urban regions through infrastructure and networks, policies need to be integrated and highlight win-win scenarios.	Areas close to cities benefit especially, not only through infrastructure but also corporate relationships, market pervasion and communication networks.
Technology and digitalisation	Fast-paced technological innovations demand dynamic policies that respond to changing demands in the labour force and policies that connect rural firms, SMEs and research institutions to developments that benefit rural regions.	Technologies associated with digitalisation create new jobs, new ways to deliver services and provide transportation and change the way of life in rural regions in ways that can improve their attractiveness and value creation.
Demographic changes	New policy areas arise from the need to provide long-term and sustainable solutions taking into account ageing and population growth as well as the need for attracting and retaining young people and newcomers. Greater focus needs to be placed on healthcare, physical and digital connectivity and skills.	Developing the silver economy and investigating ways to keep the elderly integrated into economic and community activities. Social innovations can be used as a tool to find new solutions to societal challenges with the goal of enhancing societal well-being.
Climate change and the transition to a low-carbon economy	New priority areas and objectives for rural policy to limit temperature increases to 1.5°C above pre-industrial levels and foster transitions using and safeguarding rural assets (i.e. land, biodiversity, etc.).	Development potential arising from green industries that contribute to climate change mitigation and adaptation. Rural places can take advantage of investment and technologies associated with renewable energy and the circular economy.

A number of priority areas for rural regions

The analysis and the global context create a number of opportunities and challenges for rural regions spanning economic, social and environmental dimensions. To address these challenges and harness the opportunities, Rural Well-being Policy Framework identifies a number of priority areas to prepare rural regions for the future.

Raise productivity

Rural regions face challenges generating productivity due to their lack of density and economies of scale. Such low-density regional economies have seen decreased and fragmented internal demand, coupled over the past two decades with competitive pressures from low-wage emerging economies. Moreover, because low-density regions produce a limited range of goods and services, they are more vulnerable to industry-specific shocks than the more diversified economic base of larger and denser regions.

Upgrading skills and knowledge is a priority to deal with upcoming changes in technology, demography and climate as well as to increase the attractiveness of rural regions to balance out-migration through improving quality of life across all three dimensions. The share of workers with tertiary education (i.e. a university degree) is currently lower in regions characterised by low-density economies. Moreover, students in rural schools tend to underperform in secondary education outcomes in comparison to students in cities.

To mobilise their assets and overcome productivity generation challenges, rural economies need to fully use opportunities related to digitalisation, enhance their links with urban areas and further increase their added value in tradeable activities. Better links with urban regions can unleash benefits from the proximity to agglomeration economies, including innovation spill-overs and greater movement of workers and ideas. Increased exports are an especially important source of productivity gains for remote regions. Notably, greater participation in high value-added tradeable activities offers the opportunity for rural economies to overcome challenges associated with their small market size and to trigger innovation based on exposure to global competition and GVCs.

Key strategies for rural economies include:

- **Adding value to tradeable activities by:**
  - Supporting smart specialisation strategies through greater diversification among related sectors or activities in rural economies.
  - Enhancing innovation by strengthening the links of rural economies with urban regions and GVCs, and generating common environments that concentrate firms, entrepreneurs and research institutions by considering the special potential of digital technologies.
  - Increasing productivity of rural SMEs by improving the local business environment (e.g. simplified administrative process), supporting co-operation of SMEs with large firms and providing specific support and training for women in enhancing entrepreneurship capacities.
- **Internationalising SMEs** by improving networks and connections with external markets (e.g. participation in international fairs and with business organisations).
- **Retaining more value in rural communities** by ensuring competitive regulation for local economies to reap benefits from foreign investment and promoting local benefit-sharing policies (monetary and non-monetary), including capacity-building activities for local firms, promoting quality standards and training programmes.
- **Strengthening rural skills** by improving collaboration between public authorities, local businesses and not-for-profit organisations to ensure local education and training match the current and future needs of rural firms and harness digital technologies to support lifelong learning for rural youth and experienced workers.

Design forward-looking policies to increase resilience

Megatrends such as digitalisation, demographic and climate change as well as ongoing COVID-19 pandemic effects are creating new challenges and opportunities for rural communities. To increase rural resilience, innovation and technological change can be leveraged to create new solutions for rural regions so they can overcome their remoteness to markets, higher transportation costs and lack of critical mass. Innovation in rural economies often occurs through adaptive measures that try to negate market and policy failures (in terms of government service provision), with entrepreneurs in rural regions often creating innovative products and processes through an aggregation of smaller changes, such as incrementally learning by doing.

Among other initiatives to promote resilience, policy makers should take into account that innovation occurs differently and has a different impact in rural areas than in densely populated areas. Future-looking policies should focus on skills forecasting and development, reducing market frictions, strengthening the adaptability of workers and ensuring the social safety net. Likewise, regulations should allow local communities to take advantage of technological changes (drones, 3D printers) and focus on providing the conditions to encourage networking and diffusion of practices, rather than creating precise targets. These policy targets should be reviewed on a regular (pluri-annual) basis incorporating consultation, particularly with civil society, trade unions and businesses from rural communities. Importantly, a concerted effort to communicate forward-looking support mechanisms to rural entrepreneurs and communities can improve the effectiveness of a forward-looking environment.

Make the most of connectivity and digitalisation to harness rural opportunities

Though there has been a strong reduction in the gap of broadband coverage between rural and urban areas in recent years, the quality (primarily speed) of the connections remains significantly weaker in rural areas. In addition, data available across European countries reveals that individuals living in rural regions strongly lag behind their peers in cities with regard to their level of digital skills. Addressing this digital gap is key because the economic and social challenges of many rural regions are fundamentally linked to economic remoteness.

The deployment of information and communication technology (ICT) and digital infrastructure can play a key role in bringing rural regions closer to markets and services. While in some countries, including Iceland, Luxembourg, the Netherlands and Switzerland, access to high-speed broadband in rural areas is similar to the national average, a significant gap remains present in other countries such as Finland, Italy, Spain and Sweden.

Beyond accessibility, to fully leverage technology for economic opportunities and improve well-being, many rural regions will also need to overcome a gap in digital skills. The ongoing COVID-19 pandemic could accelerate the need for digitalisation and give rise to a new urgency in addressing shortcomings of ICT infrastructure as more people than ever are working from home and students around the globe engage in distance learning. This can be a unique opportunity for rural regions to bridge the digital divide and seize new opportunities for their economies and people.

Deliver sustainable services to ensure inclusive rural places for all

Driven by migration patterns, population changes are shaped by regional differences in fertility and mortality. Remote regions face a strong depopulation trend, which reduces the economies of scale needed for delivering quality services (health and education) in a viable way. This has been reflected in the closures of rural hospitals and the consolidation of rural schools.

A growing elderly population also increases the need for age-related goods and services in rural regions. By 2050, nearly 30% of the population in European regions outside of metropolitan areas is expected to be 65 years old or older. Current elderly dependency ratios in rural regions – the share of the population aged 65 and over as a percentage of the population aged 20-64 – stands already at 29% on average and is higher in rural remote regions. Furthermore, many people in rural places already face greater difficulties in accessing health and social care services. Geographical distances and less developed transportation services amplify these challenges as people's mobility or cognitive function often decreases with age.

Integration of public services is thus key to enhance the availability of high-quality public services and thus the attractiveness of rural regions. Furthermore, the COVID-19 pandemic demonstrated the usefulness of access to digital health and education services. Different forms of integration include colocation, collaboration, co-operation, and co-production:

- *Colocation*: integration that locates many services or agencies in one building.
- *Collaboration*: agencies work together as part of a network to share information and training.

- *Co-operation*: entails different levels of government communicating and working together on multi-agency teams.
- *Co-production*: involves community and non-profit groups in providing services. By partnering with citizens and local organisations, public service providers can ensure products and programmes reflect the needs of the community.

Make rural communities attractive for youth, the elderly and newcomers

Rural communities face challenges in attracting newcomers and in retaining the people who live there and making the most of their talents. While OECD remote rural regions experience the highest fertility rates among all type of regions, young people tend to leave and those who remain, including traditionally underrepresented groups such as Indigenous Peoples, face lower levels of employment than their peers in cities. Population projections for Europe show that more than half of regions are expected to lose population by 2050 and half of EU countries will have to manage population decline in remote regions. Population losses shrink the local tax base and make it more difficult to provide public services. Attracting skilled migrants, young people and especially women to rural communities requires a strategic and a tailored policy approach. People will only come and stay in places if they offer the potential for personal and professional development.

In addition, ensuring the social well-being of elderly people offers opportunities for economic development. While rural economies are facing a shrinking labour force, developing and testing "silver" services in rural places is an opportunity to increase the economic inclusion of the elderly population and can attract investment to rural economies. The consumer spending power of elderly people is significant. Technological innovations focused on living well as we age are at the heart of this market.

Elderly people also bring personal and professional assets that are important for rural regions. Older workers bring institutional knowledge, social maturity and stability and can pass on business relationships to younger workers. This is important for newcomers who want to set up businesses in rural places and need help navigating new environments. Furthermore, retirees, who have free time, can be vital in contributing to voluntary work and help mitigate gaps in regional support structures including childcare or integration of migrants.

Key strategies to ensure rural places are both attractive and inclusive for all ages include:

- **Developing targeted immigration programmes that help promote rural life to newcomers**, connect them with employment opportunities and provide local support services to assist with their integration into the community and retention.
- **Enhancing the quality and availability of ICT**. New technologies can provide an alternative employment pathway for young people and migrants through new forms of economic activities and jobs in rural regions. These include tourism, services (marketing, design), niche manufacturing and food production.
- **Developing services related to maternal health, childcare and integration** to help young parents and especially (migrant) women remain active in the workforce.
- **Improving communications on the benefits of rural amenities such as lower cost of living and closeness to nature**. Working towards building a brand that highlights the progressive and modern aspects of rural places.
- **Providing special teaching and leadership to young rural populations** from different backgrounds and supporting co-business and development of networks.
- **Developing "silver" services** that address challenges faced by the elderly population including in health, transportation and social isolation.

- **Providing pathways for older people to continue to make contributions to rural communities** and economies making use of their knowledge and business relationships, including through volunteering opportunities where needed.
- **Investing and supporting in social innovations** that help to find solutions to societal challenges and enhance social support networks and trust amongst population groups at the same time.

Put rural regions at the centre of the transition to a low-carbon economy

Rural economies are pivotal in the transition to a low-carbon economy because of their natural endowments and specialisation in resource-based industries. Climate change is already affecting the agriculture, forestry, fisheries, mining and energy sectors due to dislocation and costs associated with responding to the increasing frequency and intensity of extreme weather events. To adhere to the goal of the Paris Agreement – limiting global average temperatures rising to only 1.5°C degrees compared to pre-industrial times – emission reductions need to go hand in hand with safeguarding the world's carbon sinks and creating and investing in new methods of carbon removal.

Rural land is fundamental to absorbing carbon from the atmosphere. Forests and wetlands function as natural carbon sinks – trees and other vegetation absorb large amounts of carbon dioxide from the atmosphere (equivalent to almost one-third of carbon dioxide emissions from fossil fuels and industry). Reforestation, soil carbon sequestration, as well as bioenergy with carbon capture and storage can facilitate shifts to sustainable land use. Linking these efforts to rural development strategies can help generate benefits for local communities and create incentives to facilitate the transition to a low-carbon economy.

Policy makers need to consider environmental sustainability along with economic and social policy objectives. The concept of a "just transition" is that developments towards an environmentally sustainable economy need to be managed in a way that contributes to job creation, job upgrading, social justice and poverty eradication. The International Labour Organization (ILO) estimates that a transition to more sustainable economies could generate up to 60 million new jobs worldwide over the next 2 decades.

Rural places can employ a number of proactive strategies to support a just transition to a low-carbon economy. This can include developing new industries such as ecosystem services and resource extraction needed for renewable energy technologies. Rural places can also identify new ways to add value to natural resources and waste products through circular and bio-economy approaches.

Key strategies to make the most of the transition to a low-carbon economy in rural places include:

- **Facilitating the development of renewable energy** that can benefit rural economies by integrating it within a local development strategy, identifying synergies with other sectors (e.g. agriculture and forestry) and linking it with local supply chains.
- **Identifying ways to capture the value of positive externalities such as ecosystem services** including fresh water supply, storm and flood protection, and pollination. This also includes payments for environmental management and carbon offsets.
- **Promoting sustainable land use and resource extraction as part of the circular and bioeconomy** including grants and loans to support capital investment, changes to regulatory frameworks, brokering and facilitating relationships between producers and consumers, investing in research and development with local universities, as well as effective land use policies, mechanisms for local benefit-sharing and working with local communities.
- **Rethinking transportation for rural dwellers**. Considering population density and reliance on cars, solutions need to focus on alternative and technological innovations to reduce emissions as well as infrastructure development.

- **Working with regions dependent on carbon-intensive sectors to develop new economic opportunities and managing social consequences**, including support for SMEs, investing in digital infrastructure, retraining and employment pathways for affected workers and setting up social support groups.

Implementing rural policies

As rural policy making is cross-cutting by nature, the governance of the different governmental and non-governmental actors is fundamental. Policy interventions that target administrative boundaries or economic sectors in silos miss opportunities to unlock synergies and meet broad policy objectives for rural regions and countries. Recovery from external shocks, such as the 2020 COVID-19 crisis, calls for a greater multi-level governance and stakeholder co-ordination as identified in the OECD Principles on Rural Policy adopted in 2019 by the Regional Development Policy Committee.

A multi-level governance framework encourages different levels of government to engage in vertical (across different levels of government), horizontal (among the same levels of government) or networked co-operation in order to design and implement better policies.

Horizontal co-ordination across levels of government involves an approach in which policy makers mainstream rural issues across all policies to ensure rural needs are taken into account. A sound rural proofing approach should involve not only deliberately reviewing new policy initiatives through a rural lens but also ensuring policy complementarities among different policy strategies. Other important aspects to take into account for successful co-ordination among governments include:

- **Identifying the right scale** of intervention by adapting policies and governance to functional geographies. According to the 2018-19 OECD institutional survey, for most OECD countries (80% of surveyed countries), the rural definition for policy making recognises the heterogeneity of rural areas. About 51% of OECD countries consider at least 3 types of rural areas (mixed rural/urban areas, rural areas close to cities and remote rural areas).
- **Setting a clear leadership role for policy co-ordination** on rural issues to better integrate rural policies, promoting synergies and upgrading the concept of rural development at all levels within the country and beyond. While OECD countries tend to have more than one ministry in charge of rural development, in most cases (62% or 21 out of the 34 surveyed countries), the lead ministry on rural policy is related explicitly to agriculture. To overcome a sectoral bias and siloed policy making, many OECD countries have established an inter-ministerial committee or body to define rural development policies. Most OECD countries (85% or 29 out of 34 surveyed countries) have established an inter-ministerial committee in the form of advisory councils, platforms, networks or presidential committees.
- **Strengthening inter-municipal co-operation arrangements** between regions or municipalities, including cross-border co-operation. For this, some OECD countries have established institutionalised municipal co-ordinating bodies at the regional level or voluntary inter-municipal co-operation mechanisms. Other countries have developed inter-municipal development agencies to support municipal governments in improving the business environment and well-being locally.
- **Promoting rural-urban partnerships** to take advantage of functional links. These links include economic and demographic linkages, delivery of public services, exchange of amenities and environmental interactions.

Vertical co-ordination refers to the linkages between higher and lower levels of government, including their institutional, financial and informational aspects. While institutional co-ordination mechanisms vary among countries, all types of approaches aim for more effective sharing of information and objectives. In many OECD countries, a first step of co-ordination is through the development of national development plans or national plans for regional or rural development. Other instruments can include contracts between levels of government, including internationally (i.e. in regions that cross national boundaries), national-level regional development agencies, national representatives in regions, co-funding agreements or consultation fora.

Multi-stakeholder engagement and a "bottom-up" approach for rural policy are key ingredients to ensure sustainability and local ownership of rural policies. With the deepening of globalisation, rural regions increasingly feel that their requirements are overlooked in policy making. New technologies, fiscal consolidation efforts, socio-political changes, declining levels of trust and the COVID-19 crisis have increased demand for government transparency, accountability and a movement beyond a provider role towards a partnering relationship with citizens and the private sector.

Greater involvement of local actors in policy design and implementation requires recognising a different vision of development for rural places and in turn adapting the strategies to involve citizens, private sector and civil society in policy making process. Countries and regions have adopted different approaches to engaging local actors, varying from basic communication to full-co-production and co-delivery of policies. Engagement strategies include:

- **Citizen engagement**: participative and open budgeting, co-production of social service delivery, fora or policy summits.
- **Private sector engagement**: public-private partnerships and platforms for dialogue.
- **Collaboration with higher education institutions**: partnerships to co-produce regional and local plans, programmes to support skills of public staff and support the local innovation strategy.

2 A roadmap for delivering well-being in rural regions

This chapter outlines long-term trends in socio-economic development in OECD regions, with a focus on the effects of the 2008 financial crisis and the implications of the current COVID-19 crisis. The first section introduces a new way of classifying regions based on their density and access to cities. The second section discusses key demographic trends across rural regions, focusing on distinctive challenges brought about by population losses and ageing. The third section describes the changing economic conditions facing rural regions after the financial crisis and their effects on regional inequality. The chapter closes with a discussion on the role of skills and human capital, Internet connectivity and innovation as enabling factors of regional development.

Key messages

- Around 30% of the OECD population lived in rural regions in 2019, of which three-quarters lived in regions with close connections to cities. Still, in seven OECD countries, one-fifth of the population or more live in remote, sparsely populated regions.

- Annual population growth in metropolitan regions has more than doubled versus rural regions in the past two decades. Among rural regions, remote regions gained more population than regions with or near a small/medium city, where population growth slowed down after the 2008 financial crisis.

- Demographic pressures are stronger in regions far from cities. Half of OECD countries with remote regions and about one-third of countries with regions with or near a small/medium city dealt with population decline in the last two decades.

- In 2019, the elderly as a percentage of the working population was above 30% across rural regions and was highest in rural regions near to large cities at 33%. Seventy-three regions had elderly dependency ratios above 50%, and were above 60% in 11 regions. The ageing dependency ratio has increased fastest in remote regions in the past two decades.

- The gap between top and bottom regions and between metropolitan regions and regions far from large cities widened in the aftermath of the global financial crisis in most OECD countries.

- Regional inequality, measured as the difference between the top 20% and bottom 20% of regions in gross domestic product (GDP) per capita, increased in 24 out of 28 OECD countries with available data in the post-crisis period and as compared to the pre-crisis period. In countries where regional inequality increased, changes were driven by improvements in top regions, except in the case of Greece and Italy.

- The income level, productivity level and employment rate of regions near a large city are around 18, 10 and 8 percentage points below OECD average levels respectively. The gaps for regions with or near a small/medium city are even bigger, at 28, 20 and 14 percentage points below the OECD average, while the gap for remote regions is 21, 14 and 3 percentage points below the OECD average.

- Larger and denser places were more resilient to the shock of the 2008 financial crisis. After the financial crisis, regions far from large cities grew slower than all other region types. Meanwhile, regions near a city grew faster than other region types and employment creation was concentrated largely in metropolitan regions.

- The importance of the service sector increased in metropolitan and rural regions. Some 71% of jobs were in the service sector in remote regions while the percentage in metropolitan regions was 75% in 2017. While top-performing rural regions in terms of GDP per capita levels are specialised in high-value-added services, bottom-performing rural regions have not diversified away from traditional primary sectors and low value-added services.

- Rural regions struggled to create new jobs after the global financial crisis. In the post-crisis period, rural regions contributed less than 10% to employment growth, down from a contribution of over 20% in the pre-crisis period.

- Innovation performance, based solely on patent activity, is lower in rural regions compared to metropolitan regions. At the same time, evidence for Europe suggests individuals living in rural regions strongly lag behind their peers in cities with regard to their level of digital skills, paramount for many modern workplaces. Addressing the rural-urban digital divide in connectivity, education and skills is crucial to boost innovation in rural regions.

Introduction

In recent decades, OECD countries and regions have faced a number of structural transformations affecting their development trajectories. Globalisation, digitalisation and the shocks of the global financial crisis and current COVID-19 crisis are deeply shaping the economic landscape of rural economies. Today more than ever, the distance between "winners" and "losers" feels ever-widening. The 2008 global financial crisis exacerbated the divergence between regions endowed with the key ingredients for high-income generation and those lacking them (Iammarino, Rodriguez-Pose and Storper, 2018[1]). Persistent inequality has divided societies, leading large swaths of the population to feel they belong to "places that do not matter" (Rodríguez-Pose, 2018[2]). This discontent has recently fuelled populist and anti-establishment sentiments in some OECD countries, underscoring the failure of traditional "place-insensitive" solutions to ensure prosperity and convergence (McCann, 2019[3]). Inequalities within countries will likely widen with the current COVID-19 crisis as both virus incidence and socio-economic consequences are highly asymmetrical across places. The financial and economic consequences of the ongoing COVI-19 pandemic threaten to become a catalyst for further discontent.

It is in this context that many rural communities will face further ageing, outmigration, service provision challenges and a shift in population compositions following international migration in the next decades. Rural economies will also continue to face sweeping megatrends including global shifts in production, new technological breakthroughs and environmental pressures from climate change. These megatrends offer new opportunities to rural economies, including the transition to renewable energy, benefitting from tourism and ecosystem services, and adopting artificial intelligence technologies to improve well-being. The same trends may on the other hand generate uncertainty stemming from job losses from increased digitalisation, environmental disasters, higher fiscal pressure tied to declining tax revenues, and uncertainty about adequate public service provision.

Making the most of these changes requires a forward-looking view of a sustainable, inclusive and balanced development path. Policies need to shift from space-blind to place- and people-based, from the passive use of transfers and subsidies to active efforts to make the best use of resources. By focusing on rural places, this chapter sheds light on the distinctive shifts taking place outside urban areas, the needs of different types of rural regions and the importance of rural-urban linkages.

The next section discusses the definition of rural in the context of regions and introduces an alternative typology of regions based on their density and level of access to cities. The second section discusses demographic trends amid increasing urban concentration, focusing on distinctive challenges for rural regions. The third section analyses economic trends across OECD regions, with an emphasis on the effect of the economic crisis in 2008. The final section discusses the role of skills and human capital, Internet connectivity and innovation as enabling factors of regional development.

Rural and regional definitions and their importance for policy

The term "rurality" is generally recognised as a multidimensional concept, embodying different meanings for different purposes. Debates on the definition of rural spaces focus on how best to define the concept – e.g. as a geographical/spatial concept, a land use concept, a socio-economic or socio-cultural descriptor, a functional concept related to, for instance, labour market flows, or simply as "not urban".

In March 2020, the United Nations (UN) Statistical Commission endorsed a new global definition of cities, urban and rural areas called the Degree of Urbanisation (UN Statistical Commission, 2020[4]). The Degree of Urbanisation is the first global definition of rural areas to be endorsed by the UN and it goes beyond the traditional rural-urban dichotomy by proposing concrete measures of places in the rural-urban continuum. What is more, the Degree of Urbanisation also provides a refined definition of moderate and low-density areas that include towns, villages, dispersed area and mostly uninhabited areas (Box 2.1). This new definition of the space outside cities opens new possibilities for measuring diversity within rural and emphasise the role of rural-urban linkages in future work. As a definition built for international comparability, the Degree of Urbanisation is not designed to replace national definitions. National definitions can incorporate more indicators, can be tailored to reflect specific circumstances and better serve the needs of national policies.

Box 2.1. The Degree of Urbanisation level 1 and level 2

Six international organisations – the European Commission, the UN Food and Agriculture Organization (FAO), the UN Human Settlements Programme (UN-Habitat), the International Labour Organization (ILO), the OECD and the World Bank – have worked closely together to develop a harmonised methodology to facilitate international statistical comparisons, called the Degree of Urbanisation.

The Degree of Urbanisation was designed to create a simple and neutral method that could be applied in every country in the world. It relies primarily on population size and density thresholds applied to a population grid with cells of 1 km by 1 km. The different types of grid cells are subsequently used to classify small spatial units, such as municipalities or census enumeration areas. The Degree of Urbanisation was endorsed by the UN Statistical Commission in March 2020.[1] The Degree of Urbanisation level 1 classifies the entire territory into: i) cities; ii) towns and suburbs; and iii) rural areas. At level 2, towns and suburbs are split into: i) dense towns; ii) semi-dense towns; and iii) suburbs. Rural areas are split into: i) villages; ii) dispersed rural areas; and iii) mostly uninhabited areas.

- Cities have a population of at least 50 000 inhabitants in contiguous grid cells with a density of at least 1 500 inhabitants per km^2.

- Dense towns have a population of between 5 000 and 50 000 inhabitants in contiguous grid cells with a density of at least 1 500 inhabitants per km^2.

- Semi-dense towns have a population of at least 5 000 inhabitants in contiguous cells with a density of at least 300 inhabitants per km^2 and are at least 2 km away from the edge of a city or dense town.

- Suburbs have most of their population in contiguous cells with a density of at least 300 inhabitants per km^2 that are part of a cluster with at least 5 000 inhabitants but are not part of a town.

- Villages have between 500 and 5 000 inhabitants in contiguous cells with a density of at least 300 inhabitants per km^2.

- Dispersed rural areas have most of their population in grid cells with a density between 50 and 300 inhabitants per km^2.

- Mostly uninhabited areas have most of their population in grid cells with a density of fewer than 50 inhabitants per km^2.

Source: UN Statistical Commission (2020[4]), "A recommendation on the method to delineate cities, urban and rural areas for international statistical comparisons", https://unstats.un.org/unsd/statcom/51st-session/documents/BG-Item3j-Recommendation-E.pdf.

Traditional definitions of "rural" have relied on a number of noticeable characteristics including: i) classifying the entire territory as either urban or rural; ii) focusing the definition primarily on urban characteristics by defining rural as the residual of urban; iii) not differentiating among different types of rural areas; and iv) not recognising mixed areas with strong urban and rural interactions (OECD, 2014[5]).

An evolution of these definitions identified density as the differentiating factor conceptualising rural regions. In 2006, the New Rural Paradigm (OECD, 2006[6]) separated the concept of rural from the concept of urban by using actual rural characteristics. The New Rural Paradigm recognised the diversity of rural regions in terms of access to markets, economic competitiveness and structure that sets them apart from each other and urban regions (OECD, 2016[7]), and introduced the narrative of rural as places of opportunities.

Since context and geography matter, it is no surprise that OECD member countries have adopted a wide range of definitions delimiting and adapting urban and rural borders to their geographic characteristics (see Box 2.2). The wide diversity of rural definitions (see Table 3.A.3.1 in (OECD, 2016[7])) also reflects different criteria that exist to elaborate definitions including density, economic activity, size or distance to services, among others. Beyond the definition of rural, it should be emphasised that a strong rural development policy requires actions not only by local but also by regional and national levels of government.

Box 2.2. Examples of rural definition in OECD countries

Rural definitions adapted to local realities

OECD countries have moved away from traditional definitions of rural as simply the remaining "leftover" space that is not urban, to delimitations of rural that can help identify common challenges and opportunities to design better policy responses.

The design of new and territorial definitions is possible today more than ever thanks to the advancement of Geographic Information System (GIS) tools and better availability of data. The revisions of definitions have incorporated new criteria such as distance, commuting and accessibility to services, and are now recognising areas with strong urban and rural interactions. For instance:

- France is advancing on a definition considering accessibility. The National Institute of Statistics and Economic Studies has developed an indicator that examines the accessibility of services and amenities that are important to daily life for communities of varying population densities (Barbier, Toutin and Levy, 2016[8]).

- New Zealand has adopted a definition that distinguishes between rural areas with high, moderate or low urban influence and those deemed rural-remote, by drawing on both population density, place of employment and commuting data (Statistics New Zealand, 2004[9]).

- Italy has developed a definition based on service accessibility and policy objectives. Rural areas in Italy are split into three categories: intensively cultivated and plain areas; intermediate rural areas; and areas with lagging development. This classification is based on population density indicators and share of agricultural land. Italy has also adopted a classification of rural areas based on policy objectives. It characterises "inner areas" as groups of municipalities facing "inadequate access to essential services", including healthcare, education and transportation.

- The Australian Bureau of Statistics (ABS) developed a typology of regions and cities that aims to capture the particularities of Australian geography, such as a small density of settlements and large portions of empty territory. It defines geographic areas including metropolitan, inner regional, outer regional, remote and very remote areas, and urban areas and localities of various sizes. The ABS geography also includes an accessibility and remoteness index.

Source: Barbier, M., G. Toutin and D. Levy (2016[8]), "L'accès aux services, une question de densité des territoires", https://www.insee.fr/fr/statistiques/1908098; Statistics New Zealand (2004[9]), New Zealand: An Urban/Rural Profile, http://archive.stats.govt.nz/browse_for_stats/Maps_and_geography/Geographic-areas/urban-rural-profile.aspx#gsc.tab=0; European Network for Urban Development (n.d.[10]), Strategy for Inner Areas - Italy, https://enrd.ec.europa.eu/sites/enrd/files/tg_smart-villages_case-study_it.pdf; Australian Bureau of Statistics (n.d.[11]), The Australian Statistical Geography Standard (Asgs) Remoteness Structure, https://www.abs.gov.au/websitedbs/D3310114.nsf/home/remoteness+structure; Australian Bureau of Statistics (2018[12]), 1270.0.55.005 - Australian Statistical Geography Standard (ASGS): Volume 5 - Remoteness Structure, July 2016, https://www.abs.gov.au/ausstats/abs@.nsf/mf/1270.0.55.005.

Key dimensions defining rural

The geography of a place is effectively defined by a combination of physical ("first-nature") and human ("second-nature") geographies. The more people inhabit a place, the more its character will be defined by second-nature geography – by human beings and their activities. In contrast, less human presence implies a larger role for natural factors in shaping economic opportunities.

Economic remoteness or "peripherality" has three distinct features:

- The first is the *physical distance to major markets*. Distance increases travel times and shipping costs, which must be borne by the buyer (in the form of higher prices) or seller (in the form of lower margins).
- The second is the degree of *economic connectedness*. Lack of economic integration not only reduces current trade opportunities but also the ability of agents in a place to identify new opportunities. Thus, there are both static and dynamic associated costs.
- The third is the degree of *sector specialisation*. Production is concentrated in relatively few sectors since it is impossible to achieve "critical mass" in more than a few activities. A narrower economic base implies greater vulnerability to sector-specific shocks, whether positive or negative.

In this context, rural places have "low-density economies", specialised in niche markets or those linked to natural resources (e.g. agriculture, tourism, etc.). Geographical features and settlement patterns set rural areas apart from urban areas, as they differ in terms of local workforce size, sensitivity to transport costs, level of competition with similar regions, and reliance on innovations developed elsewhere. Because of their size and reliance on external markets, rural economies may be more vulnerable to external changes affecting economic and natural conditions. At the same time, many rural places have rich social capital resulting from community cohesion and strong informal and formal social networks capable of promoting social trust.

The *Geography of Opportunities* paradigm extends this diversity and acknowledges the existence of a rural-urban continuum so that it is not the presence of characteristics but rather the degree of a factor – rurality for example – which differentiates places. In addition to density as a central concept to rural economies, accessibility has taken a central role as a defining characteristic of places. While common perception suggests that all rural places typically face larger physical connectivity barriers to markets and services than cities, the level of access depends on the location of rural places relative to urban nodes. This will also determine the degree of interdependencies between rural and urban areas through different types of linkages that often cross traditional administrative boundaries.

Urban and rural places are highly interconnected across economic, social and environmental dimensions (Figure 2.1), and these linkages tend to be stronger in rural places that are closer to cities. Linkages can occur in many dimensions including amongst other commercial ties, environmental goods and population flows.

Rural places that are in close proximity to cities have much stronger linkages in transportation networks, commuting flows, spatial planning and the provision of goods and services. Furthermore, these rural places can also benefit from good access to markets, services and agglomeration of talent present in urban areas. These benefits are often referred to as "borrowed" agglomeration effects. In turn, rural places close to cities also enjoy environmental amenities and lower housing costs than cities making them attractive and liveable places.

Linkages are not limited to city-centred local labour market flows and include bi-directional relationships. Each type of interaction encompasses a different geography or "functional region". Flexibility is required in the space considered for governing these complex relationships. Remote areas in contrast face the largest connectivity barriers due to their geographical location far away from transportation nodes. This distinction matters because lack of connectivity entails higher transportation, infrastructure and service provision costs that affect the well-being of rural residents.

Figure 2.1. Linkages between rural and urban areas within functional regions

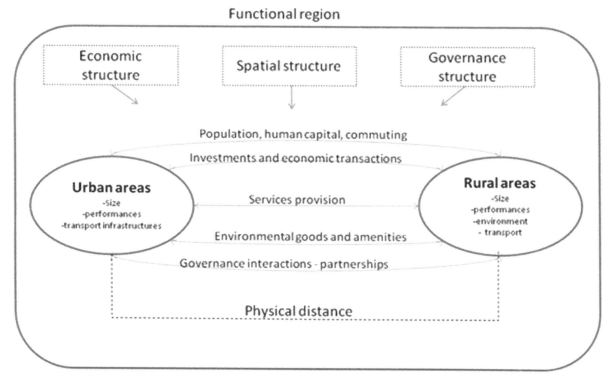

Source: OECD (2013[13]), *Rural-Urban Partnerships: An Integrated Approach to Economic Development*, https://dx.doi.org/10.1787/978926420 4812-en.

This complexity can be represented by an urban to rural continuum. While there are no sudden breaks in these spatial relationships, there is great diversity in the size and types of interconnections. Figure 2.2 depicts a continuity of urban and rural places based on location, proximity and density characteristics – moving from more to less concentrated settlements, with multiple connections and interactions among them. Such distinctions are important for public policy, with implications for jobs, services and infrastructure development, among other considerations. It also implies that the barriers between urban and rural are not dichotomous and clear-cut because territories display different degrees of interaction between urban and rural.

Rural in this continuum plays an important complementary role to urban. This means that the development path of most rural places is not to become themselves cities but instead to provide goods and services that are best produced in a rural setting and then delivered to national and international markets.

From the perspective of regions, the main difference is where the driving source of economic dynamism is located. In highly urbanised regions, it is clearly in the city, whereas in remote regions, it is in rural areas. The vast majority of rural territory falls into an "intermediate" situation where the urban and rural components of a region are more balanced in capacity and there are potentially substantial gains from co-ordination.

Figure 2.2. Urban to rural continuum

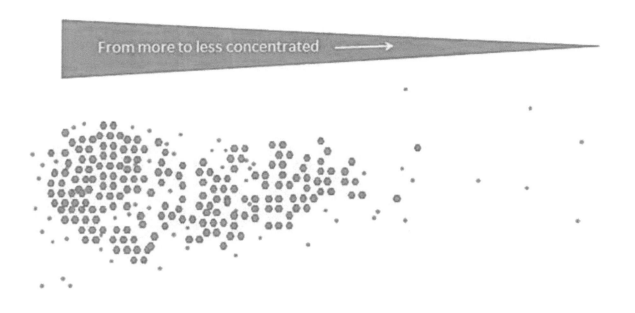

Source: OECD (2016[7]), *OECD Regional Outlook 2016: Productive Regions for Inclusive Societies*, https://dx.doi.org/10.1787/9789264260245-en.

Within this complex configuration, there are three types of rural places, each broadly defined with different characteristics and policy needs:

- *Rural within a functional urban area (FUA)* – These types of rural places are part of the catchment area of the urban core and their development is fully integrated into the metropolitan strategy. The main challenges of these types of rural places are accessibility of services within the FUA, matching of skills to the wide range of supply and managing land use policy brought by increasing pressures of the urban core.

- *Rural close to cities* – The main challenges in these types of places are: improving two-way connectivity and accessibility between the cities and rural territory; building short supply chains that link urban and rural firms; balancing population growth while preserving quality of life and green spaces; and enhancing the provision of secondary goods and services.

- *Remote rural* – Remote places depend largely on the primary activities of the area. Growth relies on absolute and comparative advantage, improving connectivity to export markets, matching skills to areas of comparative advantage and ensuring the provision of essential services (e.g. tourism). In more densely settled but remote regions where farms are distributed across the open countryside, some small cities and towns serve the farm population as market points.

Classifying regions according to their level of access to cities of different sizes

To bring these conceptual ideas into measurement, the OECD typology of regions based on their level of access to cities builds on previous territorial definitions (see Box 2.3) to introduce the idea of spatial continuity between urban and rural. TL3 regions cover the entire territory within countries, while FUAs only capture a sub-sample of the territory.

The OECD typology based on the level of access to cities aims at taking into account the relative location of rural places with respect to FUAs. This typology is meant to be relevant for rural policies while ensuring international comparability. As such, it differentiates amongst different types of rural regions – those close to cities and those that are remote. Rural places close to cities require a much stronger integration of policies with cities in areas such as transportation, land use labour market or housing amongst others. Furthermore, the definition differentiates rural with access to large cities *vis-à-vis* small/medium places allowing for a better understanding and capturing differences in linkages.

The typology used in this document identifies five types of (TL3) regions based on the share of population living in metropolitan areas and an accessibility criterion. The 5 types of regions include 2 types of metropolitan regions – large metropolitan (with an FUA of more than 1 million people) and metropolitan regions (with an FUA of less than 250 000 people) –, and 3 types of rural regions – regions near a large city (i.e. regions with access to an FUA of more than 250 000 people within a 60-minute drive), regions with a small/medium city or near one (i.e. regions with an FUA of less than 250 000 people or with access to one within a 60-minute drive), and remote regions.

Throughout this report, reference will be made to "rural regions" when referring to the group of non-metropolitan regions. The term "rural regions" is not a synonym for "predominantly rural regions" as defined in the OECD regional typology developed in 2011 (see Box 2.3). The terms "city" and FUA will be used interchangeably. The document uses the term "large city" to signify a city (FUA) with more than 250 000 inhabitants and "very large" city when referring to a city with more than 1 million inhabitants. The term "areas outside FUAs" is meant to be comprehensive of territories with settlements with intermediate or low-density levels, such as towns and suburbs as defined by the Degree of Urbanisation. On the other hand, terms such as "rural economy", "rural places" and "rural communities" are used conceptually for policy purposes and are not meant to reflect any particular territorial definition.

Box 2.3. A short account of OECD territorial definitions

Three decades of territorial definitions for international comparisons

Country rural definitions are adapted to their specific needs and are mainly used for policy implementation. The OECD has developed regional typologies to allow for international comparisons and to be able to compare regions with similar characteristics.

The first OECD regional typology was elaborated in 1991 in collaboration with the European Commission (EC). It classified Territorial Level 3 (TL3) regions as predominantly urban, intermediate or predominantly rural using simple and commonly accepted criteria based on a three-step procedure:

1. Identify rural communities according to population density. A community is defined as rural if its population density is below 150 inhabitants per km² (500 inhabitants per km² for Japan).

2. Classify regions according to the percentage of the population living in rural communities. A TL3 region is classified as predominantly rural if more than 50% of its population lives in rural communities.

3. Adjust the classification of "predominantly rural" and "intermediate" regions based on the size of the urban centres.[2]

This typology was further developed in 2011 introducing an accessibility criterion sub-classifying rural regions into two sub-groups: rural close to cities and rural-remote regions based on a driving distance to urban centre criterion.[3] The result is a fourfold classification of TL3 regions: predominantly urban (PU), intermediate regions (IN), predominantly rural regions close to a city (PRC) and predominantly rural-remote regions (PRR) (Brezzi, Dijkstra and Ruiz, 2011[14]). This extension already included two of the types of rural areas outlined above.

In 2014, the European Union (EU) modified the rural-urban typology, using one-km² population grids as building blocks to identify rural or urban communities with the aim of improving international comparability by changing the previously arbitrarily defined local units (Dijkstra and Poelman, 2014[15]). The OECD updated this classification only for EU-OECD countries.

In parallel to the regional typology, in 2011, the OECD elaborated an FUA definition of cities and their broader area of influence based on commuting patterns. An FUA is constructed by concatenating grid cells with high population density (above 1 500 inhabitants per km²) into an urban core (Fadic et al., 2019[16]). These cells are then connected with surrounding lower-density cells when the flows of commuting between the 2 types of cells exceed a given threshold (i.e. at least 15% of the labour force commutes to the urban core). The set of the urban core and the hinterland compose the FUA.[4]

In 2018, the OECD developed an alternative definition of regions based on their level of access to cities of different sizes (see Box 2.4).

Source: Fadic, M. et al. (2019[16]), "Classifying small (TL3) regions based on metropolitan population, low density and remoteness", https://dx.doi.org/10.1787/b902cc00-en; Brezzi, M., L. Dijkstra and V. Ruiz (2011[14]), "OECD Extended Regional Typology: The Economic Performance of Remote Rural Regions", https://dx.doi.org/10.1787/5kg6z83tw7f4-en; Dijkstra, L. and H. Poelman (2014[15]), "A harmonised definition of cities and rural areas: The new degree of urbanisation", *European Commission Regional Working Papers*, European Commission.

The alternative regional typology helps uncover the many existing shades of rural: while large metropolitan regions are clearly more "urban" and remote regions clearly more "rural", other region types differ in their degree of rurality (i.e. the share of the regional population outside FUAs) (Figure 2.3). It also highlights the role of access in setting apart regions with a high degree of rurality with and without access to cities.

Figure 2.3. Regions come in all shades of rural

Density plot based on region-level estimates of the degree of rurality

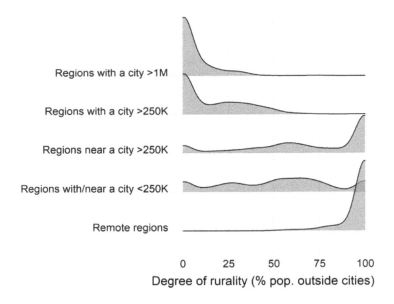

Note: City refers to an FUA.
Source: OECD (2020[17])*OECD Regional Statistics (database)*, http://dx.doi.org/10.1787/region-data-en, EC (n.d.[18]), *Global Human Settlement Layer 2015*, https://ghsl.jrc.ec.europa.eu/

The regional classification based on access allows measuring socio-economic differences between regions, across and within countries. It takes into consideration the presence of and access to FUAs.

Access is defined in terms of the time needed to reach the most proximate urban area, a measure that takes into account not only geographical features but also the status of physical road infrastructure.

Box 2.4. A typology of TL3 regions based on their level of access to cities of different sizes

The first tier adopts as a threshold of 50% of the population of the TL3 (small) region living in an FUA of at least 250 000 people; the second tier uses a 60-minute driving-time threshold, a measure of the access to an FUA.

The new methodology classifies TL3 regions into metropolitan and non-metropolitan according to the following criteria:

Metropolitan TL3 region, if more than 50% of its population live in an FUA of at least 250 000 inhabitants. Metropolitan regions are further classified into:

- **Large metropolitan TL3 regions**, if more than 50% of its population lives in an FUA of at least 1.5 million inhabitants.

- **Metropolitan TL3 regions**, if the TL3 region is not a large metropolitan region and 50% of its population lives in an FUA of at least 250 000 inhabitants.

Non-metropolitan TL3 region, if less than 50% of its population live in an FUA. These regions are further classified according to their level of access to FUAs of different sizes into regions:

- **With access to (near) a metropolitan TL3 region**, if more than 50% of its population lives within a 60-minute drive from a metropolitan area (an FUA with more than 250 000 people); or if the TL3 region contains more than 80% of the area of an FUA of at least 250 000 inhabitants.

- **With access to (near) a small/medium city TL3 region**, if the TL3 region does not have access to a metropolitan area and 50% of its population has access to a small or medium city (an FUA of more than 50 000 and less than 250 000 inhabitants) within a 60-minute drive; or if the TL3 region contains more than 80% of the area of a small or medium city.

- **Remote TL3 region**, if the TL3 region is not classified as NMR-M or NMR-S, i.e. if 50% of its population does not have access to any FUA within a 60-minute drive.

Source: Fadic, M. et al. (2019[16]), (2019), "Classifying small (TL3) regions based on metropolitan population, low density and remoteness", https://dx.doi.org/10.1787/b902cc00-en.

Key demographic trends across regions

Rural places have common features: low density, peripherality and remoteness. In other words, they all lack economies of agglomeration that attract firms and workers to a given location. Firms tend to locate close to other firms and densely populated areas due to lower transportation costs, proximity to markets and wider availability of labour supply. People are also attracted to densely populated areas for the wider availability of job opportunities, goods and services. These mutually reinforcing forces yield economic premia for both consumers and firms through economies of scale, better matching and functioning of labour markets, spill-over effects and more technological intensity (Duranton et al., 2004[19]). To no surprise, productivity and wages tend to be on average higher in densely populated areas. The benefits, however, must be weighed against the costs of agglomeration – often referred to as diseconomies of scale – including congestion, higher land and housing prices, rising inequality and environmental pressures.

Yet, even without economies of agglomeration from high-density, rural economies can also benefit from agglomeration effects indirectly or at lower scales. Pockets of density outside large cities including villages, market towns and smaller cities can represent important development hubs for the broader rural economy. Rural places located near urban areas can also *borrow* agglomeration benefits and, at the same time, enjoy lower diseconomies of scale.

In other rural places, however, demographic decline might constitute an unavoidable long-term trend driven by structural factors. In these cases, rural policies should not fight against demographic patterns but rather respond with strategic, sustainable forward-looking policies to manage population decline.

Population distribution across regions

According to the OECD regional typology, 25% of OECD population lived in predominantly rural regions in 2017, 20% of which lived in rural regions close to cities and 5% in rural-remote regions. This means that 80% of the OECD rural population live in close proximity to cities and only 20% in remote regions. This definition, however, does not rely on functionality and classifies many rural places as intermediate regions. According to the alternative regional typology, in 2019, 42% of the OECD population lived in regions with a large city. Amongst the reminding 58%, approximately three-quarters lived in regions near cities, while one-third lived in remote regions (accounting for 8% of the total population). This evidence confirms that the bulk of residents of regions have a strong interaction with cities, or differently said, only a small share of the total population lives in remote areas with no interaction to nearby cities.

Table 2.1. Population shares by OECD regional typology and regional typology based on access to cities

Percentage of the total population, 2019

OECD regional typology (%)		OECD regional typology based on access to cities (%)	
Predominantly urban regions	48	Regions with a city >1M	42
Intermediate regions	27	Regions with a city >250K	29
Predominantly rural regions	25	Regions near a city >250K	12
Close to cities regions	20	Regions with/near a city <250K	9
Remote	5	Remote regions	8

Note: City refers to an FUA. Based on available data for 2 152 TL3 regions in 33 OECD countries. 2018 values for Australia, Ireland, Japan and the United States.
Source: OECD (2020[17]), *OECD Regional Statistics (database)*, http://dx.doi.org/10.1787/region-data-en.

StatLink https://doi.org/10.1787/888934176283

The distribution of the population of regions according to the alternative typology (Figure 2.4) captures some similarities of countries according to their geographic characteristics:

- Although only 8% of the OECD population live in remote regions, in 7 OECD countries one-fifth or more of the national population live in remote regions. These include Norway (31%), Finland (28%) and Sweden (24%) from Scandinavia with sparsely populated regions, Greece (31%) with an island and mountainous geography, and 2 of the largest OECD countries in terms of area, Canada (23%) and Australia (20%).

- In 15 OECD countries, more than one-fifth of the national population live in regions with or near a small/medium city. Countries with the highest shares of population in these types of regions include Iceland (84%), and former East European and Baltic countries including the Slovak Republic

(63%), Latvia (57%), the Czech Republic (43%), Hungary (36%), Estonia (34%) and Lithuania (33%).

- Regions near a large city are home to one-fifth of the national population or more in 10 OECD countries. These include small- and medium-sized European countries, namely Austria (21%), Belgium (50%), Denmark (30%), Germany (23%), Italy (22%), the Netherlands (25%), Portugal (20%), Slovenia (40%), Switzerland (40%) and the United Kingdom (22%).

Figure 2.4. A relatively large share of the population lives in regions far from large cities in many OECD countries

Population in 2019 (percentage)

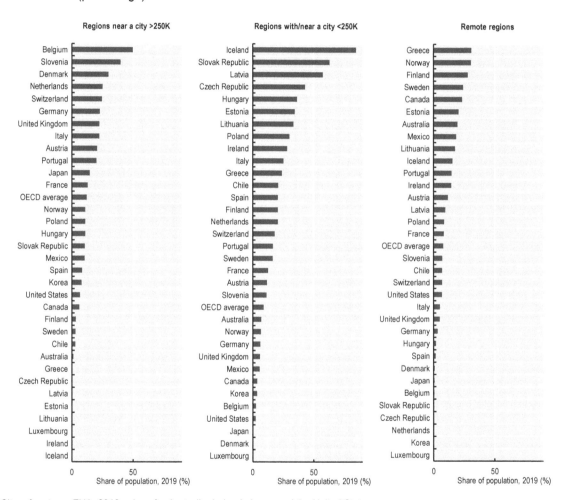

Note: City refers to an FUA. 2018 values for Australia, Ireland, Japan and the United States.
Source: OECD (2020[17]), *OECD Regional Statistics (database)*, http://dx.doi.org/10.1787/region-data-en.

StatLink 🔗 https://doi.org/10.1787/888934176302

Demographic dynamics in rural regions

A common characteristic of cities is their ability to attract people and firms to their location in a sustained form. This occurs since firms like to locate where other firms and/or suppliers are located given the lower transportation costs. They also like to locate where consumers and densities are higher, especially service-oriented firms. Workers in turn also like to locate close to firms, given the higher job opportunities available. Studies of this phenomenon include Perroux's notion of "growth poles" (1995[20]). Myrdal's analysis of "circular and cumulative causation" (Myrdal and Sitohang, 1957[21]) and Hirshman's concept of "forward and backward linkages" (1958[22]).

Demographic patterns across OECD countries over the past two decades confirm these circular and cumulative causation dynamics. The share of population living in metropolitan regions against the share of rural regions increased in all but three OECD countries (Greece, Korea and the Netherlands).

Figure 2.5. The share of the population in metropolitan regions increased in the last two decades

Change in the share of metropolitan regions between 2001 and 2019 (percentage)

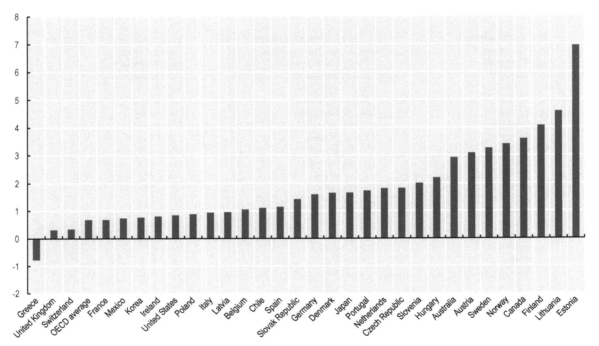

Note: Metropolitan regions include regions with a city of at least 250 000 inhabitants. Based on available data for 2 147 TL3 regions.
Source: OECD (2020[17]), *OECD Regional Statistics (database)*, http://dx.doi.org/10.1787/region-data-en.

StatLink ᵐˢᵖ https://doi.org/10.1787/888934176359

Greece was the only OECD country that experienced absolute population losses in the aftermath of the financial crisis, with most of outmigration flows originating in metropolitan regions. Most countries concentrated even more population in metropolitan regions in the aftermath of the crisis, especially small countries such as Estonia and Lithuania and those with large sparsely populated areas such as Canada, Finland and Norway. As most of the largest increases happened in relatively small countries, the increase in the share of metropolitan regions is close to half a percentage point across 31 OECD countries.

Between 2001 and 2019, the population in metropolitan regions grew annually twice as fast (0.70%) as in rural regions (0.33%), driven by growth in large metropolitan regions (0.79%). Outside metropolitan regions, remote regions experienced the fastest growth rate (0.45%) and the second-largest absolute increase (7 million people) after regions near a large city (8 million) (Table 2.2).

Population growth slowed down after the crisis across all rural region types, except in remote regions where population growth slightly accelerated. After the crisis, population growth slowed down by

0.13 percentage points (p.p.) in regions near a large city. In regions with a small/medium city or near one, the slow-down was even sharper at 0.14 p.p.

Table 2.2. Population growth slowed down in rural regions after the crisis

Region type	Change (millions of people)	Population growth rate 2001-19 (%)	Population growth rate 2001-07 (%)	Population growth rate 2008-19 (%)
Regions with a city >1M	68	0.79	0.85	0.75
Regions with a city >250K	34	0.57	0.63	0.52
Regions near a city >250K	8	0.30	0.38	0.25
Regions with/near a city <250K	5	0.28	0.35	0.21
Remote regions	7	0.45	0.41	0.45

Note: City refers to an FUA. Based on available data for 2 147 TL3 regions in 33 OECD countries.
Source: OECD (2020[17]), *OECD Regional Statistics (database)*, http://dx.doi.org/10.1787/region-data-en.

StatLink https://doi.org/10.1787/888934176321

Although the population in rural regions has grown at a slower pace than in metropolitan regions, around two-thirds of rural regions in each of the three types is gaining population. Still, population decline hit some remote regions the hardest in 2001-19: 36% of all OECD remote regions experienced population decline, with the population falling at a rate of 1% or more in 26 regions in Canada, Chile, Estonia, Germany, Latvia, Lithuania and Portugal.

Table 2.3. One-third of rural regions experienced population decline in the last two decades

	Population growth (number of regions)	Population decline (number of regions)
Regions with a city >1M	239	37
Regions with a city >250K	416	110
Regions near a city >250K	269	132
Regions with/near a city <250K	214	116
Remote regions	394	220
Total	1 532	615

Note: City refers to an FUA. Based on available data for 33 OECD countries.
Source: OECD (2020[17]), *OECD Regional Statistics (database)*, http://dx.doi.org/10.1787/region-data-en.

StatLink https://doi.org/10.1787/888934176340

Over 2001-19, metropolitan regions displayed the highest population growth rates and remote regions the slowest rates in the majority of OECD countries. Among 24 countries with at least 1 large metropolitan region, large metropolitan regions grew faster than other region types in 19 countries – in the remaining 5 countries, metropolitan regions grew faster. In contrast, in 19 out of 28 OECD countries with remote regions, population growth was lowest in that type of region. Half of OECD countries with remote regions (14 out of 28) and 9 out of 31 countries with regions with or near a small/medium city dealt with population decline in those types of regions in 2001-19 (Figure 2.6). Meanwhile, only 5 OECD countries (Japan, Hungary, Germany, Poland and Portugal) dealt with population decline in regions near a large city.

Available population projections for Europe show that, as a whole, regions with or near a small/medium city will have absolute population loses within a decade as early as 2040 and will continue to do so afterwards. The same will happen in metropolitan regions and regions near a large city by 2060. By 2060, regions with or near a small/medium city in Europe will have lost nearly 700 000 people compared to 2015, while metropolitan regions and regions near a large city will have gained nearly 22 million.

Figure 2.6. The population grew in regions near large cities in most countries in the last two decades

Population growth rates 2001-19

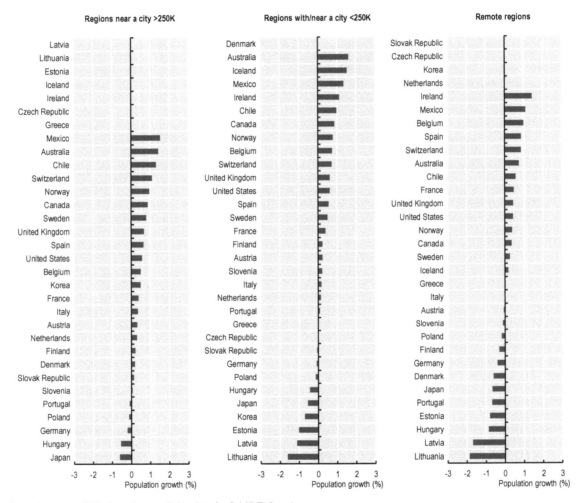

Note: City refers to an FUA. Based on available data for 2 147 TL3 regions.
Source: OECD (2020[17]), *OECD Regional Statistics (database)*, http://dx.doi.org/10.1787/region-data-en.

StatLink https://doi.org/10.1787/888934176378

Figure 2.7. The population is projected to decline in all rural region types in European countries

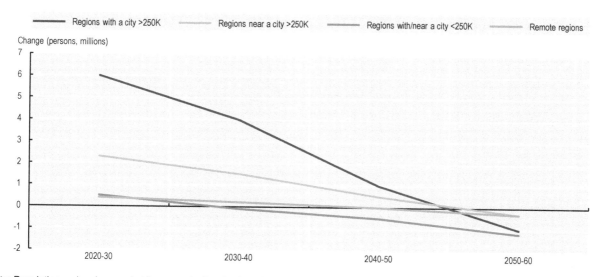

Note: Population series downscaled from country level to NUTS3 level, consistent with the 2018 EC Ageing Report, https://ec.europa.eu/info/sites/info/files/economy-finance/ip065_en.pdf.
Source: Batista e Silva, F. et al. (2016[23]), *Regionalisation of Demographic and Economic Projections*, https://op.europa.eu/fr/publication-detail/-/publication/f6155238-3f4e-11e6-af30-01aa75ed71a1.

StatLink 📊 https://doi.org/10.1787/888934176397

Population growth is mainly driven by three factors: migration, fertility and mortality. Metropolitan areas appear to be drivers of migration. In both metropolitan regions and regions near a large city, net migration was positive in 2015, whereas they are negative in regions with or near a small/medium city and in remote regions. This suggests that larger cities and their surrounding areas are important hubs attracting migrants, whereas smaller cities do not have the same level of attractiveness.

Table 2.4. Net outflows of young people are larger in rural regions

Net (young) migration rate defined as the median value of inflows minus outflows of (young) people over total population, 2015

	Net migration rate (%)	Net migration rate (15-29 year-olds) (%)
Regions with a city >1M	0.070	0.028
Regions with a city >250K	0.098	0.019
Regions near a city >250K	0.128	-0.059
Regions with/near a city <250K	-0.065	-0.085
Remote regions	-0.058	-0.087

Note: Based on available information for 1 493 TL3 regions in 25 countries. Inflows defined as the group of new residents in the region coming from another region of the same country; outflows defined as the group of persons who left the region to reside in another region of the same country.
Source: OECD (2020[17]), *OECD Regional Statistics (database)*, http://dx.doi.org/10.1787/region-data-en.

StatLink 📊 https://doi.org/10.1787/888934176416

The comparison of net migration rates of total population versus young people reveals that: i) large metropolitan regions attract young people; ii) migration into regions near a large city corresponds to an older profile, as net migration flows for the 15-29 age bracket in this type of region are actually negative; and iii) compared to other age groups, young people disproportionally leave remote regions and regions with or near a small/medium city.

Regarding fertility, the relationship between the proportion of children to women and migration is not simple. Not all age groups and genders migrate at the same rate as different places bring different demands and changes in lifestyles that might affect fertility decisions. Still, child-woman ratios are higher in metropolitan regions across 15 out of 22 countries with available data and lower in rural regions in 8 countries (Figure 2.8).

These findings on higher fertility rates in remote places than in larger cities are consistent with previous studies in the literature (Kulu, 2013[24]). The studies identify compositional effects and contextual ones as the main drivers of the variation:

- The compositional effects are due to the higher proportion of highly educated people in cities than in remote areas, and higher fertility tends to be lowest for university education and highest for individuals with only compulsory education (Andersson et al., 2009[25]; Hoem, 2005[26]). The variation may also result from the larger share of students in metropolitan regions and their surrounding areas than in remote regions (Hank, 2001[27]).

- The over-representation of married people in small towns and rural areas may explain the higher fertility rates there, in particular the higher likelihood of family formation (Hank, 2001[27]). Couples who intend to have a child (or another child) may move from cities to small towns and villages because the latter are perceived as better suited to raising children and as offering more affordable and spacious child-friendly housing (Kulu, 2013[24]).

Figure 2.8. Child-woman ratios are higher in metropolitan regions in two-thirds of OECD countries

Children (0-4 years old) over women (15-49) in regions with a large city relative to regions without a large city, 2019.

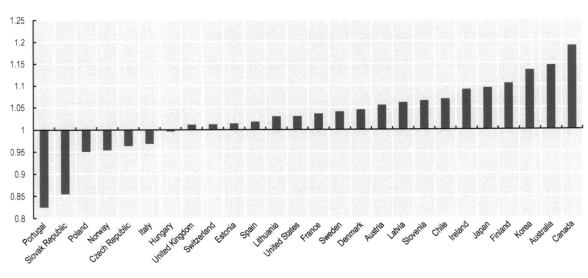

Note: Based on available data for 1 407 TL3 regions.
Source: OECD (2020[17]), *OECD Regional Statistics (database)*, http://dx.doi.org/10.1787/region-data-en.

StatLink https://doi.org/10.1787/888934176435

In turn, mortality rates are expected to be lower in better-performing regions that attract population because of the effect of higher incomes and health infrastructures. The analysis across region types does not reveal a one-to-one correspondence between death rates and density (Figure 2.9) and regions near a large city have the highest maximum average age over the last decade (82 years in 2015). In fact, remote regions have similar death rates than metropolitan regions and both regions have displayed similar trends over time.

Figure 2.9. Death rates are similar in metropolitan and remote regions

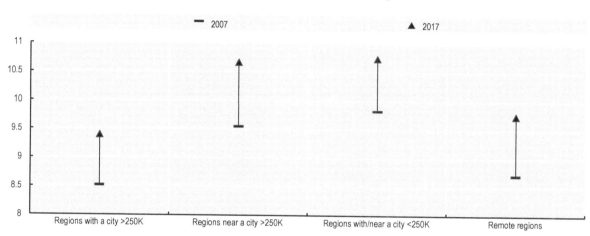

Note: The death rate is the number of deaths per 1 000 inhabitants. Based on available information for 1 729 TL3 regions in 29 countries.
Source: OECD (2020[17]), *OECD Regional Statistics (database)*, http://dx.doi.org/10.1787/region-data-en.

StatLink ᵐˢᵖ https://doi.org/10.1787/888934176454

Nevertheless, people in remote regions experience the lowest life expectancy on average by living two years less while in regions with or near a small/medium city live one year less. From a national perspective, only Swiss rural regions have a lower death rate than the metropolitan regions. Countries with the largest regional differences include Canada, Denmark, Estonia, Japan, Korea, Portugal and Sweden.

Rural regions face structural challenges of an ageing population

OECD countries are facing structural challenges of an ageing population. Current elderly dependency ratios – the share of the population aged 65 and over as a percentage of the population aged 20-64 – stands at 28.6%. This share is expected to increase to 35% by 2025 and to 53% by 2050 on average in OECD countries (Figure 2.10). Greece, Italy, Japan, Korea, Portugal and Spain are all expected to have elderly dependency ratios of over 70% by 2050.

These national figures, however, mask important regional variations within countries. The rates of change and impacts vary greatly from place to place, resulting in significant changes to both labour markets and the settlement pattern across types of regions. Ageing is a stronger structural phenomenon in rural regions *vis-à-vis* metropolitan regions. In only one OECD country (Poland), ageing dependency ratios are significantly lower in rural regions compared to metropolitan regions. In the large majority of countries (27 out of 31 countries with available data), the elderly dependency ratio is higher in rural regions by at least 1 percentage point. The countries with the largest gap in elderly dependency ratios in 2019 include Japan, Finland, Australia, United Kingdom, Sweden, Canada and Korea, all with a gap above 9 percentage points.

Figure 2.10. Elderly dependency ratio is projected to increase across all OECD countries

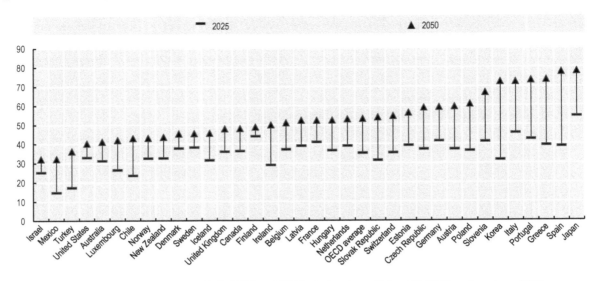

Source: OECD (2017[28]), *Pensions at a Glance 2017: OECD and G20 Indicators*, https://doi.org/10.1787/pension_glance-2017-en.
Note: Elderly dependency ratio defined as the number of individuals aged 65 and over per 100 people of working age defined as those aged between 20 and 64.

In 2019, regions near a large city had the highest average elderly dependency ratios (33%), followed by remote regions (31%) and regions with or near a small/medium city (31%). Remote regions experienced, on average, the largest increases between 2003 and 2019 (a 0.9 percentage point increase). In 2019, 73 regions had elderly dependency ratios above 50% and, in 11 regions (including Evrytania from Greece and Akita, Kochi, Shimane and Yamaguchi from Japan), they were above 60%.

Figure 2.11. Elderly dependency is increasing faster in remote regions

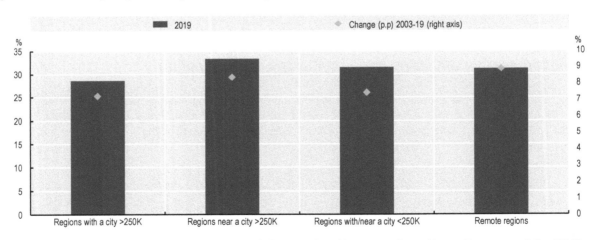

Note: Elderly dependency ratio defined as the average share of +65 population with respect to the working working-age population (15-64 years old). Based on available data for 2 147 TL3 regions in 33 countries.
Source: OECD (2020[17]), *OECD Regional Statistics (database)*, http://dx.doi.org/10.1787/region-data-en.

StatLink ᐧᐧᐧ https://doi.org/10.1787/888934176473

Rural regions will need to prepare to face the growing pressures of ageing. While elderly dependency ratios are highest in regions near a large city, many countries face growing pressures of ageing in regions far from large cities. In about two-thirds of OECD countries with remote regions (23 out of 32), elderly dependency ratios were the highest in remote regions and in 20% (6 out of 30), they were the highest in regions with or near a small/medium city. The gap of age dependency ratios between remote regions and other rural regions is particularly substantial in Denmark (15 percentage points) and Portugal (12 p.p.).

Figure 2.12. Elderly dependency ratios are larger in remote regions in most OECD countries

Share of +65 population with respect to the working-age population (15-64 years old), 2019

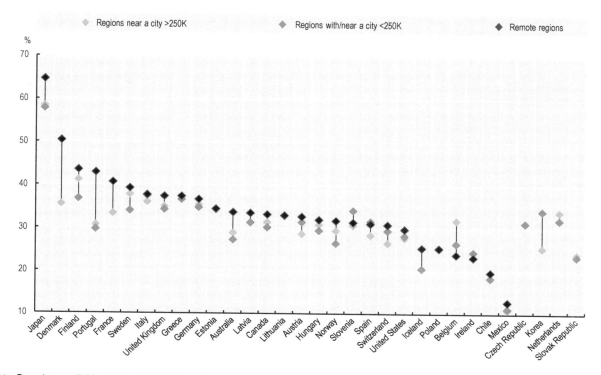

Note: Based on available data for 2 147 TL3 regions.
Source: OECD (2020[17]), *OECD Regional Statistics (database)*, http://dx.doi.org/10.1787/region-data-en.

StatLink https://doi.org/10.1787/888934176492

Ageing also has gender variations across types of regions. Remote regions comprise a lower share of females amongst the elderly (0.83 elderly males per elderly female) than other rural regions (0.76). Overall, females are over-represented amongst the elderly age group given their longer longevity but less so in remote places.

In conclusion, most of the population in rural regions have a strong interaction with urban economies. The share of metropolitan *vis-à-vis* rural regions has been increasing in almost all OECD countries. Yet in half of OECD countries, remote regions are losing population and one-third of regions near a city are losing population. Fertility rates appear to important drivers of the population for remote regions and migration flows for metropolitan regions and their surrounding areas. Rural regions face stronger ageing pressures than metropolitan regions. The highest pressures are in remote regions.

A changing economic landscape for rural economies

OECD countries and regions have faced a number of structural transformations over the past decades creating opportunities and challenges. The intensification of globalisation has delocalised many production tasks to emerging economies where labour costs are cheaper against capital-intensive ones contributing to the emergence of complex global value chains (GVCs). This delocalisation has contributed to the tertiarisation of economic activities across OECD countries, in which the relative share of services increased. Services nowadays represent around 80% of value-added across OECD countries increasing by 15 percentage points relative to the share of services 15 years ago.

These two interconnected forces have not been neutral in space. Manufacturing ceased to be the economic base of large cities against service-oriented activities because they require a pool of specialised labour, access to capital and knowledge networks that are found in cities, especially large ones. This transformation benefitted cities while low-density regions faced increased competition in tradeable goods over the past decades.

Beyond this structural transformation, territories are facing the effects of a number of economic shocks including the 2008 global financial crisis and the COVID-19 pandemic. Low-density regions that produce a limited range of goods and services have a greater vulnerability to economic shocks, whether positive or negative. All things equal, in a very large, dense economy, the greater range of activities typically offers a greater degree of resilience to external shocks.

This section examines the economic performance of TL3 regions since the early 2000s. It focuses particularly on the effect of the crisis on incomes, employment and productivity and examines the effects of these structural transformations on spatial inequality and the economic structure of regions.

The global financial crisis accentuated regional disparities in most OECD countries

The effects of growing and sustained inequalities have come to the forefront of the policy debate. In the past, spatial inequalities were regarded as a natural process of development, given that denser areas benefit more from economies of agglomeration yielding higher levels of productivity, wages and living standards than lower-density areas. Policy responses have focused on mitigating inequalities within cities (OECD, 2016[29]) but recently, the attention switched to the effects of growing and sustained territorial inequalities that bring about a "geography of discontent" especially during the aftermath of the global financial crisis (Dijkstra, Poelman and Rodríguez-Pose, 2018[30]; Hendrickson, Muro and Galston, 2018[31]; McCann, 2019[3]). Analysis in this section is limited to data availability at the regional level, up to 2017, thus capturing only the effects of the aftermath of the global financial crisis.

In 2017, regional disparities, measured as the difference between the top 20% and bottom 20% of regions in GDP per capita level, are substantial across many OECD countries. The absolute gap between incomes in top versus bottom region was highest in France, Germany, Norway and the United Kingdom and lowest in Hungary, New Zealand and Portugal (Figure 2.13). In 16 out of 26 countries with available data, per capita incomes in top regions were more than double that of bottom regions.

Regional inequality increased in 24 out of 28 OECD countries with available data in the post-global financial crisis period (2008-17) compared to the pre-crisis period (2000-07). The relative decline in regional performance in Greece, Italy and Portugal occurred in a context of severe austerity measures in the years following the crisis. The distributional impacts of public spending cuts may have affected bottom-performing regions the most because many regions with high unemployment tend to have relatively high concentrations of public sector jobs.

In absolute terms, the change in regional inequalities was largest in Slovakia, Poland, Lithuania and Czech Republic and the United Kingdom, where the gap in per capita incomes between top and bottom regions increased by at least USD 6 000 between 2000-07 and 2008-17. High levels of regional inequality coincide with a substantial number of high-growing regions of all types. This is due to substantial differences in regional growth rates, as well as the varied composition of top and bottom regions across countries. For instance, in Norway, 5 out of 6 bottom regions are remote, while in Germany only 9 out of 106 bottom regions are remote (and 52 are metropolitan). Across all countries, 30% of metropolitan regions, 24% of regions near a large city, 18% of regions with or near a small/medium city, and 28% of remote regions are bottom regions. (Figure 2.14). Importantly, however, an increase or a decrease in spatial inequality by itself is not necessarily a negative outcome. If spatial inequalities increase because the top regions become better off and the rest of regions remain as they were, the increase is not necessarily a negative outcome. If, on the other hand, inequalities increase because bottom or top regions fall further behind, the rise in inequality signals a problem.

In the case of the 24 countries where regional inequality increased, changes were driven by improvements in top regions in most cases. The exception was Greece, where bottom regions were worst off in terms of income per capita in 2017 compared to 2000. Amongst the four countries reducing inequality, it was in one case (Portugal) due to top regions falling behind. In Austria, Belgium and Finland, larger inequalities went along with an improvement of the bottom regions and, in Switzerland, with a worsening of both top and bottom regions' per capita incomes.

Figure 2.13. Income per capita in top regions more than doubles that of bottom regions across most OECD countries

GDP per capita gap between top and bottom regions, 2017

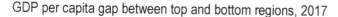

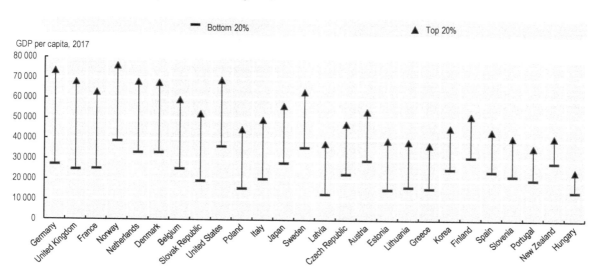

Note: Top (bottom) refers to top (bottom) 20% regions with the highest (lowest) GDP per capita levels with populations adding up to at least 20% of the national population. 2016 values for France and Japan. Based on available data for 1 512 TL3 regions.
Source: OECD (2020[17]), OECD Regional Statistics (database), http://dx.doi.org/10.1787/region-data-en.

StatLink ᴍᴤ̇ᴸ https://doi.org/10.1787/888934176511

The relative decline in regional performance in Greece, Italy and Portugal occurred in a context of severe austerity measures in the years following the crisis. The distributional impacts of public spending cuts may have affected bottom-performing regions the most because many regions with high unemployment tend to have relatively high concentrations of public sector jobs.

In absolute terms, the change in regional inequalities was largest in Slovakia, Poland, Lithuania and Czech Republic and the United Kingdom, where the gap in per capita incomes between top and bottom regions increased by at least USD 6 000 between 2000-07 and 2008-17. High levels of regional inequality coincide with a substantial number of high-growing regions of all types. This is due to substantial differences in regional growth rates, as well as the varied composition of top and bottom regions across countries. For instance, in Norway, 5 out of 6 bottom regions are remote, while in Germany only 9 out of 106 bottom regions are remote (and 52 are metropolitan). Across all countries, 30% of metropolitan regions, 24% of regions near a large city, 18% of regions with or near a small/medium city, and 28% of remote regions are bottom regions.

Figure 2.14. Regional inequalities increased after the crisis in most OECD countries

Worse off means GDP per capita levels in 2017 are lower than in 2000

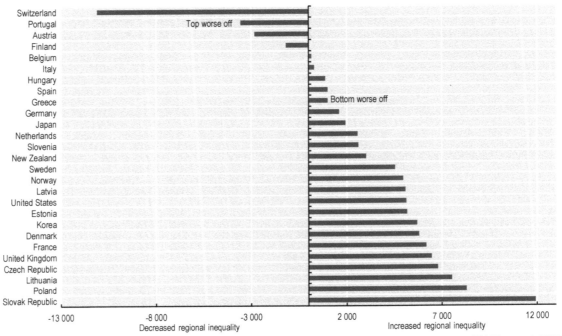

Note: 2017 extrapolated values for France and Japan based on 2001-16 regional growth rates. Based on available data for 1 629 TL3 regions. Unlabelled cases are better off (top or bottom). Top (bottom) refers to top (bottom) 20% regions with the highest (lowest) GDP per capita levels (PPP) with populations adding up to at least 20% of the national population.
Source: OECD (2020[17]), *OECD Regional Statistics (database)*, http://dx.doi.org/10.1787/region-data-en.

StatLink 🔗 https://doi.org/10.1787/888934176530

The distance penalty widened after the global financial crisis

The global financial crisis occurred more than a decade ago. Although the crisis affected all regions, the recovery has been much slower for rural economies. Low population growth, slow employment creation and sluggish productivity appear to be working against the recovery in hard-hit rural regions. This trend has been especially stark in regions far from large cities, which are diverging from other regions in terms of productivity and incomes, and in regions with a small/medium city or near one, where employment rates have fallen behind.

A well-established fact is that per capita income and productivity levels are higher in higher density areas across OECD countries due to the benefits associated with economies of agglomeration (OECD, 2015[32]; OECD, 2016[29]) The alternative TL3 typology provides further evidence on this well-known fact. It shows how incomes per person, productivity and employment rates decrease as distance to high-density areas increases (Table 2.5). The gaps between regions near a large city and the group of regions far from large cities are substantial:

- Regions near a large city have a gap in GDP per capita with respect to metropolitan (large) regions of nearly USD 4 600 (USD 18 000). Their productivity levels and employment rate are around 10 and 8 percentage points below OECD average levels respectively.
- The gaps for regions with or near a small/medium city are even larger. With respect to GDP per capita, they are 28 percentage points below the OECD average. In terms of productivity and employment rates, the gap is also still significant, at 20 and 14 percentage points.
- For remote regions, the gap is 21 percentage points below the OECD average in GDP per capita, 14 percentage points in labour productivity and 3 percentage points in employment rates.

Table 2.5. Distance from density relates to all dimensions of regional performance

2017 values

	GDP per capita (USD)	Share GDP per capita to OECD (%)	Gross value added (GVA) per worker (USD)	Share GVA per worker to OECD (%)	Employment rate (%)	Share employment rate to OECD (%)
Regions with a city >1M	55 965	119.7	97 906	111.5	82.9	106.5
Regions with a city >250K	42 935	91.8	82 224	93.6	76.8	98.6
Regions near a city >250K	38 280	81.9	78 937	89.9	71.4	91.8
Regions with/near a city <250K	33 641	72.0	70 536	80.3	67.2	86.4
Remote regions	36 850	78.8	73 400	83.6	75.6	97.1

Note: GDP per capita based on data available for 1 496 TL3 regions in 26 countries. GVA per worker based on data available for 1 410 TL3 regions in 23 countries. Employment rates based on data available for 1 574 TL3 regions in 29 countries. GDP is in USD PPP with the base year 2015. 2016 GDP values for France and Japan. 2016 GVA values for France, Japan and New Zealand. 2016 employment values for France, Japan and Switzerland. Employment rates based on employment at place of work over working-age (15-64 year-old) population.
Source: OECD (2020[17]), *OECD Regional Statistics (database)*, http://dx.doi.org/10.1787/region-data-en.

StatLink ᯿ https://doi.org/10.1787/888934176549

Convergence was brought to a halt by the crisis

The current gap between metropolitan and rural regions in GDP per capita is the result of long-standing differences that accentuated after the financial crisis of 2008, especially for regions far from large cities (Figure 2.15). Regions near a large city, in contrast, maintained and even marginally reduced their gap in GDP per capita gap with respect to the OECD average.

The global financial crisis had an asymmetric impact across region types and brought regional convergence to a halt. Before the crisis, regions far from large cities were growing faster than other region types. The crisis clearly slowed down growth rates across all region types (as seen by comparing the slope of the lines in Figure 2.16). The decline, however, was much higher in regions with or near a small/medium city and remote regions (as seen by comparing the slope of the lines connecting the dotted and full bubbles). Meanwhile, metropolitan regions and their surrounding regions weathered the effects of the crisis better than the rest of the regions.

One of the factors contributing to the resilience of metropolitan regions is the presence of skilled labour (Crescenzi, Luca and Milio, 2016[33]). On the other hand, the disproportionate effect of the crisis in regions far from large cities is related to their thinner and less diversified economic base (OECD, 2016[7]). To the effect of decreased and fragmented internal demand, low-density economies have faced competitive pressures from low-wage emerging economies over the past two decades. Without increased exports, the sources of productivity gains have remained limited for remote regions. Moreover, because low-density regions produce a limited range of goods and services, they are more vulnerable to industry-specific shocks that are neutralised by a broader and more diversified economic base in larger and denser regions.

Figure 2.15. The income per capita gap of regions far from large cities widened after the crisis

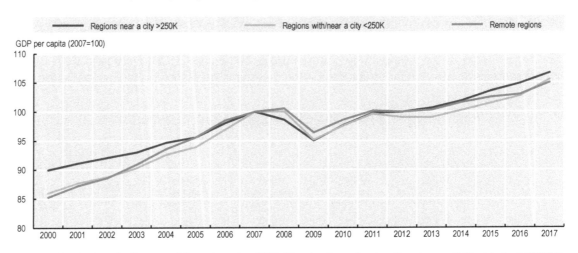

Note: 2017 extrapolated values for France and Japan based on 2001-16 regional growth rates. Based on available data for 1 536 TL3 regions in 28 countries. GDP is in USD PPP with the base year 2015.
Source: OECD (2020[17]), *OECD Regional Statistics (database)*, http://dx.doi.org/10.1787/region-data-en.

StatLink 🔗 https://doi.org/10.1787/888934176568

Figure 2.16. The global financial crisis brought convergence to a halt

Size of the bubble proportional to population in the initial and final year

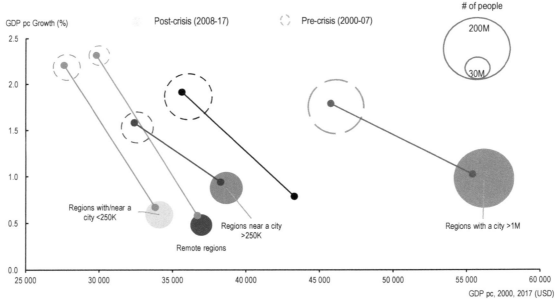

Note: 2017 extrapolated values for France and Japan based on 2001-16 regional growth rates. Based on available data for 1 530 TL3 regions in 28 countries. GDP is in USD PPP with the base year 2015.
Source: OECD (2020[17]), *OECD Regional Statistics (database)*, http://dx.doi.org/10.1787/region-data-en.

StatLink 🔗 https://doi.org/10.1787/888934176587

The global financial crisis brought about a starker division between winners and losers in terms of GDP per capita growth across rural regions. Before the crisis, most regions experienced growth in income per capita and there was convergence within each type as evidenced by higher growth rates in regions with initially lower income per capita levels (Figure 2.17). After the crisis, the variability in growth performance increased across all rural region types. A considerable number of regions far from large cities achieved relatively high growth in a broader context of sluggish economic growth.

In aggregate terms, as of 2017, 85% of large metropolitan regions, 87% of the metropolitan regions and 83% of regions near a large city had already recovered to pre-crisis levels in GDP per capita (Table 2.6). In contrast, only 69% of regions with or near a small or medium city and 74% of remote regions had recovered.

Table 2.6. A lower share of regions far from large cities have recovered their pre-crisis GDP per capita levels

	Regions with a city >1M	Regions with a city >250K	Regions near a city >250K	Regions with/near a city <250K	Remote regions
Share of regions with GDP per capita in 2017 larger than in 2000-07 (%)	85	87	83	69	74

Note: 2017 extrapolated values for France and Japan based on 2001-16 regional growth rates. Based on available data for 1 530 TL3 regions in 28 countries. GDP is in USD PPP with the base year 2015.
Source: OECD (2020[17]), *OECD Regional Statistics (database)*, http://dx.doi.org/10.1787/region-data-en.

StatLink 🔗 https://doi.org/10.1787/888934176625

While the success recovery stories accrued all types of regions, they were highly concentrated in Germany and Poland. About 71% of regions in which GDP per capita in 2017 was at least 25% larger than in the pre-crisis period were from these 2 countries (Table 2.7). Germany concentrated about three in four high-growth regions near a large city and one out of two high-growth remote regions.

Table 2.7. Fast-growing and declining regions concentrate in a few countries

High growth means a 25% or higher GDP per capita in 2017 compared to 2000-07; declining means 10% or lower GDP per capita in 2017 compared to 2000-07

Country	Regions with a city >250K	Regions near a city >250K	Regions with/near a city <250K	Remote regions	Share of population in high/low-growth regions (%)
Number of high-growth regions	120	95	78	61	
Number of high-growth regions by country (top contributors)					
Germany	71	45	22	23	34
Poland	17	22	25	9	100
Korea	2	7	6	1	100
Number of declining regions	30	9	40	35	
Number of declining regions by country (top contributors)					
Italy	17	5	18	5	38
Greece	0	5	1	10	75

Note: 2017 extrapolated values for France and Japan based on 2001-16 regional growth rates. Based on available data for 1 530 TL3 regions in 28 countries. GDP is in USD PPP with the base year 2015.
Source: OECD (2020[17]), *OECD Regional Statistics (database)*, http://dx.doi.org/10.1787/region-data-en.

StatLink 🔗 https://doi.org/10.1787/888934176644

Figure 2.17. Post-global-financial-crisis growth rates across rural regions are more dispersed

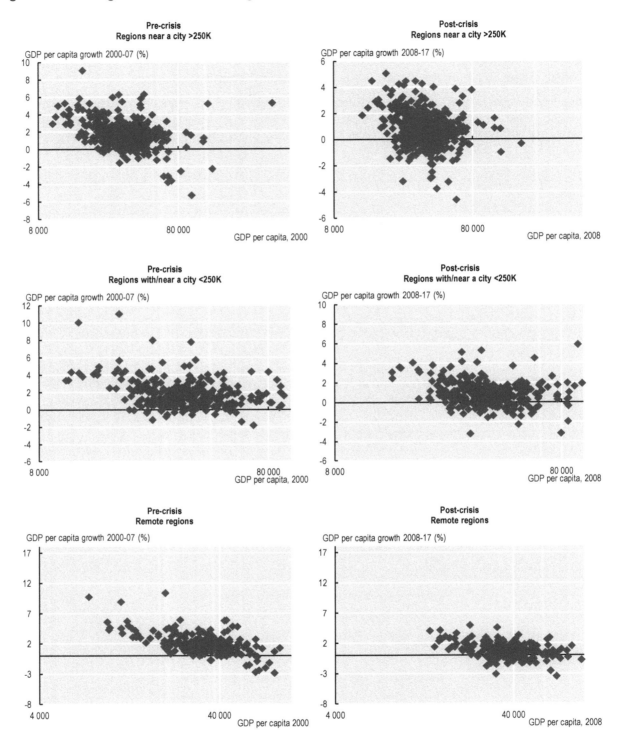

Note: 2017 extrapolated values for France and Japan based on 2001-16 regional growth rates. Based on available data for 28 countries. GDP is in USD PPP with the base year 2015.

Source: OECD (2020[17]), *OECD Regional Statistics (database)*, http://dx.doi.org/10.1787/region-data-en.

StatLink 🔗 https://doi.org/10.1787/888934176606

In contrast, regions suffering the highest economic decline were mostly rural regions, and most of them were in Greece or Italy. Three-quarters of the population of Greece (75%) and 38% of the population of Italy lived in regions where income per capita in 2017 was still 10% lower than during the pre-crisis period (Table 2.7). Overall, the lack of recovery was more frequent in regions far from large cities.

Productivity in remote regions drifted away after the crisis

After the shock of the financial crisis, labour productivity started to converge slowly in regions near cities but drifted away in remote regions (Figure 2.18). One explanation for this divergence is that productivity in regions with a small- and medium-sized city or near one may have benefitted from agglomeration benefits, though not on the same scale as metropolitan regions. In contrast, further concentration of productive industries in cities translated into productivity losses in remote regions that were highly dependent in a few industries with lower than average productivity performance.

Higher productivity levels in metropolitan regions compared to rural regions is the norm across OECD countries. Aside from Korea, all OECD countries with available data show higher productivity in metropolitan regions compared to rural regions (Figure 2.19). The difference is especially stark in small East European and Baltic countries with relatively low productivity levels (Latvia, the Slovak Republic, Lithuania and Estonia), where productivity in metropolitan regions is at least 50% higher than in rural regions. In contrast, the productivity gap is narrow in countries with diverse productivity levels, including Spain, Hungary, Denmark, Japan, Slovenia and Austria.

Figure 2.18. Productivity diverged in remote regions after the global financial crisis

OECD average = 100, the value indicates the percentage gap

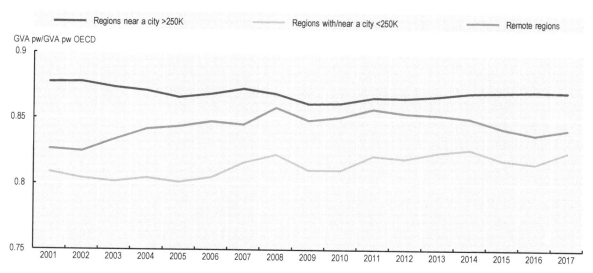

Note: 2017 productivity measured as GVA per worker. GVA extrapolated values for France, Japan and New Zealand based on 2001-16 regional growth rates. 2017 employment extrapolated values for France, Japan and Switzerland based on 2001-16 regional growth rates. Based on available data for 1 346 TL3 regions in 22 countries. GVA is in USD PPP with the base year 2015. Employment at place of work.
Source: OECD (2020[17]), *OECD Regional Statistics (database)*, http://dx.doi.org/10.1787/region-data-en.

StatLink https://doi.org/10.1787/888934176663

Figure 2.19. Productivity levels are higher in metropolitan regions in most OECD countries

Productivity measured as GVA per worker, 2017.

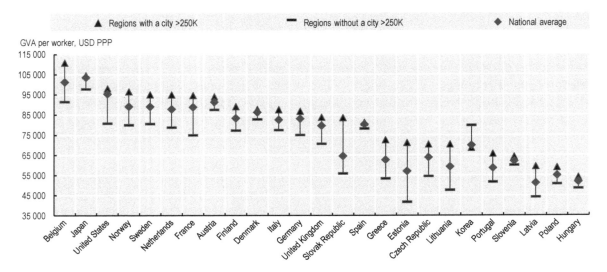

Note: 2017 GVA extrapolated values for France, Japan and New Zealand based on 2001-16 regional growth rates. 2017 employment extrapolated values for France, Japan and Switzerland based on 2001-16 regional growth rates. Based on available data for 1 491 TL3 regions. GVA is in USD PPP with the base year 2015. Employment at place of work.
Source: OECD (2020[17]), *OECD Regional Statistics (database)*, http://dx.doi.org/10.1787/region-data-en.

StatLink ᘈᑕᛋ https://doi.org/10.1787/888934176682

Rural economies struggle to create employment in the new service economy

The contribution of rural regions to employment growth declined significantly after the crisis. In 2001-07, rural regions contributed 22% to an employment growth rate of 7.5%, similar to their contribution to GDP and GVA, and above their contribution to population growth (18%) (Table 2.8). After the crisis, the contribution of rural regions to employment growth fell to 7%, meaning that more than 90% of employment growth was contributed by metropolitan regions in the post-crisis period. The drop in contribution was particularly big for regions with or near a small/medium city, which moved from a contribution of 8% to a negative contribution of 0.9% after the crisis.

The closing of the productivity gap in regions with or near a small/medium city after the crisis is at odds with a diverging trend in employment rates. Even before the crisis in 2008, employment rate levels in regions with or near a small/medium city drifted away from other types of rural regions (Figure 2.20). In 2013, the employment rate gap reached a minimum of 16% below OECD levels. In contrast, in the same year, employment rates in large metropolitan regions were 7% above OECD levels.

The stark difference between remote regions and regions with or near a small/medium city may be due to the mobility and size of the working-age population. Small and medium cities have relatively smaller pools of workers and a different demographic composition, which means more competition for existing job posts. With slow employment creation, workers in small and medium cities may decide to wait for employment opportunities instead of migrating, as cities allow them to access health, education and other services. Policy responses can focus on addressing some structural challenges in smaller cities to tackle the lack of new employment opportunities.

Table 2.8. The contributions of rural regions to GDP, GVA and employment growth decreased substantially after the crisis

The contribution is measured as the share of OECD growth explained by the region type over the OECD growth rate

	Population (%)		GDP (%)		GVA (%)		Employment (%)	
	2001-07	2008-17	2001-07	2008-17	2001-07	2008-17	2001-07	2008-17
OECD growth rate	4.0	4.9	15.7	11.5	15.8	10.8	7.2	6.2
Regions with a city >1M	51.8	58.8	50.1	66.3	50.6	67.1	49.4	70.2
Regions with a city >250K	30.4	27.3	28.0	21.1	27.9	20.5	29.0	22.3
Regions near a city >250K	9.0	8.4	8.7	7.8	8.6	7.8	8.2	6.6
Regions with/near a city <250K	5.3	1.8	7.6	2.5	7.3	2.6	8.0	-0.9
Remote regions	3.4	3.8	5.7	2.3	5.7	2.0	5.4	1.7

Note: 2017 GVA extrapolated values for France, Japan and New Zealand based on 2001-16 regional growth rates. 2017 employment extrapolated values for France, Japan and Switzerland based on 2001-16 regional growth rates; employment data for Poland not available. Based on available data for 1 345 TL3 regions in 22 countries. GVA is in USD PPP with the base year 2015. Employment at place of work.
Source: OECD (2020[17]), *OECD Regional Statistics (database)*, http://dx.doi.org/10.1787/region-data-en.

StatLink 🖳 https://doi.org/10.1787/888934176701

Figure 2.20. Employment rates in regions near a small city drifted apart relative to other rural regions after the crisis

OECD average = 100, the value indicates the percentage gap

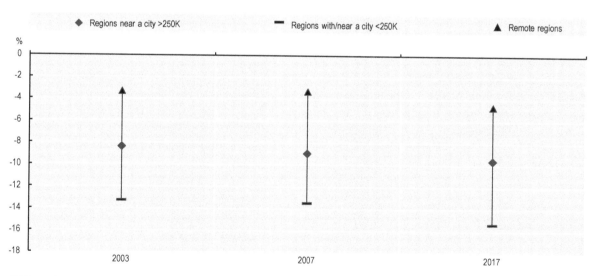

Note: 2017 employment extrapolated values for France, Japan and Switzerland based on 2001-16 regional growth rates. Based on available data for 1 395 TL3 regions in 23 countries. Employment at place of work. Employment rates based on employment at place of work over working-age (15-64 year-old) population.
Source: OECD (2020[17]), *OECD Regional Statistics (database)*, http://dx.doi.org/10.1787/region-data-en.

StatLink 🖳 https://doi.org/10.1787/888934176720

The territorial disparities in employment performance have occurred in the context of a general and steady increase in the importance of services against manufacturing and agriculture. The share of total employment in services grew across all region types after 2008 but remote regions experienced faster tertiarisation (Figure 2.21). In fact, in 2017 the share of employment in services in remote regions was only 4 percentage points below the corresponding share for metropolitan regions with a city of 250 000 people or more (71% versus 75%).

Figure 2.21. The share of employment in services is steadily increasing in most rural regions

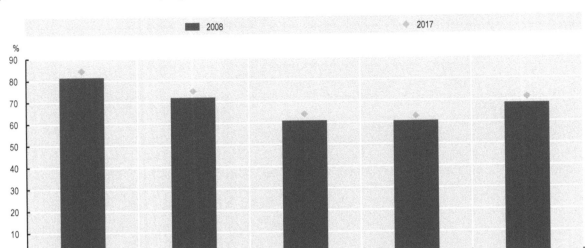

Note: 2017 employment extrapolated values for France based on 2001-16 regional growth rates. Based on available data for 1 403 TL3 regions in 24 countries.
Source: OECD (2020[17]), *OECD Regional Statistics (database)*, http://dx.doi.org/10.1787/region-data-en.

StatLink https://doi.org/10.1787/888934176739

Bottom-performing regions remain over-specialised in primary sectors agriculture

Despite a strong tertiarisation trend, rural regions continue to be specialised in primary sectors, including agriculture, forestry and fishing. Although the share of primary sector employment is over-represented across all rural region types, a larger proportion of regions far from large cities show relatively high levels of employment specialisation (i.e. a specialisation index larger than 2) (Figure 2.22). On the other hand, rural regions have similar patterns of specialisation in manufacturing, which are in line with the median levels of specialisation in metropolitan regions.

Regions with very large cities are in the best position to reap the benefits of specialisation in high-value-added services. The productivity of services tends to increase in large cities with access to a pool of specialised labour and knowledge networks. Furthermore, many service-oriented businesses are less vulnerable to offshoring and therefore protected from international competition. To no surprise, large metropolitan regions are more specialised in high-value-added services that lower-density areas (Figure 2.22).

The slow-down in trade brought about by the financial crisis made regions far from cities more dependent on internal markets, as they cater a more limited range of the goods and services. These features make rural regions less prone to specialise in high-value-added services. In fact, bottom rural regions are overly specialised in primary sectors, while top rural regions are specialised in high-value-added services (Figure 2.23).

Figure 2.22. Sector specialisation in employment by type of TL3 region, 2017

A specialisation value above one indicates the share of employment in the region is higher than the corresponding share across all types

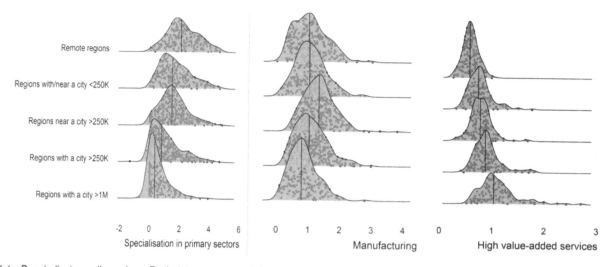

Note: Bars indicate median values. Each dot represents a TL3 region. High-level value-added services include information and communication, financial and insurance activities, and professional, scientific, technical, administrative, support service activities. Data for 19 OECD countries with available data (16 for high value-added services).
Source: OECD (2020[17]), *OECD Regional Statistics (database)*, http://dx.doi.org/10.1787/region-data-en.

Figure 2.23. Sector specialisation employment by type of top and bottom rural TL3 regions, 2017

A specialisation value above one indicates the share of employment in the region is higher than the corresponding share across all types

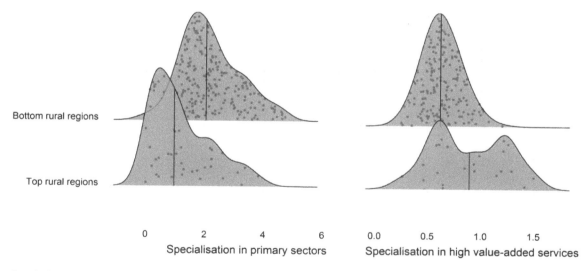

Note: Bars indicate median values. Each dot represents a TL3 region. High-level value-added services include information and communication, financial and insurance activities, and professional, scientific, technical, administrative, support service activities. Top and bottom regions refer to the 20% highest and lowest-ranked regions in terms of GDP per capita in each country, accounting for at least 20% of the population. Data for 22 OECD countries with available data (19 for high value-added services).
Source: OECD (2020[17]), *OECD Regional Statistics (database)*, http://dx.doi.org/10.1787/region-data-en.

Women increasingly participate in rural labour markets

The evolution of employment after the crisis has favoured occupations that disproportionally employ women. While female employment rates had recovered their pre-crisis levels across all rural region types by 2014, male employment rates continue to be below 2007 levels across all region types (Figure 2.24). Employment rates of males were particularly slow to pick up in regions far from metropolitan regions. In regions with access to a small/medium city, female employment rates were 4 p.p. above 2007 levels, while male employment rates were 5 p.p. below.

These diverging trends relate to broad structural changes that have had localised impacts on rural labour markets. In general, rural labour markets tend to be divided by gender, with women more represented in lower-wage services sector jobs (e.g. health and social care services) and men more represented in higher wage primary sectors and associated manufacturing (e.g. agriculture, forestry and mining). Ongoing structural change in primary sectors and rural manufacturing have contributed to increasing differences between employment rates for men and women in regions far from large cities.

Figure 2.24. Female employment rates increased faster than male employment rates across all types of rural regions after the crisis

Employment rate values index to 2007

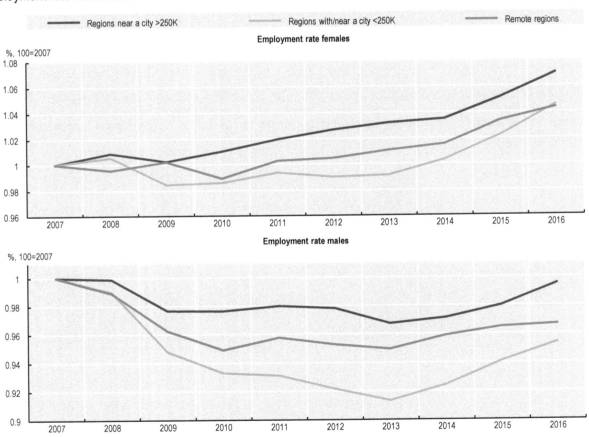

Note: Based on data available for 776 TL3 regions in 14 countries. Employment rate calculated as employment at place of residency over the working-age (15-64 year-old) population of each gender.
Source: OECD (2020[17]), *OECD Regional Statistics (database)*, http://dx.doi.org/10.1787/region-data-en.

StatLink https://doi.org/10.1787/888934176758

The productivity paradox intensified in rural regions after the crisis

Productivity gains can be powerful engines of social transformation but can also be a vehicle for wider gaps across regions if they occur in a context of job-less growth (OECD, 2018[34]). The reasons why productivity gains do not translate into employment gains are manifold. One reason is a more difficult adjustment in the labour market following re-adjustments across and within industries. This is the case if the economic crisis brought about a reorientation towards industries intensive in highly specific skills (e.g. programming and data science) that are difficult to acquire for certain workers. Another reason is the structural unemployment arising from the exit of unproductive firms and unproductive workers that are not absorbed by more productive local firms that may source labour abroad or replace labour with capital.

Across OECD countries, 60% of employment concentrated in regions that experienced productivity and employment gains simultaneously. This "gain-gain" situation was far more common in metropolitan regions than in rural regions (Figure 2.22). Meanwhile, the mismatch between employment and productivity gains became more prevalent in all types of regions after the crisis but more pervasive in regions far from large cities. In the post-crisis period, about half of employment in regions with or near a small/medium city (51%) and remote regions (57%) concentrated in regions with employment and productivity gains.

The "productivity paradox", a scenario of productivity gains with low employment, intensified outside metropolitan regions after the crisis. Indeed, in 2008-17, 18% of employment was concentrated in regions that experienced employment losses in the presence of productivity gains. While this touches all region types, it was more prevalent in regions with or near a small/medium city (concentrating 25% of employment) and in remote regions (28%).

Figure 2.25. The productivity paradox intensified in rural regions after the crisis

Share of employment in regions by productivity and employment performance, measured as the difference between 2008-17 and 2000-07 values

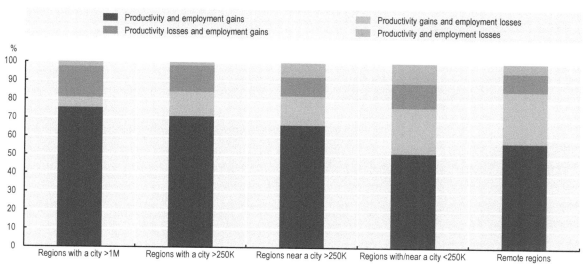

Note: Based on available data for 1 225 TL3 regions in 20 countries. Productivity measured as GVA per worker.
Source: OECD (2020[17]), *OECD Regional Statistics (database)*, http://dx.doi.org/10.1787/region-data-en.

StatLink 🔗📊 https://doi.org/10.1787/888934176777

Moreover, employment and productivity losses combined affected total employment more strongly in rural regions. Within rural regions, remote regions had the biggest drop in productivity of almost a full percentage point the average negative rates of regions near a large city. Regions with or near a small/medium city (accounting for 10% of regions of this type) had the biggest drop in employment.

The relationship between regional productivity and employment growth varies widely across OECD countries. Table 2.9 shows the split of regions in each country between different scenarios in terms of employment and productivity growth in the post-crisis period. Several conclusions emerge:

- The win-win situation of productivity growth paired with employment creation occurred in most regions of Austria, Belgium, Germany, the Netherlands, New Zealand, Sweden and East European countries, including the Czech Republic, Poland and the Slovak Republic. This is consistent with the evidence of concentration of rapid recovery from the economic crisis of 2008 in Germany, Eastern Europe and in northern European regions (OECD, 2018[35]).

- In Hungary, Latvia, Lithuania, Portugal and Spain, more than half of employment occurred in regions where productivity gains occurred without employment gains. In the most extreme case, all regions in Portugal experienced productivity gains paired with employment losses.

- Greece and Italy stand out as the countries concentrating the bulk of regions in decline. In Italy, about one-quarter of employment (27%) occurred in regions that experienced employment and productivity losses. In Greece, 46% of regions had both employment and productivity losses.

Table 2.9. Distribution of employment according to employment and productivity changes in TL3 regions

Change measured as the difference between average employment and productivity in 2008-17 compared to 2000-07

Share of employment in regions with:	Regions with employment and productivity gains (%)	Regions with employment losses, productivity gains (%)	Regions with employment gains, productivity losses (%)	Regions with employment and productivity losses (%)
New Zealand	100	0	0	0
Slovak Republic	100	0	0	0
Belgium	97	0	3	0
Sweden	89	11	0	0
Czech Republic	89	11	0	0
Netherlands	87	11	2	0
United States	83	5	10	2
Austria	73	0	27	0
Germany	71	9	19	0
United Kingdom	68	13	18	1
Slovenia	65	35	0	0
Finland	61	2	34	3
Denmark	58	38	4	0
Estonia	52	48	0	0
Latvia	46	54	0	0
Spain	39	61	0	0
Lithuania	32	68	0	0
Greece	6	29	18	46

Share of employment in regions with:	Regions with employment and productivity gains (%)	Regions with employment losses, productivity gains (%)	Regions with employment gains, productivity losses (%)	Regions with employment and productivity losses (%)
Italy	5	9	59	27
Portugal	0	100	0	0
Luxembourg	0	0	100	0
New Zealand	100	0	0	0
Slovak Republic	100	0	0	0

Note: Based on available data for 1 225 TL3 regions. Productivity measured as GVA per worker.
Source: OECD (2020[17]), *OECD Regional Statistics (database)*, http://dx.doi.org/10.1787/region-data-en.

StatLink https://doi.org/10.1787/888934176796

In conclusion, regions far from large cities were growing faster than the national average before the crisis, but the crisis brought convergence to a halt. In contrast, regions near a large city have shown more resilience and have performed as well as metropolitan regions after the crisis. The increases in productivity in regions far from large cities were accompanied by labour shedding in many cases. Regions with access to smaller cities experienced the largest drops in employment, with effects likely coming from the effect of international competition on tradeables. As ongoing trade tensions between countries can disproportionately affect these types of regions, there is an urgent need to restructure their economies toward sectors that can create local employment while adding value. On the other hand, large cities and their surrounding regions have weathered the effects of the crisis better than the rest of the regions.

The economic consequences of the ongoing COVID-19 pandemic threaten the incipient recovery of lagging regions in countries badly hit by the financial crisis. The negative shock of the ongoing health crisis will impact rural industries including tourism and agriculture and disproportionally affect the most vulnerable, including temporary and self-employed rural workers. Appropriate and timely place-based policy responses should go in the direction of bridging gaps and containing the increase in inequality across people and places, in order to ensure social cohesion and stability.

Enabling factors

Innovation is today a major driving force for economic growth across OECD countries. The speed of innovation generation is constantly increasing, making innovation a basic requirement for national and regional competitiveness. Skilled human capital along with sound information and communication technology (ICT) and civil infrastructure are cornerstones to developing an ecosystem that sparks innovation at the local level.

Skills and human capital

Human capital and skills are critical drivers of regional growth and this is particularly challenging for rural regions that may suffer from "brain drain" (OECD, 2012[36]). Cities attract high-skilled workers from over the globe due to their amenities, presence of economies of agglomeration and higher paid jobs especially in services. In contrast, the market for low and technical skills is much more locally driven. This suggests that the productivity of rural economies depends on the successful upgrading of low-skill workers and an increase in workers with technical skills. Research finds strong benefits of reducing the share of low-skilled workers in the regional labour force supports economic growth (OECD, 2012[36]).

The quality and accessibility of rural education have a double role to play in addressing gaps in skills: starting from children's early years, high-quality education and care can help raise outcomes in education and the labour market. At the same time, access to public services, such as childcare and schools, is a locational factor shaping the attractiveness of rural places, including for highly skilled workers. This also means that a lack of access to high-quality education and training provision in rural places can aggravate the rural-urban divide with regard to skill levels.

Low levels of high-skilled workers can be a bottleneck for growth in low-density economies. For instance, across European countries, individuals living in rural regions strongly lag behind their peers in cities with regard to their level of digital skills, paramount for many modern workplaces (Figure 2.26). Educational attainment provides another indicator of the average skill level in the labour force. The share of workers with tertiary education, i.e. a university degree, is lower in regions characterised by low-density economies, while the share of workers that do not have education beyond primary education (a proxy for low-skilled workers) tends to be higher in these regions (OECD, 2016[7]). Across all countries considered, the share of workers with tertiary education in the most urbanised regions is higher than in low-density regions ranging from 57 percentage points higher in the Czech Republic to 2.8 in the United States (US). All OECD countries have a higher share of primary educated workers in low-density regions except for Germany and the US. In Germany, this partly reflects the historic east-west divide and the significantly lower shares of workers with only primary education in the (less-densely populated) east of Germany and, for the US, the difference can be driven by states that are mostly urbanised and have a large percentage of foreign-born residents.

Figure 2.26. Share of the individuals living in rural areas and cities in Europe with basic or above digital skills

2019 values

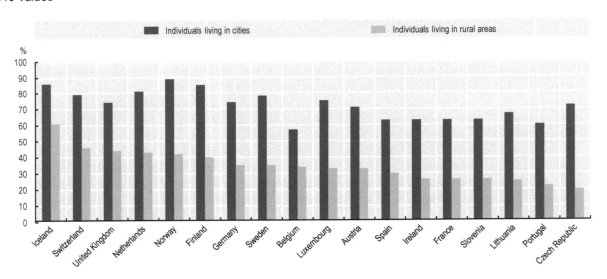

Note: Not all OECD countries covered by the data source. For further information on the Eurostat classification of areas by degree of urbanisation, see https://ec.europa.eu/eurostat/web/degree-of-urbanisation/background.
Source: Eurostat (2020[37]), *European Social Survey*, https://ec.europa.eu/eurostat/cros/content/european-social-survey_en.

StatLink https://doi.org/10.1787/888934176815

In terms of the level of skills of students, results from the Programme for International Student Assessment (PISA) show that students in rural schools, defined as villages, hamlets or rural areas with fewer than 3 000 people, tend to underperform in secondary education outcomes in comparison to cities that have more than 100 000 inhabitants (Echazarra and Radinger, 2019[38]). On average, students in city schools across OECD countries scored 48 points higher in reading than their peers in rural schools, according to the PISA 2018 data – more than the equivalent of a year of schooling (new analysis of PISA 2018 data adapted from Figure 2.27). Yet, when the comparison accounts for the socio-economic status of students and schools, the performance gap between rural and city schools was no longer statistically significant. This means that differences in the socio-economic composition of the population tend to explain the rural-urban gap in academic performance.

Figure 2.27. The rural-urban gap in reading performance

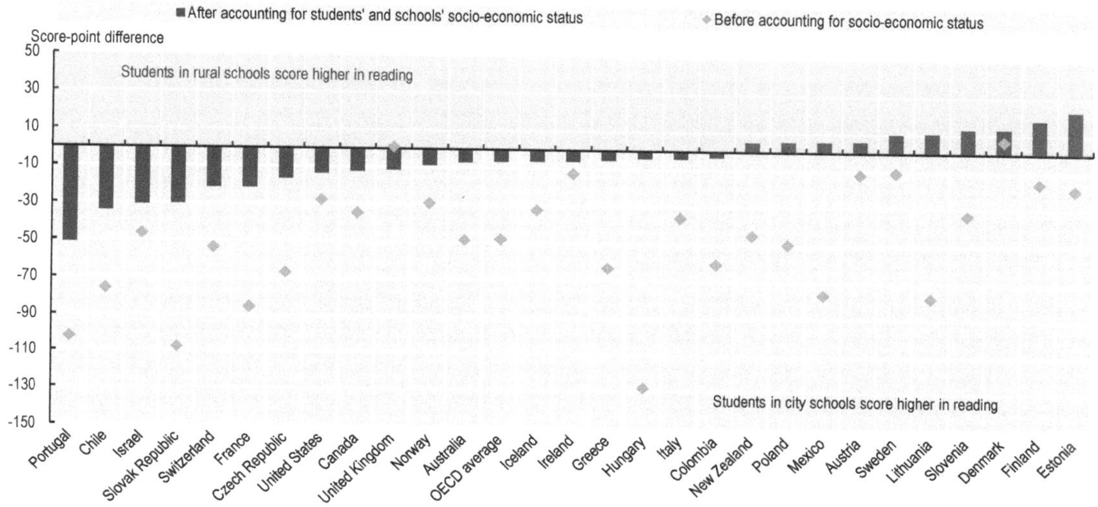

Note: Rural schools are schools in villages, hamlets or rural areas with 3 000 or fewer inhabitants; city schools are those in places with a population of more than 100 000. Results based on linear regression models. Statistically significant coefficients are marked in a darker tone. Source: OECD PISA 2018 database, adapted from Echazarra, A. and T. Radinger (2019[38]), "Learning in rural schools: Insights from PISA, TALIS and the literature", https://doi.org/10.1787/8b1a5cb9-en.

StatLink ⫘⫘ https://doi.org/10.1787/888934176834

The rural-urban education gap is even more visible when analysing rural students' educational expectations. Based on a survey among 15-year-old students carried out by PISA 2018, on average across OECD countries, students in rural schools are half as likely to expect completing a university degree as those in city schools (new analysis of PISA 2018 data adapted from Echazarra and Radinger (2019[38])). This reflects students' self-assessment of their opportunities and capacities regarding higher education (OECD, 2017[39]). In that sense, beyond financial facilities, other factors might discourage students in rural areas to advance further in their studies, including geographical barriers, lack of career role models and highly skilled jobs in their home areas.

Attracting highly skilled teachers to rural areas is key to improve student outcomes. While differences in the highest level of education are on average not statistically significant between rural and city schools OECD countries, there tends to be a greater share of new teachers and a higher turnover rate in rural schools (OECD, 2020[40]). As teachers in rural schools also tend to be more satisfied with their salaries and tend to report less stress than their peers in cities, policy makers need to take a broader approach to measures to attract and retain teachers to those locations that go beyond financial incentives. Those trends vary across countries but they highlight that a spatial lens is warranted when considering the support teachers need to deliver high-quality education in different locations, for instance, to enable collaborative professional learning when schools are small.

Policies related to skills development and education cannot be spatially blind across countries' territories and must address rural regions' specific challenges related to lower densities and longer distances in developing a strong skill base for the future local economic development.

Internet connectivity is key for the future of rural regions

Advances in technology and particular Internet infrastructure are quite relevant for low-density regions. Improvements in Internet connectivity can overcome some of the core challenges they face including isolation, high transportation costs, high costs to delivery services and distance to markets. Most Internet infrastructure investments were initially deployed in urban areas given their higher densities and commercially viable solutions. Over the past years, further improvements in ICT technology will have a proportionally higher impact in low-density regions since most urban areas are already well connected.

Furthermore, confinement measures during the Covid-19 crisis have fomented the use of teleworking, remote learning and e-services. These practices will accelerate the usage of these digital tools beyond the crisis period. With changing habits and more willingness to embrace these digital tools, government and private operators may increase investments to realise their potential benefits. In rural economies, the increased connectivity of services can further unlock opportunities for future work, synergies and regional integration between rural places and their surroundings.

In order to benefit from Internet infrastructure deployments, a multidimensional response is needed (as will be argued in Chapter 5); deployment by itself is a necessary but not sufficient condition to reap the potential benefits of Internet connectivity and the potential benefits for rural regions. These range from attracting new economic activity and skills, improving the productivity of firms, raising the quality and reducing costs of service delivery, connecting to a new market and overcoming isolation.

Economic remoteness, or peripherality, has three distinct features:

- The first is simple *physical distance to major markets*. This increases travel times and shipping costs, which must be borne by the buyer (in the form of higher prices) or seller (in the form of lower margins).

- The second dimension of peripherality is the degree of *economic connectedness*. Lack of economic integration not only reduces current trade opportunities but it also reduces the ability of agents in a place to identify new opportunities. Thus, there are costs in both static and dynamic perspectives.

- Third, the economic structures of such places often have *specific features*. Production is concentrated in relatively few sectors since it is impossible to achieve "critical mass" in more than a few activities. Whatever the respective roles of the primary, secondary and tertiary sectors, a narrower economic base implies greater vulnerability to sector-specific shocks, whether positive or negative.

Broadband access is today a needed asset for economic progress and well-being. Quality broadband is instrumental to harness the benefits from new technologies, including the Internet of things, blockchain, artificial intelligence, big data and 5G networks (see Chapter 5).

Broadband access in rural areas has increased across OECD countries. Since 2010, the gap of broadband access between rural and urban areas, as defined for this measure, has decreased by half in almost all OECD countries (OECD, 2019[41]). In 2018, the average share of rural households with broadband connection in a sample of 31 OECD countries reached 82%, slightly below the 89% in urban areas (Figure 2.28).

Figure 2.28. Households with broadband connections 256 Kbps or greater, urban and rural

As the percentage of households in each category, 2010 and 2018

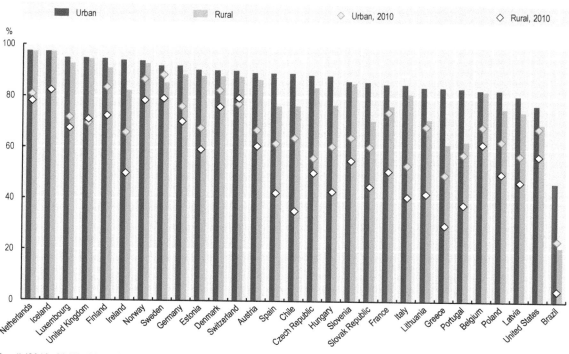

Note: Brazil (2010, 2016), Chile (2017, 2012), Switzerland (2017, 2012), United States (2010, 2017). For EU countries, rural areas are those with a population density less than 100 per km². For Canada, rural areas are those with a population density less than 400 per km². For the United States, rural areas are those with a population density less than 1 000 per square mile or 386 people per km².
Source: OECD (2019[42]), *Measuring the Digital Transformation: A Roadmap for the Future*, https://dx.doi.org/10.1787/9789264311992-en; OECD (2018[43]), *ICT Access and Usage by Households and Individuals (database)*, http://oe.cd/hhind.

In terms of speed capacity, there is still a gap between rural and urban regions. Based on data of 27 OECD countries for 2017, just 56% of rural households have access to fixed broadband with a minimum speed of 30 Mbps (speed required to support many consumer applications such as streaming high-definition video), in comparison to over 85% in urban areas (Figure 2.29). In countries like Finland for instance, while the share of rural households with an Internet connection is almost 90%, just 8.3% of households in rural areas had a connection to quality broadband. Slow or intermittent broadband connection reduces the opportunities for people to participate and benefit from economic gains and quality of life in the digital age.

Figure 2.29. Broadband quality is lower in rural areas across most OECD countries

Households in areas where fixed broadband with a contracted speed of 30 Mbps or more is available, as a percentage of households in the total and rural categories, 2017

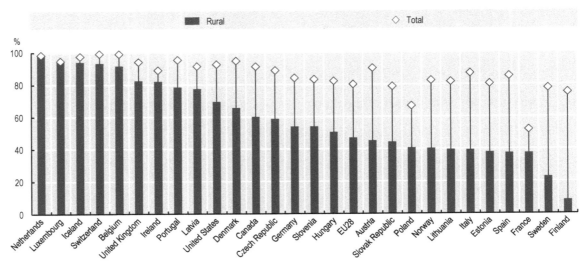

Note: 2016 data for the United States.
Source: OECD (2019[42]), *Measuring the Digital Transformation: A Roadmap for the Future*, https://dx.doi.org/10.1787/9789264311992-en; OECD calculations based on CRTC (2017[44]), *Communications Monitoring Report 2017*, https://crtc.gc.ca/eng/publications/reports/policymonitoring/2017/cmr.htm; EC (2017[45]), *Study on Broadband Coverage in Europe 2017*, European Commission; FCC (2018[46]), *2018 Broadband Deployment Report*, https://www.fcc.gov/reports-research/reports/broadband-progress-reports/2018-broadband-deployment-report; https://doi.org/10.1787/888933915050.

Rural economies lag in innovation as measured by patent activity

Innovation encompasses a wide range of activities from research and development (R&D) to organisational changes, training, testing, marketing and design. The Oslo Manual recognises four types of innovation: product innovation, process innovation, marketing innovation and organisational innovation (OECD, 2015[32]). Despite this broad definition, due to the availability of data patent application, a type of intellectual property rights (IPs) remains the most common indicator to measure innovation performance. Not only do they focus on a subset of innovation (science and technology) but there are measurement biases driven by the location of where the patent is recorded against where it was conceived.

Innovation performance, based solely on patent activity, is lower in rural regions compared to metropolitan regions (Figure 2.30). In 2016, the average number of patents per 10 000 inhabitants in metropolitan regions (1.9) almost doubled the number in regions near a large city (1.0) on average across OECD countries. Patent activity is even lower in regions with or near a small/medium city (0.6) and remote regions (0.5). However, out of 30 OECD countries with metropolitan areas, 6 countries (Chile, Hungary, Italy, Mexico, Slovenia, United Kingdom) exhibit more patent activity in at least one type of rural region compared to metropolitan regions. In the United Kingdom, for instance, regions near a large city, including those with university towns such as Cambridge and Oxford, display higher patent intensity than metropolitan regions.

Better data to measure innovation performance at the local level is needed to assess the different regional dynamics. Patents mainly measure the front-end – or invention – of the innovation process, giving less indication on the back-end or the commercialisation. Thus, patent data tends to overlook the firms that only apply existing technologies to their operations, without engaging in technological development that leads to a patentable invention (OECD/Eurostat, 2018[47]). Furthermore, not all technological development activities result in patentable inventions and firms do not seek patent protection for all of their inventions.

Thus, measuring innovation through patents or IPs can penalise rural places since these metrics do not fully measure grassroots or user-developed innovation, which may be more important to rural firms (Whitacre, Meadowcroft and Gallardo, 2019[48]; Wojan and Parker, 2017[49]). Therefore, there is a need to come up with tailored indicators that are able to canvas how rural business innovate or use technologies in innovative ways.

Figure 2.30. Patent activity is lower in rural regions in most OECD countries

Patent counts per 10 000 inhabitants, 2016

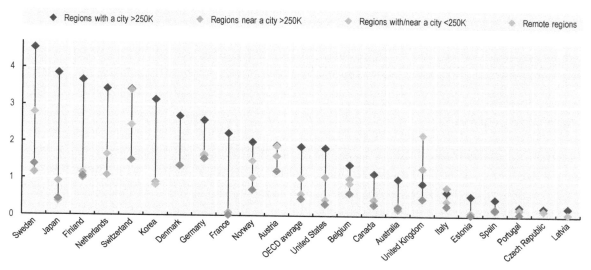

Note: Variable constructed using total population and fractional count of patents.
Source: International Energy Agency (2018[50])CO2 Emissions from Fuel Combustion 2018; OECD (2020[17]), OECD Regional Statistics (database), http://dx.doi.org/10.1787/region-data-en; OECD (2019[41]), Going Digital: Shaping Policies, Improving Lives, https://doi.org/10.1787/9789264312012-en.

StatLink ᴍᴤᴸ https://doi.org/10.1787/888934176853

Box 2.5. US study on Rural Establishment Innovation Survey (REIS)

USDA undertook a broad study to better understand innovation in rural areas using a variety of data sets, including a large-scale survey that compares innovation in urban and rural areas based on some 11 000 business establishments with at least 5 paid employees in tradeable industries in rural and metropolitan areas. The survey divides business into either: i) substantive innovators, which amount to 30% of business launching new products and services, making data-driven decisions and creating intellectual property worth protecting; ii) nominal innovator, which comprise 33% of firms and engage in the more incremental improvement of their products and processes; or iii) non-innovators, amounting to 38% of firms showing little or no evidence of innovation. The study finds:

- Establishments in metropolitan areas are slightly more innovative – around 20% of rural firms are substantive innovators, compared to 30% of firms in metropolitan areas.

- Rural areas have a slightly higher overall rate of substantive innovation for large firms (those with 100 employees or more), while urban areas win out in their rate of substantive innovation by small- and medium-sized firms.

Rural areas have a slight advantage over their metropolitan counterparts in the rate of substantive innovation by the most innovative firms (those that are patent-intensive). That is because innovation in rural areas tends to be a product of patent-intensive manufacturing in industries like chemicals, electronics and automotive or medical equipment, while urban areas have higher rates of innovation in services.

Source: Wojan, T. and T. Parker (2017[49]), *Innovation in the Rural Nonfarm Economy: Its Effect on Job and Earnings Growth, 2010-2014*, http://dx.doi.org/10.22004/ag.econ.264596 (accessed on March 2020).

Digitalisation and automation are the main global trends that will affect rural economies. The effects of these trends can radically transform life and work for rural inhabitants (see Chapter 5). Detailed data and indicators to measure the impacts of digital transformation at the local level will be instrumental for policies to adapt and make the most of the technological change.

Concluding remarks

This chapter has outlined population and economic trends shaping rural development and the status of skills, human capital, digital connectivity and innovation as enabling factors for rural development.

A policy roadmap for delivery of well-being in rural regions has to take into account the variety of development profiles of rural regions in OECD countries. The alternative typology of regions has uncovered the differentiating role of access to density in the economic performance of rural regions, particularly after the 2008 global financial crisis. In more remote regions, policies will have to place emphasis not only on bridging the "distance penalty" through the provision of quality and affordable digital access for people and entrepreneurs but on designing overarching policies targeting rural attractiveness that nurture existing and new economic activities. These plans can take advantage of new economic opportunities generated by the transition to a low-carbon economy, new business opportunities in the care sector and social innovation initiatives. Furthermore, although the effects of the COVID-19 crisis will likely deepen territorial inequalities, they will also potentially accelerate some megatrends, in particular digitalisation.

Confinement measures have brought changing habits and more willingness to embrace digital tools. Government and private operators will likely increase investments to realise their potential benefits. In rural areas, the increased connectivity of services can further unlock opportunities for future work, synergies and territorial integration.

In regions close to cities, policy strategies can leverage the natural attractiveness of proximity to dense labour and consumer markets by focusing on high-quality affordable housing and services, the attraction of high-value-added service industries and co-ordination solutions to maximise rural-urban linkages. Across all rural regions, ambitious and urgent strategies to increase digital skills and connectivity are required to bridge development gaps with metropolitan regions.

References

Andersson, G. et al. (2009), "Cohort fertility patterns in the Nordic countries", *Demographic research*, Vol. 20, pp. 313-352, http://dx.doi.org/10.4054/DemRes.2009.20.14.   [25]

Australian Bureau of Statistics (2018), *1270.0.55.005 - Australian Statistical Geography Standard (ASGS): Volume 5 - Remoteness Structure, July 2016*, https://www.abs.gov.au/ausstats/abs@.nsf/mf/1270.0.55.005.   [12]

Australian Bureau of Statistics (n.d.), *The Australian Statistical Geography Standard (Asgs) Remoteness Structure*, https://www.abs.gov.au/websitedbs/D3310114.nsf/home/remoteness+structure. [11]

Barbier, M., G. Toutin and D. Levy (2016), "L'accès aux services, une question de densité des territoires", *Insee Première*, No. 1579, Insee, https://www.insee.fr/fr/statistiques/1908098. [8]

Batista e Silva, F. et al. (2016), *Regionalisation of Demographic and Economic Projections*, Joint Research Centre, European Commission, https://op.europa.eu/fr/publication-detail/-/publication/f6155238-3f4e-11e6-af30-01aa75ed71a1. [23]

Brezzi, M., L. Dijkstra and V. Ruiz (2011), "OECD Extended Regional Typology: The Economic Performance of Remote Rural Regions", *OECD Regional Development Working Papers*, No. 2011/6, OECD Publishing, Paris, https://dx.doi.org/10.1787/5kg6z83tw7f4-en. [14]

Crescenzi, R., D. Luca and S. Milio (2016), "The geography of the economic crisis in Europe: National macroeconomic conditions, regional structural factors and short-term economic performance", *Cambridge Journal of Regions, Economy and Society*, Vol. 9/1, pp. 13-32, http://dx.doi.org/10.1093/cjres/rsv031. [33]

CRTC (2017), *Communications Monitoring Report*, Canadian Radio-television and Telecommunications Commission, https://crtc.gc.ca/eng/publications/reports/policymonitoring/2017/cmr.htm. [44]

Dijkstra, L. and H. Poelman (2014), "A harmonised definition of cities and rural areas: The new degree of urbanisation", *European Commission Regional Working Papers*, European Commission. [15]

Dijkstra, L., H. Poelman and A. Rodríguez-Pose (2018), "The geography of EU discontent", *Regional Studies*, Accesed on 15 July 2019, https://doi.org/10.1080/00343404.2019.1654603. [30]

Duranton, G. et al. (2004), "Micro-foundations of urban agglomeration economies", pp. 2063-2117. [19]

EC (2017), *Study on Broadband Coverage in Europe*, European Commission. [45]

EC (n.d.), *Global Human Settlement Layer 2015*, European Commission, https://ghsl.jrc.ec.europa.eu/. [18]

Echazarra, A. and T. Radinger (2019), "Learning in rural schools: Insights from PISA, TALIS and the literature", *OECD Education Working Papers*, No. 196, OECD Publishing, Paris, https://doi.org/10.1787/8b1a5cb9-en. [38]

European Network for Urban Development (n.d.), *Strategy for Inner Areas - Italy*, https://enrd.ec.europa.eu/sites/enrd/files/tg_smart-villages_case-study_it.pdf. [10]

Eurostat (2020), *European Social Survey*, European Commission, https://ec.europa.eu/eurostat/cros/content/european-social-survey_en. [37]

Fadic, M. et al. (2019), "Classifying small (TL3) regions based on metropolitan population, low density and remoteness", *OECD Regional Development Working Papers*, No. 2019/06, OECD Publishing, Paris, https://dx.doi.org/10.1787/b902cc00-en. [16]

FCC (2018), *2018 Broadband Deployment Report*, Federal Communications Commission, https://www.fcc.gov/reports-research/reports/broadband-progress-reports/2018-broadband-deployment-report.   [46]

Hank, K. (2001), "Regional fertility differences in western Germany: An overview of the literature and recent descriptive findings", *International Journal of Population Geography*, Vol. 7/4, pp. 243-257, http://dx.doi.org/10.1002/ijpg.228.   [27]

Hendrickson, C., M. Muro and W. Galston (2018), *Countering the geography of discontent: Strategies for left-behind places*, https://www.brookings.edu/research/countering-the-geography-of-discontent-strategies-for-left-behind-places/ (accessed on 26 July 2019).   [31]

Hirshman, A. (1958), "The strategy of economic development", *The Annals of the American Academy of Political and Social Science*.   [22]

Hoem, J. (2005), "Why does Sweden have such high fertility?", *Demographic Research*, Vol. 13, pp. 559-572, http://dx.doi.org/10.4054/DemRes.2005.13.22.   [26]

Iammarino, S., A. Rodriguez-Pose and M. Storper (2018), "Regional inequality in Europe: Evidence, theory and policy implications", *Journal of Economic Geography*, Vol. 19/2, pp. 273-298, http://dx.doi.org/10.1093/jeg/lby021.   [1]

International Energy Agency (2018), *CO2 Emissions from Fuel Combustion 2018*.   [50]

Kulu, H. (2013), "Why do fertility levels vary between urban and rural areas?", *Regional Studies*, Vol. 47/6, pp. 895-912, http://dx.doi.org/10.1080/00343404.2011.581276.   [24]

McCann, P. (2019), "Perceptions of regional inequality and the geography of discontent: Insights from the UK", *Regional Studies*, pp. 1-12, http://dx.doi.org/10.1080/00343404.2019.1619928.   [3]

Myrdal, G. and P. Sitohang (1957), *Economic theory and under-developed regions*, Duckworth, London.   [21]

OECD (2020), *OECD Regional Statistics (database)*, OECD, Paris, http://dx.doi.org/10.1787/region-data-en.   [17]

OECD (2020), *TALIS 2018 Results (Volume II): Teachers and School Leaders as Valued Professionals*, TALIS, OECD Publishing, Paris, https://dx.doi.org/10.1787/19cf08df-en.   [40]

OECD (2019), *Going Digital: Shaping Policies, Improving Lives*, OECD Publishing, Paris, https://dx.doi.org/10.1787/9789264312012-en.   [41]

OECD (2019), *Measuring the Digital Transformation: A Roadmap for the Future*, OECD Publishing, Paris, https://dx.doi.org/10.1787/9789264311992-en.   [42]

OECD (2018), *ICT Access and Usage by Households and Individuals (database)*, OECD, Paris, http://oe.cd/hhind.   [43]

OECD (2018), *Productivity and Jobs in a Globalised World: (How) Can All Regions Benefit?*, OECD Publishing, Paris, https://dx.doi.org/10.1787/9789264293137-en.   [35]

OECD (2018), *The Productivity-Inclusiveness Nexus*, OECD Publishing, Paris, https://dx.doi.org/10.1787/9789264292932-en.   [34]

OECD (2017), *Pensions at a Glance 2017: OECD and G20 Indicators*, OECD Publishing, Paris, https://doi.org/10.1787/pension_glance-2017-en. [28]

OECD (2017), *PISA 2015 Results (Volume III): Students' Well-Being*, PISA, OECD Publishing, Paris, https://dx.doi.org/10.1787/9789264273856-en. [39]

OECD (2016), *Making Cities Work for All: Data and Actions for Inclusive Growth*, OECD Publishing, Paris, https://dx.doi.org/10.1787/9789264263260-en. [29]

OECD (2016), *OECD Regional Outlook 2016: Productive Regions for Inclusive Societies*, OECD Publishing, Paris, https://dx.doi.org/10.1787/9789264260245-en. [7]

OECD (2015), *The Innovation Imperative: Contributing to Productivity, Growth and Well-Being*, OECD Publishing, Paris, http://dx.doi.org/10.1787/9789264239814-en. [32]

OECD (2015), *The Metropolitan Century: Understanding Urbanisation and its Consequences*, OECD Publishing, Paris, https://dx.doi.org/10.1787/9789264228733-en. [51]

OECD (2014), *OECD Rural Policy Reviews: Chile 2014*, OECD Rural Policy Reviews, OECD Publishing, Paris, https://dx.doi.org/10.1787/9789264222892-en. [5]

OECD (2013), *Rural-Urban Partnerships: An Integrated Approach to Economic Development*, OECD Rural Policy Reviews, OECD Publishing, Paris, https://dx.doi.org/10.1787/9789264204812-en. [13]

OECD (2012), *Promoting Growth in All Regions*, OECD Publishing, Paris, https://dx.doi.org/10.1787/9789264174634-en. [36]

OECD (2006), *The New Rural Paradigm: Policies and Governance*, OECD Rural Policy Reviews, OECD Publishing, Paris, https://dx.doi.org/10.1787/9789264023918-en. [6]

OECD/Eurostat (2018), *Oslo Manual 2018: Guidelines for Collecting, Reporting and Using Data on Innovation, 4th Edition*, The Measurement of Scientific, Technological and Innovation Activities, OECD Publishing, Paris/Eurostat, Luxembourg, https://dx.doi.org/10.1787/9789264304604-en. [47]

Perroux, F. (1995), "Note sur la notion de pôle de croissance", *Économie appliquée*. [20]

Rodríguez-Pose, A. (2018), "The revenge of the places that don't matter (and what to do about it)", *Cambridge Journal of Regions, Economy and Society*, Vol. 11/1, pp. 189-209, http://dx.doi.org/10.1093/cjres/rsx024. [2]

Statistics New Zealand (2004), *New Zealand: An Urban/Rural Profile*, http://archive.stats.govt.nz/browse_for_stats/Maps_and_geography/Geographic-areas/urban-rural-profile.aspx#gsc.tab=0. [9]

UN Statistical Commission (2020), "A recommendation on the method to delineate cities, urban and rural areas for international statistical comparisons", https://unstats.un.org/unsd/statcom/51st-session/documents/BG-Item3j-Recommendation-E.pdf. [4]

Whitacre, B., D. Meadowcroft and R. Gallardo (2019), "Firm and regional economic outcomes associated with a new, broad measure of business innovation", *Entrepreneurship & Regional Development*, Vol. 31/9-10, pp. 930-952, http://dx.doi.org/10.1080/08985626.2019.1630486. [48]

Wojan, T. and T. Parker (2017), *Innovation in the Rural Nonfarm Economy: Its Effect on Job and Earnings Growth, 2010-2014*, http://dx.doi.org/10.22004/ag.econ.264596 (accessed on March 2020).   [49]

Notes

[1] See https://unstats.un.org/unsd/statcom/51st-session/documents/BG-Item3j-Recommendation-E.pdf.

[2] A region that would be classified as "predominantly rural" in the second step is classified as "intermediate" if it has an urban centre of more than 200 000 inhabitants (500 000 for Japan) representing no less than 25% of the regional population. Similarly, a region that would be classified as "intermediate" in the second step is classified as "predominantly urban" if it has an urban centre of more than 500 000 inhabitants (1 million for Japan) representing no less than 25% of the regional population.

[3] The distance from urban centres is measured by the driving time necessary for a certain share of the regional population to reach an urban centre with at least 50 000 people.

[4] The OECD Metropolitan Database contains a range of socio-economic indicators at the FUA level and can be accessed at https://measuringurban.oecd.org/.

3 Putting well-being at the forefront

A changing socio-economic landscape highlights the need for rural policies to shift towards a well-being oriented, people-centred approach. This chapter presents a Rural Well-being Policy Framework to support rural policy makers to succeed in a dynamic environment and address a number of interconnected challenges and opportunities, aiming to shape rural as places of opportunities. The chapter starts with an overview of the structural changes that have had implications on rural policy, making the case for a differentiated approach. It then outlines the OECD's evolving rural development framework and summarises key elements of the new framework. The final section presents the policy strategies to enhance rural well-being in its three dimensions – economic, social and environmental – to unlock development opportunities and a sustainable future for people and business in rural places.

Key messages

A number of structural transformations, including the three megatrends (digitalisation, demographic and environmental change), are **creating new opportunities and challenges for rural regions**.

- **Global shifts in production and the rise of the service industry** have increased competition from emerging economies and led policies to focus on product differentiations, niche markets and upscaling in global value chains (GVCs). Yet, openness to foreign investment and promotion of linkages between local firms and multinational enterprises may strengthen the growth of high-value-added tradeable activities in rural regions.

- **Well-being is becoming a priority for policy making.** As communities increasingly demand higher living standards and a reduction of inequalities, rural policies need to target well-being for rural dwellers and broaden the classical frameworks for rural policy making. For instance, enabling factors like digitalisation and considerations on how to build and attract human capital are not part of traditional rural policy frameworks. These aspects need to be better integrated.

- **Rural-urban linkages** have gained relevance with increasing globalisation and improved infrastructure. Seizing the benefits of these linkages requires integrated policies and developing win-win scenarios. Rural places close to cities are likely to benefit from improved corporate relationships, exchanges in labour markets and communication and innovation networks.

- **Technology and digitalisation** innovations are fast-paced and demand dynamic policy responses that accommodate these changes and leverage them for the benefit of people and the environment. Digitalisation creates new jobs, new ways to deliver services and transport people and goods, which can improve attractiveness and value creation in rural regions.

- **Demographic changes** call for new policy objectives that provide sustainable solutions to maintain a robust labour force, attractiveness and quality services in rural regions. It requires forward-looking planning that takes into account ageing, population decline and the need to attract and retain young workers. To adapt to demographic changes, rural regions need to support a vibrant community culture for people of all ages and mechanisms to integrate the elderly in the local economy. Social innovations can be an important tool to find solutions to societal challenges and enhance well-being simultaneously.

- **Climate change and the transition to a low-carbon economy** demands that rural policies include climate objectives such as limiting the temperature increase to 1.5°C above preindustrial levels and fostering transitions using and safeguarding rural assets (i.e. land, biodiversity, etc.). Rural communities can unlock growth and well-being opportunities through the development of renewable energy projects and bio- and circular economies.

To harness the benefits of these structural changes and unlock the growth potential of rural regions, OECD's new rural development framework *Rural Well-being: Geography of Opportunities* provides a multi-dimensional view of rural policies with:

- **Three types of rural areas** – Rural inside functional urban areas (FUAs), rural close to cities and remote rural, along with the interactions between rural places and cities.

- **Three objectives** – Encompassing not only economic objectives but also social and environmental objectives and their interdependence.

- **Three different stakeholders** – Including government as well as the private sector and civil society.

This chapter identifies a number of policy recommendations regarding **economic, social and environmental dimensions across the different types of rural communities, with the ultimate goal of boosting rural well-being**:

- *Economic dimension* – Rural regions need to **enhance productivity and competitiveness** by:
  - Adding value to tradeable activities by deepening smart specialisation strategies in rural regions and promoting innovation.
  - Internationalising small- and medium-sized enterprises (SMEs) and expanding into national markets by improving networks and connections with urban, national and external markets.
  - Supporting productivity in rural firms by improving the local and regional business environment and facilitating training for entrepreneurs and SMEs.
  - Facilitating traditional and innovative sources of financing for rural firms.
  - Retaining more value in rural communities by ensuring competitive regulation for local economies and promoting local benefit-sharing policies (monetary and non-monetary), including capacity-building activities for local firms, promoting quality standards and training programmes.
  - Strengthening rural skills by improving collaboration between public authorities, local businesses and not-for-profit organisations, to ensure local education and training matches the current and future needs of rural firms.

- *Social dimension* – Rural communities need **to adapt to an ageing and declining population** by:
  - Enhancing the quality and availability of information and communication technology (ICT) and developing services related to maternal health, childcare and integration.
  - Designing sustainable services that take the long-term view, make use of economies of scope and scale where possible, and use technology to overcome higher per-unit cost where possible.
  - Improving communications about the benefits of rural amenities, such as lower cost of living and proximity to nature, to facilitate the recruitment of skills and retention of youth.
  - Providing special teaching and leadership to young rural populations.
  - Developing "silver" services that address challenges faced by the elderly population and providing pathways for older people to continue to make contributions to rural communities.
  - Investing and supporting social innovations that help to find solutions to societal challenges.
  - Developing targeted immigration programmes that help promote rural life to newcomers.

- *Environmental dimension* – Policies must support rural economies in the **shift to a low-carbon economy** by:
  - Facilitating the development of renewable energies that can benefit rural economies.
  - Identifying ways to capture the value of positive externalities such as ecosystem services.
  - Promoting sustainable land use and resource extraction as part of the bio- and circular economies.
  - Rethinking transportation for rural dwellers, including a focus on alternative and technological innovations to reduce emissions as well as infrastructure development.
  - Working with regions dependent on carbon-intensive sectors to develop new economic opportunities and managing social consequences.

Introduction

A combination of economic, social and environmental elements affects our well-being. Economic aspects determine the jobs we can find, the houses we can afford and the productivity and competitiveness of firms. Social arrangements define how social services and networks are available and support the cohesiveness of communities. Finally, environmental aspects define the quality of the air we breathe and the land we can use. Overall, these immediate living conditions define how resilient we are to shocks and what prospects future generations might have. They also influence regional attractiveness and, consequently, define where people choose to settle in the long term. The balance among these elements may vary considerably across regions and is largely impacted by structural changes and global trends.

Structural transformations have created new challenges and opportunities for rural areas. These changes include an ageing population, urbanisation, the rise of emerging economies, climate change, increasing globalisation, technological breakthroughs and global shocks, such as the global financial crisis in 2007 or the recent COVID-19 crisis. Chapter 2 has shown that rural regions have borne much of the cost of these structural transformations in recent decades. The re-orientation of OECD economies toward services has largely benefitted cities and industries have been exposed to increased competition from lower-wage countries, declines in trade and disruptive technologies.

Despite this, rural places make a vital contribution to the well-being and prosperity of OECD countries. The COVID-19 crisis has demonstrated, ever more importantly, how essential the production of food and raw materials, amenities and ecosystem services are for the functioning of our societies and economies. Rural economies, however, go beyond agro-food and natural resources nowadays and range from manufacturing hubs, service providers, logistical hubs and tourism destinations to name just a few. Understanding the new opportunities in these rural economies as well as how to exploit linkages with urban communities will be important in enhancing the well-being of rural citizens. Building resilience in rural regions has become indispensable due to their unique links to natural resources.

Over the long term, rural regions will continue to undergo a profound structural transformation. For instance, workers in regions with low density, specialised in carbon-intensive industries, will need to explore new job opportunities in the light of the much-needed energy transition and decarbonisation of economies. Policy makers in regions facing demographic decline will need to provide services that are sustainable over the medium and long terms, making the most of innovative solutions. Elderly people will need to become familiar with using online health services. Finally, rural entrepreneurs will have to find ways to stay competitive as the speed of innovations is facilitated through the Internet and as they compete with businesses around the world.

These structural changes highlight the need for rural policy makers to find ways to succeed in a dynamic environment and address a number of interconnected challenges and opportunities at once. It calls for the implementation of a new rural development framework that is centred around the well-being of individuals and encompasses economic, social as well as environmental aspects. A place-based and people-focused well-being agenda does not abandon the objective to improve rural competitiveness; rather it recognises that competitiveness is a necessary but not sufficient condition to enhance well-being. This chapter presents a broader rural development framework that is multi-dimensional and people-centred to support policy makers in shaping rural regions into places of opportunities.

To unlock the growth potential of rural regions and improve the well-being of rural dwellers, the OECD's new rural development framework *Rural Well-being: Geography of Opportunities* offers countries a people-centred approach built on:

- **Three types of rural** – Those near a large city, those with a small or medium city and remote regions.

- **Three objectives** – Encompassing not only economic objectives but also social and environmental objectives.
- **Three different stakeholders** – Including the government as well as the private sector and civil society.

The previous chapter provided a diagnosis showing different patterns of development and performance trends among the different type of rural regions, necessitating differentiating policy responses. This chapter addresses the second dimension of the framework: policy objectives. The chapter starts with an overview of the structural changes that have important implications for the design of rural policies, followed by a section that outlines the OECD's evolving rural development framework. The final section presents the policy strategies to improve the economic, social and environmental dimensions to enhance rural well-being and unlock opportunities to attain a sustainable and sustained future for people and businesses in rural regions.

Structural changes and implications for rural policy

OECD countries have faced numerous structural changes that have had strong implications for rural regions. These have been amplified by the 2008 financial crisis and by the COVID-19 pandemic. While new economic activities have flourished in rural regions (tourism, manufacturing), replacing agriculture as the primary economic engine during the great recession, some of these advances, particularly in tourism, have scaled back after the COVID-19 pandemic. In parts of the OECD, we have observed that greater infrastructure connectivity has increased linkages between cities and rural regions, creating greater interdependencies and facilitating the movement of people, goods and ideas. However, globalisation and the reduction of transport cost has also driven delocalisation of production to developing countries, adding a fierce competition to OECD rural regions. Likewise, tertiarisation has occurred in a context of greater allocation of high-value-added services in cities, increasing the income gap between cities and rural regions. As a result of such economic reshuffle, rural communities and citizens have experienced a discontent and demanded more from governments, forcing policy makers to think beyond gross domestic product (GDP) and deliver improved well-being. Today, a number of megatrends including digitalisation, demographic change, climate change and the recent health pandemic are drawing a new future for rural regions, adding new considerations for the design and implementation of rural policy. This section analyses these structural changes, arguing for the need for a new rural framework that is able to cope with current and forthcoming changes in rural regions. Table 3.1 summarises the framework outlined in this section.

Table 3.1. Putting well-being at the forefront – Structural transformations and trend overview

Structural transformations	Implications for rural policy	Opportunities for rural regions
Global shifts in production and rise of the service industry	Increased competition from emerging economies calls for policies to shift focus from low cost to product differentiations and niche markets. GVCs need to be considered in policy making.	Access to the world as a market. Openness to foreign investment and promoting linkages between local start-ups and SMEs and multinational enterprises (MNEs) may strengthen the performance and growth of high value-added tradeable activities. Exporting technical services and expertise to emerging markets may become a key growth driver for rural economies.
Well-being as a priority	Citizens demand good living standards and reduction of inequalities; this requires integrated and holistic policy responses.	Differentiated concept of well-being provides an improved understanding of rural assets, like natural environment, housing space, more social capital and greater food security.

Structural transformations	Implications for rural policy	Opportunities for rural regions
Rural-urban linkages	Globalisation increases relations between rural and urban regions, through infrastructure and networks, policies need to be integrated and highlight win-win scenarios.	Especially beneficial for rural places close to cities, not only through infrastructure links but also through corporate relationships (e.g. supply chains), market pervasion and communication networks.
Technology and digitalisation	Fast-paced technological innovations demand dynamic policies that respond to changes and connect rural firms, SMEs and research institutions to developments that benefit rural regions.	Technologies associated with digitalisation, create new jobs, new ways for services and transport, change demand in the labour force and way of life in rural regions that can improve attractiveness and value creation.
Demographic changes	New policy areas arise from the need to provide long-term and sustainable solutions taking into account ageing and population growth as well as the need for attracting and retaining young people and newcomers. Greater focus needs to be placed on healthcare, transportation, and digital connectivity and skills.	Developing the silver economy and investigate ways to keep the elderly integrated in economic and community activities. Social innovations can be used as a tool to find new solutions to societal challenges with the goal of enhancing societal well-being.
Climate change and the transition to a low-carbon economy	New priority areas and objectives for rural policy to limit a temperature increase to 1.5 C above pre-industrial levels and foster transitions using and safeguarding rural assets (i.e. land, biodiversity etc.).	Development potential arising through green industries that contribute to climate change mitigation and adaptation. Rural places can take advantage through investment and technologies associated with renewable energy and the circular economy.

The relevance of supporting rural economic diversification

While different types of rural regions exist, rural economies tend to be characterised by their low density and low level of diversification. In low-density economies, a small workforce limits the number and size of firms that can effectively operate and the distance from markets makes some rural economies sensitive to transport costs. Highly influenced by their specific natural environments, many rural economies often rely on extraction and first-stage processing of local natural resources that are exported beyond the region. This reliance on primary sectors coupled with the small size of economies leads to high vulnerability to national and global business cycles. Furthermore, in some rural regions with a higher reliance on a single sector and actor (i.e. mining regions), suppliers of goods and services, in particular when they are SMEs, tend to get trapped in lock-in supplier effects, making it hard to diversify in other sectors or markets (OECD, forthcoming[1]). After the 2009 crisis, top-performing rural regions were characterised by their specialisation on high-value-added services, while the bottom performing ones stood out by their overspecialisation in primary sectors (Chapter 2). The current projections following the COVID-19 pandemic suggest that rural economies specialised in tourism will be the hardest hit, but the effect of the crisis depends in a large part of the role of rural economies in supply chains. Rural places that heavily depend on imports in primary agricultural goods, such as food, will be hit hard by soaring food prices and lack of supply. On the other hand, rural economies that are net producers (and exporters) of agricultural goods will have more stable outcomes, if not a positive demand effect due to short-term consumption substitution patterns of surrounding regions.

Rural economic diversification is relevant to improve quality of life and meet national goals on poverty reduction. Unlike cities that enjoy the benefits of economies of scale and agglomeration, rural regions have lower-density, remote and often fragmented markets, which make it harder to unlock new business opportunities. Emerging research demonstrates that rural diversification can lead to faster poverty reduction and more inclusive growth than urbanisation (World Bank Group, 2017[2]). In Poland, for example, approximately 1 in 4 farmers live in relative poverty and 11% in extreme poverty (OECD, 2018[3]). Economic diversification that provides opportunities outside the agricultural sector contributes to increasing income and improved well-being for rural dwellers (). Overall, economic diversification is an important component of OECD economies, where SMEs account for 99% of all firms, 60% of employment and more than half of gross value added (GVA) (OECD, 2019[4]).

Economic diversification also helps to make regions more resilient to external shocks. Less diversified rural regions are vulnerable to global sector or economic activity-specific shocks. Low-density regions producing a limited range of goods and services tend to be more vulnerable to sector-specific shocks, positive or negative. Yet specialisation is a key driver for productivity and growth and should involve a type of diversification within similar activities to reduce sectoral vulnerability, so-called smart specialisation (see the economic dimension in the next section). In a very large, dense economy, the greater range of activities and services, the greater the protection. As a result, large metropolitan areas exhibit a greater degree of resilience to external shocks. As shown in Chapter 2, the effects of the crisis display a much lower growth rate in GDP per capita from 2008 to 2016 across all regional categories than before the crisis. The slow growth rate is especially present in remote regions and regions with access to a small/medium city. Metropolitan regions and those close to them have weathered the effects of the crisis much better than regions far from large cities.

Diversification means countries can no longer rely on "one-size-fits-all" economy-wide policies. Rural regions with low-density economies face different barriers to growth than their urban counterparts, so policies need to reflect the fact that regional growth patterns are not uniform (OECD, 2012[5]). Rural regions contribute significantly to aggregate growth and support to the continued diversification of these regions benefits the entire economy. Some of the opportunities for diversified rural economies, such as participation in tradeable goods production, are discussed in the section on economic well-being. Given the strong competition from emerging economies, rural regions in OECD economies can no longer compete on low-cost labour. As we will see, these economies must specialise in adding value.

Moving beyond agriculture and extractive industries

Many institutions still associate the rural economy primarily with agricultural production. Subsidies for agricultural production have directed rural policy for decades, yet support to producers in OECD countries has declined gradually over the long term (OECD, 2019[6]) The primary agency responsible for rural development in the majority of OECD countries is an agricultural or food ministry (in 57% of OECD countries) and the agriculture sector remains as a top priority in many OECD rural policies (Chapter 4). Within the European Union (EU), rural development policy constitutes the "second pillar" of the Common Agricultural Policy (CAP). Most of the budget of this policy (76% of the CAP budget) is allocated to direct payments for farmers, while the remaining funds covering a wide array of rural development activities including competitiveness, ecosystems and social inclusion. Yet, there exist other funds, such as the ERDF, ESF and Cohesion Fund, that intervene to address the wider needs of rural regions.

Traditional rural policy focused primarily on land and natural resource assets. Despite growing diversification, these assets still play an important part in resource-rich rural regions. As urbanisation concentrates larger populations into a limited number of cities and land remains a primary asset in rural regions. With low population densities and significant ecological diversity, rural spaces account for more than 75% of land in OECD countries (OECD, 2016[7]). Land availability creates opportunities for space-intensive activities and flexibility in land use. Moreover, regions with land assets experience improved well-being as a result of reduced congestion, lower environmental pressure and lower housing costs. In the Netherlands, the Environment and Planning Act (currently being updated) aims to preserve a sound balance between the use of natural resources and environmental protection by managing land development at different levels of government and with an approach drawn up in consultation with local stakeholders (OECD, 2019[8]). Policies developed in co-operation with stakeholders at the local level can identify the best way to utilise and conserve land assets.

However, the goal of diversification has increased in many countries, shifting the tide towards a more diverse set of tools intended to build capacity and improve outcomes for rural regions. The rural development approach has been evolved in many OECD countries to now include more ministries aside from only agricultural ministries. For instance, in Denmark, the responsibilities to diversify rural economies also lies within the Ministry of Enterprise and Innovation and the Ministry of Industry, Business and Financial Affairs. Likewise, rural development policies have prioritised areas beyond agriculture, including service delivery, innovation and environmental sustainability (Chapter 4). Supporting farmers and agricultural production alone does not address concerns about ageing and outmigration, accessibility and service delivery, or quality of life for rural residents. Farming jobs are often poorly protected, provide low remuneration and can be hazardous for workers. Looking for complementary policies that can function alongside policies currently targeting agricultural production is necessary to ensure programmes are effective in improving economic and well-being outcomes.

While the past few decades of structural transformation towards the services sector has benefitted cities, the most recent COVID-19 pandemic is expected to have a stronger negative impact on urban economies. The delocalisation of industrial activity from developed to developing counties has led to a growing focus on services activities, in which the relative share of services – both as a proportion of total output and employment – has increased during the past decades. Services currently account for 80% of value-added across OECD countries, representing an increase of 15 percentage points relative to the share of services 15 years ago. Although the growth of employment in services appears to offset declines in agricultural employment in the aggregate, a changing economic geography disadvantages rural region that are unable to enjoy the benefits of proximity and agglomeration – often considered prerequisites for a successful economic transition to the service sector (Chapter 2). In fact, while rural remote areas have experienced a faster transition to service sector than other rural regions in the aftermath of the financial crisis, those services are mostly from low-value-added activities that tend to be non-tradeable goods (Chapter 2). On the other hand, there have been much larger gains from the transition to the service sector in cities. The COVID-19 pandemic has disrupted supply chains for processed manufacturing intermediate and final goods for rural and urban areas. However, government restrictions on movement to contain the pandemic may dampen areas with a higher concentration of jobs in the service industry (i.e. urban areas). For rural economies, those specialising in non-tradeable goods in particular, the shock may be mitigated.

Well-being as a priority

Well-being plays an important role in contexts where income does not effectively capture the full picture. In light of growing inequalities and negative externalities stemming from increased globalisation and delocalisation of production, policy makers can no longer look to GDP to provide an accurate assessment of progress. Since the financial crisis, policy leaders have acknowledged the need for a framework that recognises broader measures of social progress alongside more traditional "production-oriented" measurements (Stiglitz, Sen and Fitoussi, 2009[9]). Today, governments are paying greater attention to dimensions of well-being, such as housing, education, access to water and civic engagement (Cornia et al., 2017[10]).

The concept of well-being recognises that economic progress works within these dimensions, encompassing a broader view of social progress beyond production and market value (Box 3.1). To drive the point, comparative measures of well-being measured by the OECD reveals that individuals who have made significant income gains often report their economic situation to be worse than much poorer rural individuals who have not achieved any income gains (Graham, 2018[11]). Individual countries have also established their own frameworks and indicators to reflect on well-being, such as those listed in Table 3.2. New Zealand has taken this a step further by seeking ways to improve quality of life for citizens through its Wellbeing Budget. The budget prioritises mental health, child well-being and Indigenous aspirations alongside more traditional economic growth goals.

Table 3.2. Selected national well-being measurement initiatives and indicator sets

Country	Measurement initiative	Leading agency	Description
Austria	How's Austria	Statistics Austria	Since 2002, Statistics Austria reports on 30 indicators focused on 3 dimensions: material wealth, quality of life and environmental sustainability.
Israel	Well-being, Sustainability and National Resilience Indicators	Central Bureau of Statistics	Since 2015, the government publishes a set of indicators focused on the following domains: quality of employment, personal security, health, housing and infrastructure, education, higher education and skills, personal and social well-being, environment, civic engagement and governance, and material standard of living.
Slovenia	Indicators of Well-Being in Slovenia	Institute of Macroeconomic Analysis and Development	Since 2015, a consortium of four institutions updates indicators on a yearly basis. These indicators are presented in three categories: material, social and environmental well-being.
Wales	Well-being of Wales	Welsh Government's Chief Statistician	Since 2015, the Well-being of Future Generations (Wales) Act is aimed at incorporating social, economic, environmental and cultural well-being into policy making. The act recognises 7 well-being goals and 46 indicators.

Source: Exton, C. and M. Shinwell (2018[12]), "Policy use of well-being metrics: Describing countries' experiences", https://doi.org/10.1787/d98 eb8ed-en (accessed on 22 July 2019).

The increased prioritisation on well-being has important implications for rural regions. Low-density economies may struggle to compete on GDP but often outpace their urban counterparts in certain quality of life measures. For example, surveys in Poland reveal life satisfaction among rural dwellers (80.6%) is higher than the national average (78.4%) (OECD, 2018[3]). With a significant portion of rural population, policies in these places can make a significant impact on national growth and well-being. Some advantages of rural communities might include greater personal security, better natural environment, more social capital and greater food security (De Muro, Degli Studi and Tre, 2010[13]). In addition to providing opportunities for firms, such advantages can attract people to live in rural regions. As well-being becomes a greater topic of concern in OECD countries, policy makers can no longer focus on competitiveness policies. Competition is a necessary aspect of development but alone is an insufficient condition. Supporting lagging regions with subsidies or investments will not address all dimensions of well-being. For these reasons, rural places need multi-dimensional policies that account for the economic, social and environmental agenda.

Box 3.1. OECD well-being framework

The OECD well-being framework provides a lens through which to consider current and future well-being through measures of quality of life, material conditions and sustainability (Figure 3.1). The first two measures – quality of life and material conditions – provide a comparison of current well-being between regions. Quality of life considers the role of health, education, environmental quality amongst other factors. The framework uses primarily objective indicators, such as voter turnout to measure civic engagement, while also including an indicator of subjective well-being through life satisfaction surveys (OECD, 2011[14]). Material conditions include measures of income and wealth, jobs and earnings, and housing. These measures rely on indicators such as disposable income, net wealth and long-term unemployment rate. Finally, future well-being represents the stock of natural, economic, human and social capital available to provide lasting well-being to future generations.

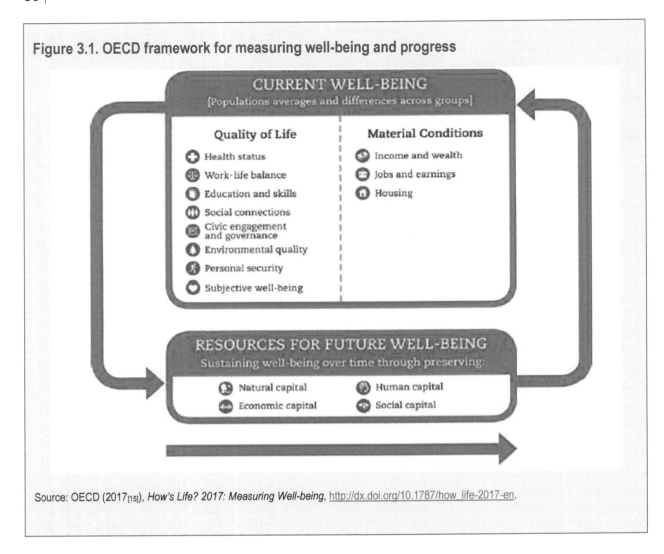

Figure 3.1. OECD framework for measuring well-being and progress

Source: OECD (2017[15]), *How's Life? 2017: Measuring Well-being*, http://dx.doi.org/10.1787/how_life-2017-en.

Rural-urban linkages

Rural and urban are more connected than ever, thanks to improved Internet accessibility and changing commuting patterns. Rural places are becoming increasingly integrated into the global economy as rural regions close to cities can participate actively in the local labour force and workers in more remote areas can participate online. The changes in connectivity have strong implications for urban areas, whose agglomeration economies see increased employment and wages, and for rural ones, where the least mobile are subject to declining wages and increased costs of living (Bosworth and Venhorst, 2017[16]). Increased urbanisation is largely seen as a positive force for economic growth and productivity on a national scale but has more mixed effects on both the economy and well-being at the local level.

The positive economic impacts of cities are not constrained by city limits. Firms and workers in rural regions close to cities can benefit from the same agglomeration benefits urban areas enjoy. Rural linkages to cities are not limited to transport connections. Some of the other benefits include the movement of people and businesses from central locations to commuting zones, looking for cheaper land cost and bigger areas (Veneri, 2017[17]), providing access to a larger market, easing firm-worker matching and improving knowledge sharing (OECD, 2018[18]). Close proximity facilitates increased flows between rural and urban areas. Rural regions close to a functioning metropolitan area can better take advantage of a city's public services or open up green spaces to urban dwellers than can rural remote regions. However, many linkages depend more on the level of embeddedness with a city rather than simply physical proximity. It includes linkages through corporate relationships, market pervasion and communication networks (Meijers and Burger, 2017[19]). As we have seen from the COVID-19 pandemic, areas with increased connectivity, in particular in telecommunications infrastructure, have been able to take temporary measures to adapt to public service delivery in education and health services, as well as provide opportunities for some types of service workers to telework.

Rural-urban linkages can take on many forms. The first and most obvious is through trade and exchange (Bulderberga, 2011[20]). Goods, services, finances and labour move constantly between rural and urban regions, with increasing levels of mobility as proximity increases. The second linkage is through institutions, as cities are more likely to host formal institutions that affect issues of governance and service delivery in rural regions. Depending on proximity, rural and urban regions may also be linked through the environment or a shared identity. For example, cultural or ethnic groups are unlikely to be separated by administrative distinctions. The implications for increased linkages depend heavily on the nature of rural-urban relationships.

Growing rural-urban linkages indicates a need to integrate rural and urban policies. Although regions across the territory may have fundamentally different goals, policy makers cannot have separate agendas for cities and rural regions that are unaligned. Implementing rural policy will require collaboration with policy makers working on rural issues, either through explicit rural-urban partnerships or through more deliberate multi-level governance or horizontal co-ordination. Chapter 4 will discuss the different strategies that OECD countries are attempting to strengthen and build on rural-urban linkages.

Technology and digitalisation

Technological change and digitalisation are bringing new challenges and opportunities for the sustainable development of rural economies (Chapter 5). The recent pandemic of coronavirus has placed high on the policy agenda the need to provide enabling conditions (infrastructure) and training for workers of all regions to work digitally (or remotely) and transition to high-value-added service activities. This crisis has also highlighted the need to further embrace digital solutions to provide public services including health and education. The overall impact of technological change on rural development will very much depend on the capacity of rural regions and policies to face changes.

On the one hand, technological change is creating opportunities to make rural economies more productive while simultaneously improving quality of life. If well-prepared, technological change can spark faster rates of economic growth and improved well-being in rural communities (Freshwater and Wojan, 2014[21]). Technology can provide improved health and education outcomes by bringing remote schooling or telemedicine to areas outside large cities as well as help rural dwellers access information about different service providers, improving the quality of supply. Other new technologies, such as 3D printing or augmented reality and virtual reality, can improve access to goods and services that would otherwise be expensive or difficult to obtain for low-density economies. Improvements in technology allow firms in rural economies to participate in international markets, keep up with global trends, find new sources of financing and recruit skilled workers (see Chapter 5). The COVID-19 pandemic also confirmed that, without access to the same technologies and services available cities, rural economies will suffer disproportionately in terms of jobs and economic activities.

While technology has the ability to improve living standards, it also carries a risk of major job reallocation. As Chapter 5 will depict, rural economies might face the higher risk of job displacement as many of these economies have a lower share of jobs in services and a higher share in manufacturing, which entails a higher share of repetitive tasks. At the same time, a single employer or industry is more likely to dominate in a rural setting, making it more difficult for displaced workers to find new opportunities as industries automate. Increased automation requires policies that carefully balance the dual challenges of high unemployment and low productivity often at play in rural economies in order to ensure technology is improving well-being overall.

The ability of digitalisation to simultaneously improve productivity and opportunities relies heavily on access to infrastructure like broadband Internet and appropriate education services. This was particularly relevant during the recent COVID-19 pandemic. Benefitting from technology not only requires good ICT infrastructure but also fast and affordable broadband connections (see Chapter 5). Providing this type of infrastructure can be challenging for some rural places, in particular remote places where low population density and large land extensions make it harder to balance cost and benefits of broadband investments (Chapter 5). In fact, Most OECD rural regions have slower Internet speed connections than urban areas (Chapter 2). OECD countries are addressing challenges in broadband access in rural regions through a variety of policy initiatives (Table 3.3). In the recent COVID-19 pandemic, access to broadband Internet was a major determinate for individuals to keep jobs, and firms to find emergency methods to temporarily adapt business models to keep firms afloat. Importantly, while digital infrastructure may help firms and (some) individuals transition to the changing occupational and sector structure of rural economies, without adequate worker upskilling and educational services, there is a disproportionately larger increased risk of long-term unemployment for workers displaced by technological advances. Continuous education and work-study arrangements are important policy levers to support the transition phase for workers.

Table 3.3. Improving broadband access and uptake

Examples of challenges and solutions from OECD countries

Challenge	Policy solution	Example
Costs exceed likely commercial returns	Universal service frameworks	Broadband Internet carriers in Canada are required to contribute towards a Universal Service Fund to support service expansion in remote regions.
Low speeds and poor quality	Minimum speed guarantees	In Australia, the country's National Broadband Network satellites provide a baseline speed of 12 Mbps across the entire country.
Lack of incentive to new market entry	Competitive tenders	Portugal launched five competitive tenders in 2009. Successful operators were required to ensure a minimum speed of 40 Mbps for 50% of the population.
Insufficient competition	Open access policies	Mexico's Red Compartida project is the OECD's first wholesale-only national wireless network.
Providers not meeting local policy objectives	Municipal networks	In Sweden, the "village fibre" approach relies on community involvement to plan, build and operate local fibre networks.
High deployment costs	Infrastructure sharing	Fibre installation projects exist on gas infrastructure in Germany and aerial power lines in Latvia, as well as along railways, roads, tunnels and bridges in other OECD countries.
Limited choice and low bandwidth	Improvement of affordability	The EU's WiFi4EU initiative, introduced in 2018, plans to use voucher schemes to promote access.
Lack of digital literacy	Training programmes	In Argentina, the Digital Country programme aims to create 300 digital inclusion centres for citizens and municipal employees and install Wi-Fi in public parks, schools and other public spaces throughout the country.

Source: OECD (2018[22]), "Bridging the rural digital divide ", https://doi.org/10.1787/852bd3b9-en (accessed on 13 May 2020).

Demographic change

As depicted in Chapter 2, rural places face increasing pressures from demographic changes. Economies of agglomeration attract firms and people to densely populated areas due to lower transportation costs, proximity to markets and a greater variety and match of supply and demand for labour. In all but three OECD countries, population growth occurs much faster in metropolitan areas than in rural regions, with one-third of rural regions experiencing population decline during the last two decades. Within rural regions, remote regions experienced the fastest population growth, driven by higher fertility rates. Outmigration of youth to pursue high degree studies or looking for new economic opportunities is one of the drivers behind this trend. A shrinking share of the younger population creates labour market shortage, reduces rates of entrepreneurship and affects local cultural life, weakening the mechanisms to integrate new inhabitants and migrants to the local community.

Coupled with outmigration, rapid population ageing accelerates the shrinking of the workforce in rural regions. In all except one OECD country, the elderly dependency ratio is much higher in rural regions than in metropolitan regions. This phenomenon hampers attractiveness of the rural business environment to meet labour demands of extent and new firms. An ageing and declining population also adds pressure on the government capacity to deliver quality public services. These challenges require co-ordinated strategies to provide economic opportunities and education alternatives to retain the young population, attract migrants and promote labour mobility.

Demographic changes drive a shift in the skill and gender of workers

Health service workers will become especially valuable in rural regions as the rising old-age dependency ratio increases demand for long-term care. A demography with a high share of elderly populations will increase demand for labour-intensive occupations, including in-person care, transportation, and other services (Autor, 2019[23]). The demand for long-term care workers is expected to double by 2050, providing an opportunity for rural regions to take the lead in improving care. A shrinking workforce population alongside an increasing share of the elderly population requires policy interventions to mitigate growth in long-term care spending and increase the supply of care (OECD, 2011[24]). Since the elderly dependency ratio is highest amongst remote rural regions in the majority of OECD countries, policy makers in these regions should aim to improve productivity and well-being for care workers.

Women have increased their participation in the economy of all types of rural regions driven by the tertiarisation of the economy. The female employment rate increased in all rural regions types after the crisis, while the male employment rate has only recovered to pre-crisis levels in regions with access to cities. In remote rural regions and regions with or near a small/medium city, the male employment rate is 5% below 2007 levels. This trend has followed an increase in service activities in rural regions and a higher level of education of women (Chapter 2). Policies adapted to women in terms of training and entrepreneurship are increasingly needed. In contrast, reskilling the male workforce is essential to compensate for the negative effect of decreasing shares of manufacturing activities and associated low-skilled employment in rural regions.

The integration of migrants is acknowledged as a mechanism for rural communities to face a natural decline in the working-age population. Migrants tend to be younger than native populations in some rural regions (OECD, 2019[8]). An inflow of young working-age people can mitigate population ageing and offer opportunities to increase economic vibrancy and diversity while balancing out the demand for public and private service provision. Further, areas outside cities can offer low housing prices and short administrative pathways, which tend to be challenges for large cities in the integration of migrants (OECD, 2018[25]). At the same time, reaping these benefits also comes with further involvement of migrants in the local community. It involves investing in language training, education and administrative support. Those actions also need to address the social challenges of a sudden high influx of new arrivals in small communities, including social tension with local excluded populations due to the special support to non-natives (OECD, 2018[25]).

Service delivery policies have gained relevance in the policy agenda as policy makers recognise the need to support well-being in rural areas. A study of 19 rural communities in Canada revealed a trend towards reductions in health, education, protection, government, business and recreation services, negatively impacting quality of life and limiting the ability of these places to attract economic development (Halseth and Ryser, 2006[26]). In the UK., a qualitative review of services particularly affected by rurality showed significantly higher costs for transportation, waste collection and disposal, social care, libraries, regulatory services, economic development and tourism, amongst other services (Ranasinghe, 2014[27]). The decline in the availability of services alongside the additional costs requires different delivery models in lower-density areas.

Supporting labour mobility is not the solution for all rural places

Many city-focused policy solutions focus on mobility as a way to solve economic problems in rural places. Even as congestion and rental costs increase drastically in large urban centres, economists laud urbanisation as the way to increase productivity. In its latest *Transition Report*, the European Bank for Reconstruction and Development recommends, "relocation opportunities for those left behind" as a policy solution for declining rural regions (EBRD, 2018[28]). Such recommendations reflect a belief that policies should target left-behind people rather than left-behind places, preferring to relocate individuals to productive places rather than investing in the declining ones. Some urban economists tend to disapprove subsidies that target transportation in low-density areas or construction in declining regions, as these interventions might be misguided and lack impact (Glaeser and Gottlieb, 2008[29]).

However, labour mobility is not a solution for many demographic groups. Suggestions that individuals facing labour market transitions simply move to a city are not feasible and, for many, do not promote well-being. Some researchers have credited insensitive policy proposals to invest only in already prosperous places with the rise of populism in the "places that do not matter" (Rodríguez-Pose, 2018[30]). For example, college education is associated with increased mobility (Malamud and Wozniak, 2012[31]), yet rural workers are less likely to be college-educated (Echazarra and Radinger, 2019[32]). At the same time, as age correlates negatively with mobility, rural communities with high elderly shares will struggle to promote policies to support commuting of older workers to other markets when the local labour market becomes unfavourable. Place-based policies that recognise the value of even those regions with historically low growth can better account for the limits to labour mobility in recent years, particularly amongst older and low-skilled workers.

Recent research suggests place-based policies can be effective if well-designed. Using place-based identifiers, such as location rather than people-based identifiers may be especially effective when designing certain types of interventions (i.e. social insurance) (Yagan et al., 2014[33]). Any policy that induces movement to the target area risk limiting the intervention's effect on the target population (Kline and Moretti, 2014[34]). If mobility increases, the additional welfare benefits to the movers lead to declines in welfare for receiver residents who may face increased housing costs and a reduced capacity for public services. Where concerns about increased mobility to declining areas exist, place-based policies may not be effective. However, where labour mobility is limited, place-based policies are especially desirable to provide targeted interventions and investments to benefit the population in a specific region.

Demographic changes have important implications for rural policy making. First, population ageing and the shrinking population indicate a need for greater focus on service delivery for rural dwellers. The needs of rural populations are changing, necessitating a greater focus on issues of healthcare, transportation and digital connectivity. Second, demographic changes require investment in human capital. With overall fewer people living in rural regions, firms require highly productive workers in order to maintain current levels of output and compete in external markets. Finally, policy makers need to address demographic changes while accounting for the limits to labour mobility (see next section for detailed policy recommendations). Place-based policies that support populations who wish to remain in low-density areas, rather than pushing for movement where the appropriate conditions may not exist, may provide the best tools to support current and future development. While interventions in low-density areas are often likely to be more expensive per head than in higher density ones, this may be the only way to ensure adequate opportunities for rural dwellers.

Climate change and the need to transition to a low-carbon economy

Signed in 2016, the Paris Agreement introduced a long-term goal to limit the increase in global average temperature to well below 2°C above pre-industrial levels. As a result, countries are seeking to develop long-term, zero- and low-emissions development strategies (OECD, 2019[35]). A number of OECD countries, including France, Germany, Norway, Portugal and The United Kingdom , amongst others, have pledged to reach net low-carbon emissions by 2050 or earlier (Committee on Climate Change, 2019[36]; Darby, 2019[37]). The European Commission's Green Deal Communication proposes reaching carbon neutrality across the EU by 2050. Increasingly, governments recognise climate action must be taken to ensure well-being, equity and long-term prospects for future generations. Although current infrastructure investment and financial flows are insufficient and poorly aligned to climate goals, a growing sense of urgency is driving countries to accelerate the transition. Yet, as policy makers strive to build more resilient cities, manage water in urban areas and strengthen spatial planning, they must not forget rural regions.

The natural resource base of many rural economies makes them particularly vulnerable to climate change. Extreme weather events, including floods, droughts, wildfires and landslides, are especially damaging and even dangerous for rural industries like agriculture, mining or forestry. Climate change will also disrupt recreational activities like hunting, fishing, and winter sports and, increasingly, forces communities to relocate because of increasing sea levels or melting permafrost soil. In addition, it is a threat to sustainable food production, as changes in temperature, rainfall and extreme weather events negatively affect crop yields and profitability. Rural communities will need help in assessing and managing these costs, risks and vulnerabilities, prioritising and co-ordinating projects, and funding and allocating resources (U.S. Global Change Research Program, 2014[38]). As a result, rural regions are critical stakeholders in global, national and regional initiatives to adapt to and mitigate climate change.

Policy efforts to transition to a low-carbon economy disproportionately affect rural regions. Carbon-intensive activities such as agriculture, mining and energy play an important role in rural economies across the OECD. Decarbonisation legislation that puts a price on carbon and aims at phasing out certain extractive industries presents a challenge to regions where firms operating in these sectors count for a large share of employment and are facing higher transport costs (Botta, 2018[39]). Further, rural economies are less resilient than urban economies in responding to these structural adjustment pressures because their economies are less diverse with lower levels of human capital. This can result in discontent and blockages to building domestic and international consensus about climate change policies. Policy makers in all countries must consider not only the sectoral but also the local impacts, taking account of the needs of the communities most severely affected by climate change mitigation and adaptation efforts, and ensuring a just transition.

Rural well-being: A geography of opportunities

Structural changes in OECD economies necessitate changing policy responses. The OECD rural development framework provides a lens through which to evaluate effective policies in light of these changes. Earlier OECD country frameworks on rural development focused on sectoral support (primarily agriculture) and subsidies to promote rural development. The New Rural Paradigm, endorsed in 2006 by OECD member countries, proposed a conceptual framework that positioned rural policy as an investment strategy to foster competitiveness in rural territories. This approach represented a radical departure from the typical subsidy programmes of the past aimed at specific sectors. The Rural Well-being Policy Framework is an extension and a refinement of this paradigm. The new framework focuses more on the mechanisms for implementation and makes well-being a leading objective.

Evolving rural development framework

The Rural Well-being Policy Framework is a continuation of the New Rural Paradigm. The OECD framework has existed for more than 40 years but has gone through significant changes. The New Rural Paradigm introduced what was at the time a bold claim – rural is not synonymous with agriculture, nor is it indicative of economic decline. This framework guaranteed adequate attention to rural issues beyond large subsidies to agriculture by seeking to empower local communities and governments.

Table 3.4. Rural Well-being: Geography of Opportunities

	Old paradigm	New Rural Paradigm (2006)	Rural Well-being: Geography of Opportunities
Objectives	Equalisation	Competitiveness	Well-being considering multiple dimensions of: i) the economy, ii) society and iii) the environment
Policy focus	Support for a single dominant resource sector	Support for multiple sectors based on their competitiveness	Low-density economies differentiated by type of rural area
Tools	Subsidies for firms	Investments in qualified firms and communities	Integrated rural development approach – spectrum of support to the public sector, firms and third sector
Key actors and stakeholders	Farm organisations and national governments	All levels of government and all relevant departments plus local stakeholders	Involvement of: i) public sector – multi-level governance, ii) private sector – for-profit firms and social enterprise, and iii) third sector – non-governmental organisations and civil society
Policy approach	Uniformly applied top-down policy	Bottom-up policy, local strategies	Integrated approach with multiple policy domains
Rural definition	Not urban	Rural as a variety of distinct types of place	Three types of rural: i) within a functional urban area (FUA), ii) close to an FUA, and iii) far from an FUA

The New Rural Paradigm was the first attempt to provide a policy roadmap that took into account the specific challenges facing rural regions. The New Rural Paradigm called for policies that could focus on places instead of sectors and investments in place of subsidies. The primary objective of the New Rural Paradigm, reflecting a shift in policies happening across OECD countries, was to increase competitiveness. Policy makers were attempting to do this by valorising local assets and exploiting unused resources. In the EU, the LEADER programme has helped rural regions capitalise on assets and resources by developing a network of local food producers in Sweden, exploiting 80 000 hectares of chestnut trees in France, and supporting cultural initiatives in Greece. The new paradigm targeted key sectors in rural economies (such as tourism, manufacturing or the ICT industry) with investments. By calling on action at all levels of government and stakeholders from the public, private and non-profit sectors, the new paradigm brought rural needs to the forefront and highlighted policies already making an impact.

The *Rural Well-being: A Geography of Opportunities* policy framework takes into account several important changes in rural development. Rural regions have evolved into more diverse and complex socio-economic systems than initially understood. Although certain major themes are common, such as ageing populations or the presence of nature-based industries, the new framework accounts for a greater degree of diversity between rural regions. Improved data and analysis have been especially crucial in providing a greater understanding of rural regions and moving away from the presumption that all rural regions are alike. The new framework also moves beyond focusing on industry sectors and growth to a broader perception of what constitutes well-being. Aside from economic aspects, it includes social and environmental dimensions as well. Finally, the updated framework recognises the strong interdependencies between different stakeholders and the need for partnerships between the government, the private sector and civil society to successfully implement policies.

Rural Well-being: A Geography of Opportunities shifts from a one-dimensional to a three-dimensional view of rural policies:

- **Three types of rural** – From a simple rural dichotomy to rural places inside FUA, close to cities and remote (and interactions between them and cities).
- **Three objectives** – The shift beyond just economic objectives to encompass social and environmental issues.
- **Three different stakeholders** – From the government acting alone to working with the private sector and civil society.

Three distinct types of rural areas

Rural places require their own definitions and categories beyond simply "non-urban". Defining rural regions by what they are not, rather than by what they are, creates challenges to policy design. Not all successful urban policy strategies have the potential to succeed in rural places and not all rural places require the same prescriptions. As the country profiles demonstrate, some OECD countries still do not have a concrete rural definition. For example, both Japan and Switzerland leave "rural" to encompass all that is not urban. Most countries define "rural" based on the size of the population or level of population density.

The OECD's new rural typology recognises the complexity of rural areas. To define rural, the OECD now looks at three layers of characteristics: the degree of linkages to cities, proximity to metropolitan regions and level of settlement. The first layer of the typology distinguishes between rural regions embedded within a metropolitan region and those resting outside. The second layer divides rural territories into those that are near or remote from a metropolitan region. The third layer further subdivides remote rural regions into uniformly settled or sparsely settled regions. A nuanced typology is necessary to understand the challenges and strengths of different regions as well as how global trends affect growth and well-being in distinct rural regions.

The three types of rural areas are structurally different. In the first two, there are strong interactions with urban areas but these interactions take different forms, whereas in remote rural regions the interactions are much weaker. All three types of regions face different challenges and opportunities (Table 3.5). Understanding these within each of the three categories leads to the possibility for shared action and more effectively targeted policy responses.

- For rural places within the commuting zone of an FUA, development is intimately linked to that of the core city. The main challenges facing them are service delivery, as services concentrate in the core area; the matching of skills to the requirements of the labour market; and managing land use policy brought on by increasing pressures of urban expansion.
- Rural places that are close to FUAs often enjoy a good industrial mix, which makes their local economies more resilient. They are also frequently able to attract new residents. The economic and social diversity of rural places that are close to an FUA can pose challenges such as competition for land and landscape in the case of economic activities, and different needs and visions between old and new residents. Conflicts over development patterns can occur between these regions and the nearby FUA.
- For remote rural places with a relatively dense settlement pattern, primary activities play a relevant role in the regional economy. Growth comes from building upon areas of absolute and comparative advantage, improving connectivity to export markets, matching skills to areas of comparative advantage and improving the provision of essential services. A strong resource base can result in high levels of income and productivity, but it can also result in cyclical (boom-bust) economies.

Table 3.5. Challenges by type of rural region

Type of region	Challenges	Opportunities
Rural inside a functional urban area (FUA)	• Loss of control over the future • Activities concentrate in the urban core • Managing land value pressures • Matching of skills	• More stable future • Potential to capture urban benefits while avoiding the negatives
Rural outside but in close proximity to an FUA	• Conflicts between new residents and locals • Avoiding sprawl • Competition for land and landscape	• Potential to attract high-income households seeking a high quality of life • Relatively easy access to advanced services and urban culture • Good access to transport
Rural remote	• Highly specialised economies subject to booms and busts • Limited connectivity and large distances between settlements • High per capita costs of services	• Absolute advantage in the production of natural resource-based outputs • Attractive for firms that need access to an urban area but not on a daily basis • Can offer unique environments that can be attractive to firms and individuals

Source: OECD (2016[7]), *OECD Regional Outlook 2016: Productive Regions for Inclusive Societies*, https://dx.doi.org/10.1787/9789264260245-en.

Understanding the growth dynamics of rural economies, such as distance to markets, the role of the tradeable sector and absolute advantages, helps to elevate burdens on rural regions that hinder growth. In the EU, for example, grant and matching requirements for investment may be too high for small businesses in low-density economies (OECD, 2019[40]). Rural regions with a smaller population and firm sizes are often ineligible for funding and investment opportunities because of policies with such minimum grant request requirements. SMEs in remote and rural regions face uneven access to finance (OECD, 2019[4]). Overcoming funding gaps will improve innovation and productivity for small firms in rural regions, thereby encouraging economic growth and resiliency throughout the market cycle.

Place-based policies offer the opportunity for policy makers to target geographic areas based on unique characteristics and address the geospatial heterogeneities of global crises. Governments often use explicit place-based programmes to encourage economic development in lagging regions (Kline and Moretti, 2014[34]). Place-based policies offer benefits to rural regions that may be otherwise disadvantaged due to a number of market imperfections: the private sector providing insufficient public goods, a lack of agglomeration or monopsony power in the labour market. In the United States, policy makers introduced one of the largest place-based policies to serve rural communities during the Great Depression (Kline et al., 2013[41]). The Tennessee Valley Authority provided public infrastructure investment to help modernise primarily rural, agricultural regions in seven states. More recently, the European Commission's "Territorial Agenda 2020" points to a place-based approach as a way to serve heterogeneous regions and rural communities (EC, 2015[42]). In places where mobility is limited, effective policies can mitigate many of the challenges inherent in living in distressed areas.

All policies have spatial consequences. Sectoral policies alone are insufficient because they affect different places differently. Based on a single, all-encompassing view of "rural", many of the traditional policy approaches fail to recognise the different typologies of rural regions as well as the importance of a rural-urban continuum in determining access to opportunities. For example, rural policies acknowledging only agriculture are likely to ignore the many rural regions where agriculture is not the dominant sector or employer. Instead, policy design must take place with specific places in mind, considering for each the assets and leading industries, limiting labour mobility and linkages to cities that make that place unique.

Three objectives

The policy focus must evolve away from short-term and sectoral support towards helping to build conditions favourable for the long-term growth of low-density economies. The fundamental economic structure of a low-density economy and its growth opportunities follow a considerably different logic than is the case in urbanised regions. Recognition that the rural economy is fundamentally different leads to the need for a new set of policy prescriptions that reflect differences in growth opportunities and constraints. These should focus on investing in human capital, infrastructure and innovation, which are enabling factors for growth, rather than short-term responses that seek to protect existing economic activities.

The Rural Well-being Policy Framework recognises that economic growth and reducing inequalities are no longer competing policy objectives. Inequality has a negative impact on growth in places with lack of access to opportunity (Aiyar and Ebeke, 2019[43]). Effective policies will address both concurrently by acknowledging the economic, social and environmental dimensions of well-being. Any approach to measuring one aspect of well-being will invariably affect the others, so policy solutions must consider both in tandem. For example, improving access to education may positively impact health outcomes and per capita incomes in addition to the overall productivity of labour. However, barriers to social mobility today run the risk of widening well-being gaps tomorrow (OECD, 2017[15]). Reducing inequalities of all kinds (economic, social and in access to opportunities) is a prerequisite to maintaining high levels of well-being across OECD countries and regions.

Growing concerns about regional inequality demand a multi-dimensional approach to well-being. OECD country surveys indicate national rural policies apply different levels of consideration for economic, social and environmental dimensions of well-being, but none are completely ignored. In large part, no dimension can be overlooked as they are so interconnected. Economic development largely drives social and environmental goals. At the same time, inclusive growth and productivity determine to what degree economic development is possible. While most national rural policies indicate economic well-being as a priority dimension (see Chapter 5), policy makers recognise achievements in this dimension require work in the others. The following sections explore the role of rural policy in attaining economic, social and environmental well-being.

The Rural Well-being Policy Framework is a people-centred approach that moves beyond focusing on industry sectors. It focuses on delivering a level of well-being to rural dwellers that is comparable to what is attainable in urban areas, even though different aspects may be emphasised. In general, quality of life has: i) economic dimensions, where household income hinges on employment in firms that are productive and competitive; ii) social dimensions whereby households have access to a broad set of services and local society is cohesive and supportive; and iii) a local environment that provides a pleasant place to live. The balance among these elements may vary considerably across rural. This broader well-being agenda does not abandon the objective to improve rural competitiveness; rather it recognises that competitiveness is a necessary, but not a sufficient, condition for well-being.

Three different stakeholders

Effective rural policies involve the engagement of a broad array of actors and multi-level governance mechanisms. Rural development extends across a wide range of policy areas and involves a variety of actors, making complete separation of policy responsibilities and outcomes difficult. A pooling of resources and capabilities across entities creates the ability to collectively accomplish what no individual actor can achieve independently. This demands the collaboration and engagement of government at multiple levels, and involvement of the private sector and third sector. Building capacity underpins the implementation of rural policy. Long-term capacity building makes rural communities more engaged in processes of development and more resilient to shocks.

Rural policies should focus on integrated investments and delivering services and programmes that are adapted to and meet the needs of rural communities. There is strong pressure to make better use of investments and more efficiently deliver services in rural places. Integrated investments have the potential to reap the benefits of complementarities when they are adapted to the needs of different types of rural areas. For that, different sectoral policies need to be co-ordinated and mutually reinforcing, and the mix between them should be rebalanced to meet differing local needs. Moreover, policy interventions that target administrative boundaries in silos can miss the strong synergies that are present between rural and urban areas. Better co-ordination between stakeholders and levels of government can help to integrate policies, for instance using rural and urban linkages.

The Rural Well-being Policy Framework provides tools to governments to better engage with stakeholders, promote rural-urban partnerships and embrace multi-level governance. It recognises that rural people and businesses know best about their own needs, suggests the use of new technologies to facilitate participation and underlines the needs for meaningful engagement. Further, it acknowledges urban regions as key partners in increasing rural well-being and highlights ways for effective partnerships and collaboration between policy makers from different levels of government.

Putting well-being at the heart in rural policy development

The analysis of contemporary rural trends suggests three priority dimensions of action for OECD countries to increase well-being. The first is how to increase productivity and foster competitiveness in the context of GVCs and digitalisation. This includes implementing incentives and mechanisms that support rural regions to identify unique assets, reduce bottlenecks and invest in enabling factors. The second is how to adapt to an ageing population and address demographic pressures. Focus areas include making rural regions more attractive through the provision of high-quality services and leveraging economic opportunities associated with an ageing population. The third is supporting rural economies in the shift to a low-carbon economy. Priorities will include facilitating shifts to more sustainable forms of land use, investment in renewable energy and proactive support for regions affected by economic restructuring.

Economic dimension

Economic well-being refers to the material living conditions that determine people's consumption possibilities and their command over resources. This includes the ability of individuals to be able to consistently meet basic needs, such as food, housing, healthcare, transportation, education as well as the ability to make choices that contribute to security, satisfaction and personal fulfilment. Income and wealth enable individuals to meet their basic needs and thus help achieve overall economic well-being. Productivity gains – the efficiency with which people and capital are combined in the output of the economy – is an essential component to generate greater income and growth and translate in improvements of living standards (Bernanke, 2005[44]).

Increasing productivity as a policy goal for rural well-being

Increasing productivity has become a key policy goal to raise rural well-being. It directly affects the resources available to improve well-being, such as investments in healthcare or environmental protection (OECD, 2018[18]). Most OECD countries see rural regions as places of opportunities for economic growth and job creation. In most of these countries (70%), economic matters are the most relevant areas when it comes to rural development policies (see Chapter 5). However, policies' pro-productivity alone is not a guarantee of an increase in income and quality of life across the population as a whole (OECD, 2018[45]). Over the last two decades, increases in productivity are largely concentrated in urban regions, leaving rural places lagging behind (OECD, 2015[46]). In fact, after the financial crisis, an increase in productivity with employment losses has been more prevalent in remote regions and regions with access to a small/medium city. It could outline a greater process of automation with a slower labour reconversion into new sectors.

Box 3.2. The "sixth industrialisation" for Japanese agricultural development

In 2011 Japan's Ministry of Agriculture, Forestry and Fisheries announced the establishment of an Industry Cooperation Network, intended to accelerate the "sixth" industrialisation. This term refers to the vertical integration of primary, secondary, and tertiary industries (1 x 2 x 3=6) to achieve greater value-added in products and services and spur growth in the agricultural, forestry and fisheries industries.

The Network offers opportunities for interaction and pooling of knowledge amongst private sector, think tanks, researchers and consumers from a variety of areas such as agriculture and forestry, fisheries, manufacturing and finance. Initially, the sixth industrialisation's activities aimed at the formation of a food system with diversification of the agriculture, forestry and fisheries industries. Later activities progressively moved to creating new businesses combining the three industries. The advantage of the sixth industrialisation is that the additional value from secondary and tertiary industries bring also benefits to the primary industry. Moreover, new businesses are created by secondary and tertiary industries that move to rural regions. This expands the economic activity in rural economies including production of primary products, sources of input materials for processing, and associated services-related businesses.

Source: NAKANO (2014[47]), "The "sixth industrialization" for Japanese agricultural development", *The Ritsumeikan Economic Review*, Vol. LXIII, No. 3.

Rural regions benefit from a number of assets with the potential to boost economic growth. Forestry, mining, oil, gas, electricity production, fishing and agriculture are almost exclusively rural industries (OECD, 2018[48]). Rural dwellers and firms can benefit from diverse natural endowments, a relatively better environmental quality, lower cost of land and larger surfaces than their urban peers. Individuals in rural places own particular know-how on managing natural resources and adapting technologies to their specific environments. For instance, Indigenous Peoples benefit from traditional knowledge that is able to support better natural resource management and innovations in food production and harvesting. Combined with other assets such as land and culture, it has led to creating competitive businesses that meet the community's objectives for development and benefit the wider region (e.g. traceable and territorially differentiated food and beverage products, ecotourism and creative industries) (OECD, 2019[49]).

Access to natural resources represents another asset for many rural communities. Unlike other assets, the natural resource assets that contribute to economic development in remote rural regions cannot be created or changed through policy (OECD, 2018[18]). Strong natural resource management creates natural capital, which can both raise incomes and help rural communities invest in other productive assets that will sustain wealth over generations (Canuto and Cavallari, 2012[50]). Efforts to regulate natural resource assets to ensure future wealth and well-being, such as through sovereign wealth funds, are especially important to rural places where fewer firms and lower overall levels of growth leave communities vulnerable to global economic shocks.

Natural endowments or "first nature" assets can indeed be a source of higher productivity level in some rural regions. In OECD countries, the most productive regions are mostly those with either a thriving extractive sector, e.g. Alberta in Canada or Antofagasta in Chile, or with a capital city (OECD, 2018[18]). However, relying solely on their natural endowment make rural regions more vulnerable to external shocks. Demand for minerals can evolve over time and resources are limited. For example, traditional rural economies in Spain that rely on coal mining are now struggling to retain people and find alternative sources of income. Policies for economic diversification are thus essential to increase resilience and reduce over-reliance in a single economic sector.

Planning for mobilising new assets

Boosting productivity in rural economies also requires a special focus on SMEs. Across the OECD, SMEs account for about 60% of employment and between 50% and 60% of value-added, as the main drivers of productivity in many regions and cities (OECD, 2019[4]). As local labour markets in rural regions, particularly more remote regions, are small, there is little likelihood of a large employer (e.g. 1 500 workers) locating to these regions (Freshwater et al., 2019[51]). Most large firms in those rural economies are focused on first-stage processing of a natural resource. Therefore, SMEs are essential to add value to the local economy while attaining greater economic diversification.

Nevertheless, the potential effect of agglomeration economies on productivity levels is lower in rural economies. Lower agglomeration economies make it harder for rural economies to benefit from agglomeration economies stemming from greater competition, deeper labour markets (better matching of workers to firms), faster spread of ideas and a more diverse intellectual and entrepreneurial environment. In fact, the vast majority of firms in rural regions are SMEs (employment of less than 250) and this population is highly skewed towards micro enterprises (which employ less than 10 people) (Freshwater et al., 2019[51]). Further, demographic trends represent an additional challenge for rural economies to close productivity gaps with urban areas. Rural regions have experienced the outmigration of talented young people looking for opportunities in high dense areas (Chapter 2).

To mobilise their assets and overcome productivity generation challenges, rural regions need to enhance the links with urban areas and further increase their added value in tradeable activities: both proximity to cities and participation in the tradeable sector can be key drivers of productivity and growth for rural economies if policy makers correctly identify and employ these assets:

- **Better links with cities lead to higher rates of GDP and population growth**. Rural regions near large cities have experienced higher productivity growth than the more remote ones (Chapter 2). This advantage is mainly explained by benefits from the proximity to agglomeration economies, including innovation spill-overs and a greater movement of workers and ideas. These rural regions can access to a larger variety of goods and services from urban centres.

- **Tradeable activities offer the opportunity for rural areas to overcome small market size**. These activities in rural economies are often the export of a high-value natural resource, which in some cases is produced by a large branch plant but in many others, originates from SMEs (Freshwater et al., 2019[51]). Rural regions benefit from participation in the tradeable sector because it provides a larger market for their goods and services. While increased exposure to international markets presents a risk for firms in tradeable sectors, the wider reach ensures growth and success is not limited to the local market (OECD, 2018[18]). A study in France revealed jobs in the tradeable sector make more significant productivity gains alongside faster wage increases than jobs in the non-tradeable sector (Frocrain and Giraud, 2017[52]).

The relevance of tradeable activities for the rural economy

The tradeable sector could be an important source of growth for rural regions. High value-added tradeable goods and services expand the links with cities, improve productivity in rural firms and help them access global markets. Many rural regions rely on tradeable activities (agriculture, manufacturing) to attain economies of scale and higher levels of income. In the post-crisis period, manufacturing growth – a key element of the tradeable sector (OECD, 2018[18]) – contributed to half of GVA in regions with access to a small/medium city, a higher share than in any other region.

The tradeable sector can spur transition toward high value-added services activities. Traditional tradeable activities in rural economies such as manufacturing, agriculture and extractive industries require a range of services to function and be sustainable. The embedded services in the production process represent a great share of the value-added of the tradeable sector. For instance, the service sector is the one with the largest backward linkages in mining activities (OECD, 2019[53]). Services represent, on average, 23% of the value-added of exports from the mining sector (based on a sample of 65 countries included in the 2018 version of the OECD Trade in Value Added (TiVA) dataset (OECD, forthcoming[54]). These services include geological services such as: surveying and sample analysis; engineering services (feasibility studies and mining design); construction services for roads, mine sites and mining camps; drilling services at both exploratory and construction phases, among others (Outokumpu). These activities offer the scope to create new jobs and new income opportunities for the local and national economy.

The tradeable sector can trigger innovation based on its exposure to global competition. Globalisation and declining transport costs has led to delocalisation of production, where different areas can contribute towards the development of a final product. Rural economies specialised in these activities have then faced fiercer competition from emerging economies. Such competition along with a greater flow of information and ideas contributes to innovation (Chapter 5). Further, participation in GVCs opens up opportunities for firms to access foreign knowledge and technology and share practices with other markets.

Rural regions in GVCs

Engagement in GVCs enhances productivity due to the efficiency-enhancing impacts of international competition and the benefits of specialisation and economies of scale (OECD, 2013[55]). It also facilitates the diffusion of knowledge spill-overs from suppliers or foreign direct investment (FDI). However, not all steps in the production chain achieve high levels of value-added. The Smile Curve, a concept proposed by Stan Shih in 1992 (Shih, 1992[56]), depicts which aspects of the value chain generate high levels of value-added (Figure 3.2). The model shows that early-stage activities, such as research and development, and late-stage activities, including marketing and sales, generate the most value-added while the manufacturing process generates the least. For this reason, economies that seek to "catch up" must engage in more knowledge-intensive and creative activities if participation in GVCs is going to lead to higher productivity and economic growth.

GVCs are not a one-size-fits-all solution to increase economic well-being. Research has shown that participation in GVCs can sometimes but not always lead to higher-paying jobs, more bargaining power or overall improvement in well-being for workers (Barrientos, 2014[57]). This can be the case of some of the regions, mainly those with access to a small/medium city, that have experienced productivity gains and employment loses, suffering by a decrease in the employment share of manufacturing. Rural regions can benefit from hosting manufacturing process or low value-added activities in a GVC by increasing the ratio of domestic value-added to these exports.

Figure 3.2. The "Smile Curve"

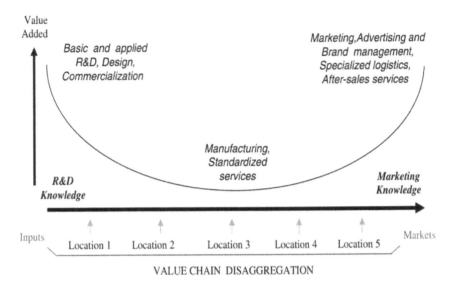

Source: Mudambi, R. (2008[58]), "Location, control and innovation in knowledge-intensive industries", http://dx.doi.org/10.1093/jeg/lbn024.

Policies to increase rural productivity

Rural regions must seek alternatives to overcome their challenges and unleash opportunities to boost productivity and attain sustainable development for people and business. Key policies for this include: i) adding value to tradeable sectors; ii) internationalising SMEs; iii) retaining value locally; and iv) strengthening rural skills (Figure 3.3).

Figure 3.3. Policy strategies to boost productivity in rural places

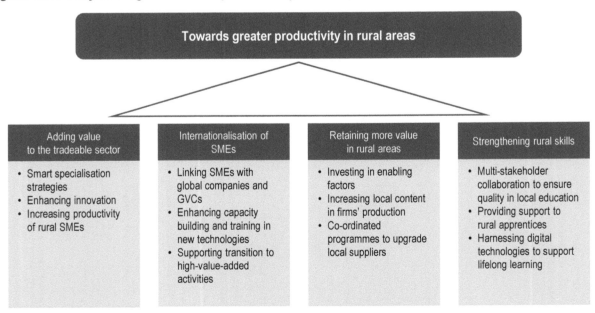

Adding value to the tradeable sector

A main challenge to ensure sustainable development in rural economies is to increase productivity in tradeable activities. These activities often depend on unique assets and resources existent in each type of rural area. Rural places close to cities can more easily leverage linkages with cities. Firms that are able to specialise within the tradeable sector can extend their network by forming linkages with nearby cities along with their participation in international markets through GVCs. In contrast, remote rural places must look to global trade for growth opportunities. Increasing the value-added of tradeable activities in rural economies requires a combination of policies including smart specialisation strategies, increasing innovation and productivity of rural SMEs as well as upskilling the labour force.

Smart specialisation strategies and economic diversification

Smart specialisation is one way for rural economies to become more competitive on international markets and aims to identify local assets in order to increase competition on international markets. It is a process of "entrepreneurial discovery" whereby market forces and the private sector discover and produce information about new activities, while the government assesses the outcomes and empowers the actors most capable of realising the potential. This strategy aims to identify the regional strengths in the form of activities – rather than sectors per se – by conducting an exploratory approach in which public decision-makers listen to market signals using a range of assessment tools (e.g. SWOT analysis, surveys) and mechanisms such as public-private partnerships, technology foresight and road mapping.

Smart specialisation within the tradeable sector is strategic for rural economies. Low-density economies cannot rely on either the services sector or primary activities to achieve long-term and sustainable productivity growth. Whereas more concentrated urban economies may be able to use vertical integration to control multiple activities in a GVC, rural economies must rely on a specialisation to focus on one aspect of the value chain where the firm has a distinct advantage (Mudambi, 2008[58]). Since manufacturing has a relatively low value-added, rural firms should seek to specialise either early in the GVC, through research and development (R&D) and design, or near the end of the GVC, through marketing, logistics and after-sale services. Policy makers can help firms specialise by focusing on the enabling factors of skills, accessibility, market intelligence, institutions and innovation.

Smart specialisation also entails specialised diversification. It means unlocking synergies among related activities to promote new growth opportunities, rather than just focusing the economy entirely into one single economic sector. This is particularly relevant for rural economies that rely on natural resource extraction or one single industry. Unleashing the new economic activities required joint work with entrepreneurs, existing firms, government and research centres. Forward-looking planning with local leadership is a key additional ingredient for a successful transition to new areas of growth. Some OECD rural regions have successfully experienced economic transitions and overcome the decline of nature-based industries (Box 3.3).

Increasing diversification for rural areas requires integrated development projects. Compensating lagging regions through farm subsidies creates dependency, not development (OECD, 2012[5]). Rather than relying on subsidies and state aid as the essential tools, policy makers can support infrastructure that benefits both agriculture and the entire region, and link funds to farming to the provision of public goods for the benefit of society as a whole. Agriculture makes up only a small share of rural GVA and employment, so focusing exclusively on this one sector fails to recognise regional assets that could drive growth in other domains, such as renewable energy, tourism or the tradeable sector. The most dynamic economies are those that are diversified amongst products (Brummitt et al., 2018[59]). Policy makers need to be thinking beyond agriculture if they hope to improve outcomes for rural economies. With the right policies, underdeveloped regions can potentially become important sources for economic growth.

Box 3.3. Transition in resource-dependent rural economies

Transition in resource-dependent economies

Specialisation in mining and extractive industries has particular impacts on rural economies. The productivity of this sector tends to be higher and provide relatively higher wages. Increased spending in mining regions can drive up prices in the non-traded sectors (e.g. accommodation, food services and housing), affecting the competitiveness of other tradeable sectors (e.g. tourism-related services, manufacturing and agriculture).

Growth cycles of these regions can differ from national economies due to shifts in commodity markets and the finite nature of non-renewable resources. There are three phases of growth in these rural regions, which are:

- The investment phase, which can lead to relatively large increases in local economic activity and employment due to the capital investment required to establish new mining and extractive activities.
- The production phase when mines are operational, which creates ongoing business and employment opportunities, often at a higher income level than other sectors.
- Decline and closure of mining and extractive operations that can then lead to significant reductions in local economic activity and employment.

A number of factors shape the resilience of resource-based economies to these transitions. They include the existence of other areas of absolute and competitive advantage (i.e. other metals, access to markets), the level of integration between mining and extractive operations and the local economy (stronger linkages boost the scope for value-adding activities) and the size of the local population that influences the diversification of the economy and its capacity to adjust to shocks.

Economic transition in Outokumpu, Finland

The municipality of Outokumpu is located within Finland's easternmost region, North Karelia. It is home to around 7 000 inhabitants (4.3% of the North Karelia's population) and is one of the most densely populated municipalities in the region.

Outokumpu was established in 1913 with the start of copper mining, which was subsequently expanded to include the refining and smelting of copper. Production of copper from the mine peaked in the 1960s and, after this point, the mine entered a long phase of declining production and closure in 1989. This process resulted in a long-term demographic decline as demand for labour at the mine was reduced. The population of the town decreased from 13 000 in 1960 to around 9 000 in 1990.

Nevertheless, the municipality proved to be resilient and shifted from a mining producing municipality to manufacturing-based economy, based on subcontracting and exports of metal technologies and mining services. Self-organisation and forward-looking planning of municipal and regional governments along with the support of national government contributed to this transition.

From the 1960s, local leaders in Outokumpu implemented a strategy to support the transition of the town to reduce its reliance on mining operations and diversify into mining services and technologies. This shift also benefitted from a circumstance of history as the Outokumpu Mining Company had to innovate copper refining methods in the context of World War 2, which led to the establishment of its technology division.

Furthermore, an industrial park was set up in Outokumpu in the late 1970s following the incentives provided by the Finnish government to attract firms to the town. From the early 1980s, the Outokumpu

Mining Company started to manufacture mining equipment in the town and, throughout this decade, manufacturing began to constitute a larger share of the local economy. While this structural shift represented a decline in population and skills mismatches, today the municipality positions itself as a modern industrial town with a focus on increasing attractiveness and improving the well-being of citizens and has potential to become an important player in the mining value chain in Finland and the EU.

Source: OECD (2019[53]), *OECD Mining Regions and Cities Case Study: Outokumpu and North Karelia, Finland*, https://doi.org/10.1787/cd72611b-en; Stimson, R., R. Stough and B. Roberts (2006[60]), *Regional Economic Development: Analysis and Planning Strategy*, Springer.

Key policies to support smart specialisation strategies:

- **Policies for entrepreneurial discovery**: The smart specialisation approach calls for an "entrepreneurial selection" of market opportunities (e.g. to minimise failures and to avoid ill-informed policy decisions). While successful companies will constitute the new specialisation of the country/region (self-discovery), the role for policy is to develop a flexible strategy focusing on measurable intermediate goals, identifying bottlenecks and market failures and ensuring feedback into policy learning processes.

- **Focusing on a pool of sectors**: Specialisation does not mean concentrating all efforts in one single sector. Diversification among related sectors or activities is essential to strengthening resilience in rural economies. Some regions (in Norway or Sweden) have decided to specialise in three relative sectors. For instance, Lapland, one of the first regions in Finland to adapt smart specialisation, based its strategy in achieving a leading position in sustainable utilisation and commercialisation of Arctic natural resources and conditions. Its smart specialisation strategy has three sectors of focus: i) mining and metal industries; ii) bioeconomy; and iii) tourism and related industries.

- **Promoting general-purpose technology platforms and networks**. Given the range of applications of general-purpose technologies, technology platforms involving public and private actors but also standard-setting organisations can help increase productivity in existing sectors and help identify sectors in which to concentrate resources.

- **Diagnostic tools and sound infrastructure**. Smart specialisation requires regions and countries to maintain an infrastructure and indicator base to monitor and evaluate performance and policies.

- **Strategic governance for smart specialisation**. Good governance and the development of local capabilities are key to identifying local strengths; aligning policy actions, building critical mass, developing a vision and implementing a sound strategy.

Enhancing innovation

Innovation has become a key factor to increase competitiveness among a more globalised and interconnected world. The tradeable sector offers untapped opportunities for constant innovation. Contact and exchange with other sectors and markets generate greater rates of innovation. Likewise, close links between cities and rural regions allow firms and entrepreneurs to benefit from knowledge spill-overs and sharing of innovation and resources (OECD, 2018[61]). Ensuring wider participation of firms and entrepreneurs in GVC and external market can unleash greater rates of local innovation (OECD, 2018[62]).

Rural regions can benefit from a broader perspective of innovation by creating ecosystems that ensure new practices and ideas in a wider range of activities. As described in Chapter 2, innovation is more than R&D and technology investment. It goes from new managerial practices to marketing innovations. Non-traditional economic activities such as culture can facilitate an innovative ecosystem in rural regions (Box 3.4). Experience across OECD countries reveals that a common environment for all key stakeholders is relevant to concentrate ideas in the same geography and enhance local innovativeness (OECD, 2011[63]). The externalities that emerge from the concentration and co-opetition of firms either within a specific industry or by the diversity of complementary industries and stakeholders in a specific area stand out as an essential component of innovation. Therefore, innovation strategies should support a wide-ranging collaboration and partnership among public, private, not-for-profit and educational organisations to spur rural innovation and create competitive business for global markets.

The innovation ecosystem should ensure the territories have the right assets in place to absorb new ideas and technologies. Innovation policy should enable firms to adopt forms of work organisation that support innovation. OECD research indicates that different models of work organisation adopted by SMEs can be related to differences in their innovation performance (OECD, 2015[64]). Investing in skills and ICT infrastructure are essential to ensure absorption capacity at the local level.

Key policies to enhance innovation:

- Strengthening the links, collaboration and knowledge sharing between urban and rural.
- Enhancing links of rural firms with GVC and global firms and promoting knowledge sharing and information exchange to encourage collaborative innovation.
- Supporting co-operation and networking among rural firms.
- Generating common environments that concentrate firms, entrepreneurs and research institutions.
- Investing in skills and ICT infrastructure to facilitate the uptake of new ideas and technologies.

Box 3.4. Promoting the arts to facilitate innovation in rural regions

Research in the United States (US) has identified the importance of the arts to innovation in rural America. Released in 2015, the Rural Establishment Innovation Survey (REIS) provides data on innovative technologies and practices. Researchers have used REIS to identify how business innovation is different in rural regions as well as how innovation and rural economies interact. The results suggest that the arts do more than simply improve quality of life. In addition to helping firms attract and retain talent, the presence of arts organisations in rural regions demonstrate a strong statistical association with innovation-oriented businesses and economic dynamism.

Arts provide two main benefits for rural communities: improved well-being and increased productivity. According to REIS data, businesses are significantly more likely to be a "substantive innovator" if they operate in a rural region with 2 or 3 performing arts organisations at 70%, compared to those with none at 60%. The probability rises to 85% in counties with 4 or more of such organisations (National Endowment for the Arts, 2017[65]). Yet, what is unclear is whether the arts are an amenity that attracts creative talent or an enabling factor to increased rates of innovation in rural regions (Wojan and Nichols, 2018[66]). Whether by attracting or enabling creative talent, promoting the arts is likely to have a positive impact on the capabilities of rural firms.

The presence of performing arts organisations is associated with higher rates of design-integrated businesses in rural economies. Design integration is an important measure for growth because innovation rises with use of design, by allowing businesses to increase market share, enter new markets and export more goods and services. REIS data indicates a business is 49% more likely to be a design-integrated business if located in a region with at least 2 performing arts organisations.

However, not all rural types benefit equally from the presence of an arts influence. Similar to urban areas, innovation concentrates into "rural creative havens", which tend to have well-established linkages to cities, contain a university or have natural amenities (Wojan, Lambert and Mcgranahan, 2017[67]). Rural regions seeking to promote the arts should therefore consider the complementary

---

policies necessary to make arts organisations successful. For example, rural-urban partnerships, as well as policies to improve transportation and access, can encourage greater arts participation and thereby bolster the impact on businesses (rural arts organisations report 31% of their audiences travel "beyond a reasonable distance" to attend events)

Source: Wojan, T., D. Lambert and D. Mcgranahan (2018[66]), *The Emergence of Rural Artistic Havens: A First Look*, http://www.uwplatt.edu/cont_ed/artsbuild/welcome.html.

While the above policy recommendations can be applied across all rural places, innovation policies should acknowledge the different characteristics of rurality:

- For regions near large cities, policies should focus on fostering the linkages with urban institutions and firms. Rural firms in tradeable activities can indeed benefit from spill-overs from agglomeration economies through direct contact, partnerships for production or integration of innovative suppliers.
- For regions with or near small/medium cities, policies should facilitate the access of firms to global markets and skill workers. Better integration with cities can boost the whole innovative ecosystem of the area.
- For remote regions, an important focus should be dedicated to ensuring the right skills and infrastructure investments to foster competition in global markets. Much of these remote areas host tradeable industries in extractive activities, forestry and agriculture.

Increasing productivity of rural SMEs and firms

SMEs are main actors in rural economies and essential for economic resilience, productivity and inclusiveness. They also maintain the industrial fabric of many regions and contribute to the identity of local communities. Yet, the vast majorities of rural SMEs (less than 250 employees) have slow employment growth and remain micro enterprises (less than 10 employees) (Freshwater et al., 2019[51]). This is explained by multiple factors including difficulty in identifying new market opportunities, limited financial capacity, labour shortages, high transport costs to external markets and owner preferences to limit growth.

A more competitive tradeable sector requires a sound business ecosystem of firms from all sizes to sustain market growth. Firms in tradeable sectors can leverage their productivity on competitive suppliers that help them cope with changing market requirements. For this, a business-friendly environment is instrumental to stimulate the development of the local private sector. It includes supporting a simplified administrative process to facilitate the opening and operation of businesses, reducing costs of complying with administrative requirements and enabling collaboration between firms, the administration and academia as well as ventures of all sizes and origins.

Linking SMEs with established firms competing in the tradeable sector can foster new business opportunities and boost SMEs' growth. As mentioned above, tradeable activities require a range of services associated with the production processes, including designs, sales, maintenance and financial management. In some cases, those services are provided remotely from the company headquarters but, in others, they need to be delivered on site. It offers an opportunity for SMEs and entrepreneurs to provide solutions to large firms. Further, large firms can contribute to the transformation of business ecosystems through business accelerators and innovation labs that provide start-ups and innovative SMEs with access to resources and markets (OECD, 2019[4]).

Innovation and new technologies are important to boost SMEs' productivity. Emerging digital technologies, including big data analytics, artificial intelligence and 3D printing, enable greater product differentiation and mass customisation, which benefit smaller and more responsive businesses (Chapter 5). Technological progress is creating new sources of financing, from peer-to-peer lending to alternative risk assessment tools, and initial coin offerings (ICOs).

Key policies to increase productivity in rural SMEs and rural firms:

- The high degree of economic and geographic diversity across rural regions means that support for rural SMEs has to be flexible, not only by the type of industry but also by the geographic setting of the firm.
- Promote a friendly business environment for SMEs. This includes supporting a simplified administrative process to facilitate the opening and operation of businesses, reducing costs of complying with administrative requirements and enabling collaboration between firms, the administration and academia as well as ventures of all sizes and origins.
- Supporting the co-operation and networking of SMEs with large firms and multinationals.
- Providing specific support and training for women in enhancing entrepreneurship capacities and developing SMEs.
- Promoting SMEs' connection to innovative sources of financing through the use of new technologies.
- Investing in skills and capacity building for SMEs to be able to uptake new technologies.

In regions with or near small/medium cities, the productivity of SMEs can be boosted through greater integration with universities and larger firms and SMEs from urban areas. When it comes to remote regions, supporting the vertical integration of SMEs into the production process of global firms as well as entrepreneurship culture should be a priority. These policies should promote entrepreneurship that unlocks the potential of existing assets in the area. For example, in North Karelia, Finland, SME support aims to enhance value-added of the smart specialisation sector, including bioeconomy and metal technologies.

Internationalisation of SMEs

The OECD's work on economic well-being suggests a need for policy solutions that support innovators, entrepreneurs and SMEs in rural economies. These stakeholders provide a valuable contribution to rural economies but may need support connecting to GVCs and making the best use of specific know-how (OECD, 2017[68]). In fact, OECD countries with a relatively high share of exports from SMEs, experience smaller differences in average salaries between SMEs and larger firms (OECD, 2019[4]).

To make the most of GVCs, policies should support SMEs in moving up the value chain, either in the pre-production or post-production process. Supporting SME participation in the services sector can lead to greater participation of the local economy in global markets. For example, displaced firms and workers from mining and extractive industries hold transferable knowledge that they can share with the global market.

Global companies connected to GVCs can be a platform to internationalise local SMEs. Linking SMEs to new markets and knowledge can lead to innovative business ideas among local companies, increase income and find diversified sources of growth (Mitchell and O'Neill, 2015[69]). Strategies to support those links include the participation of SMEs in international fairs and business rounds, quality accreditation and technological upgrades (OECD, 2016[70]). For example, governments such as Mexico have developed national SME funds to co-fund on one-to-one basis programmes and projects that addressed local problems. Some states (e.g. Queretaro) have used these funds as a vehicle to link SMEs into international supply chains through quality accreditation and the organisation of events for established transnational companies (OECD, 2019[71]).

Digitalisation can also help SMEs integrate global markets and global value chains (GVCs). The fragmentation of production worldwide has provided smaller businesses with significant scope for competing in specialised GVC segments and scaling up activities abroad (OECD, 2019[4]). In this process,

SMEs can capture international knowledge spill-overs and capitalise on more robust growth in emerging markets. Governments should provide the enabling factors (i.e. capacity building, quality broadband) to help rural SMEs benefit from new technologies (Chapter 5).

Key policies to promote the internationalisation of rural SMEs:

- Improving various types of networks – transportation, business, professional and telecommunications – since these help to reduce the penalties of distance and low density, thereby increasing access to external markets.

- Because individual SMEs in a rural region have few local peers in the same industry, local governments need to support opportunities for firms in specific industries to build professional networks through meetings and electronic means. It may also be useful to facilitate meetings of all SMEs through umbrella organisations, such as the chamber of commerce or business owner associations.

- Promoting the participation of SMEs in international fairs, quality accreditation and technological upgrades.

- Facilitating access to international markets for women-owned SMEs.

Retaining more value in rural places

Many rural economies tend to struggle with distributing the gains from tradeable activities to the entire population. Many tradeable industries rely on capital imported (machines, trucks) and in some cases provide few direct job opportunities (automated mines). In very remote regions specialised in extractive sectors, job creation does not benefit the local labour force because it relies on specialised outsiders. This reduces employment opportunities for local communities. Policies need to seek a larger integration and fit of local workers and business with industries.

Investing in enabling factors can help communities to retain benefits from large and multinational firms. A sound infrastructure, skilled labour force and conducive regulatory conditions lead to more competitive local economies able to retain value from international activities. A coherent policy will promote the reinvestment of royalties and taxes in improving those enabling factors. Collaboration with industry, communities and academic institutions can also help define the basic conditions needed to reap the benefits from private investments.

Benefit-sharing measures in tradeable activities are widespread strategies for retaining additional benefits for the local population. This measures the need to differentiate monetary and non-monetary benefits for mining communities and second to make the most out of them:

- Monetary benefit-sharing mechanisms include investment funds, equity-sharing and tax-sharing mechanisms between regional and national governments. Many countries specialised in mining and extractive activities have special tax regimes or monetary arrangements that collect the rents from extractives activities and revert them to the regions where they are extracted to different degrees (OECD, 2017[72]). In other countries, revenues from mining are mainly collected through national taxes and form part of the consolidated national revenue without a specific revenue transfer mechanism to mining regions (i.e. Finland) (Hojem, 2015[73]).

- Non-monetary benefit-sharing mechanisms include investments in education and medical facilities, local employment generation, local procurement and staff training (Söderholm, 2014[74]). These measures should consider different dimensions of well-being (income, jobs, education and training, housing amongst others) to ensure benefits match local needs. For example, quality standards and training programmes to suppliers help local companies to improve their production process and quality of the final product. Policy responses can be quite effective in upgrading or increasing local inputs into the production processes in the extractive industries. These include:

- o Reducing information and capacity gaps that diminish local firms' chances of responding to extractive firms' tender.
- o Offering technical or business assistance to suppliers and SMEs and support them in obtaining necessary certifications to respond to the needs of extractive firms.
- o Ensuring timely payment facilities for SMEs with limited cash flow.

Across OECD countries, private sector-led initiatives also implement measures for benefit sharing with local communities. Some large firms support SME capacity through a number of partnerships, including deploying specialised accelerators for start-up and individuals, setting up innovation labs with a view to encouraging "out-the-box" thinking and new collaborations within the firm (OECD, 2019[4]). Firms in extractive industries can consider capacity-building policies are needed to create a pool of competent and competitive suppliers and a workforce with the required skill level close to their operations (OECD, 2017[72]). For example, BHP Billiton has created its world-class suppliers' development programme in Chile to address its competitiveness challenges jointly with local suppliers (Box 3.5).

Key policies to retain more value in rural places include:

- Ensuring a sound infrastructure and competitive regulation for local economies to reap benefits from foreign investments.
- Promoting local benefit-sharing policies (monetary and non-monetary), including capacity-building activities for local firms, promoting quality standards and training programmes.

Box 3.5. Upgrading local suppliers

Some local and regional entities aim to reduce information and capacity gaps that diminish local firms' chances of responding to extractive firms' tender. These can include: offering technical or business assistance to SMEs; keeping databases on supplier firms; tailoring the size and scope of contracts to a level that may be more easily captured locally; aiding suppliers in obtaining necessary certifications to respond to the needs of extractive firms; and ensuring timely payment facilities for SMEs with limited cash flow.

Successful supplier development programmes, for example, have helped to create clusters of firms that provide goods and services to the mining sector. Such programmes can increase capacity and employment in local SMEs, create deep linkages and foster innovation, transfers of technology and business process knowledge.

In 2009, BHP Billiton created the World-Class Supplier Programme in Chile to address the competitiveness challenges jointly with local suppliers and create a more sophisticated, export-driven economy in Chile. The programme has successfully introduced standardisation across operations and is continuing to develop the knowledge-intensive expertise of local suppliers. This latter outcome is further serving to reduce Chile's economic vulnerability to commodity market shocks. The success of the programme attracted Codelco, to join in 2010.

The mutually beneficial programme set the goal of creating 250 world-class mining suppliers in Chile by 2020. The programme focused on five areas: water, energy, HSEC (health, safety, environment and community), human capital and operational efficiency.

The mythology of the programme is seeking tenders from local suppliers on problems or challenges identified at the operational level – rather than prescribed solutions – and using a framework to test ideas in real-time. BHP has also partnered with the government of Chile and Foundation Chile (a public-private partnership that promotes innovation) to better leverage support for the new suppliers. In the

---

first 3 years of the programme, over 100 innovation projects were submitted for consideration, 20 of which led to contracts with BHP Billiton.

Source: BHP Billiton Chile (2013[75]), *Sustainability Report 2014 - BHP Billiton Pampa Norte Minera Escondida*, https://www.bhp.com/-/media/documents/community/2014/csr-eng150518sustainabilityreport2014bhpbillitonchileoperations.pdf.

Strengthening rural skills

The gap in skill levels between rural regions and cities and the sectoral structure of rural economies imply that the former are less well-prepared to face the changing labour demand resulting from a rise in automation (OECD, 2018[76]). Skill differences between rural regions and cities are already visible at school age (Chapter 2). At the time, developing relevant skills can help rural communities harness new economic opportunities associated with technological innovation and expanding digital infrastructure. A skilled workforce is also key for rural regions to transition towards higher-value-added activities in the production chain and to attract and retain businesses more broadly. The labour force's ability to adapt to new market requirements and technologies matters in particular for ensuring the competitiveness in tradeable activities.

The resilience of the local economy as a whole also relies on the relevance and level of skills in the community. As rural economies tend to be specialised in a limited number of sectors, market shocks and shifts in demand affecting certain sectors can threaten the sustainability of local economies more broadly. Policies to support the reallocation of labour are essential to mitigate the negative effects of employment changes across industries with high GVC participation in OECD countries (OECD, 2016[77]). It can be particularly relevant for the male workforce that has struggled to cope with the trend of tertiarisation in rural regions.

At the same time, digital technologies can facilitate measures to help rural regions catch up. For instance, digitalisation opens up new ways to foster adult basic education through distance learning (Gungor and Prins, 2011[78]). Indicative research from Australia suggests that digital technologies could also facilitate Indigenous students' access to and retention in higher education, even though important physical, literacy and content barriers need to be overcome (Watson, 2013[79]) (see Chapter 5).

Vocational education and training can be another key vehicle for developing relevant rural skills. However, rural sectors may face specific challenges associated with the provision of training opportunities, such as transportation. The balance between costs and benefits of offering apprenticeships depends on the size of the firms, for instance, because larger firms are to a greater extent able to retain former apprentices as skilled workers as a return on their investment in training. It is therefore key to foster strong co-ordination between rural firms, not-for-profit organisations and government programmes to ensure that investments in training provision are worthwhile for both smaller and larger companies. Smaller employers can, for instance, be supported by policies to encourage the development of models allowing them to share risks and responsibilities related to apprenticeship provision, structures to support with the administrative burden and training delivery itself (OECD, 2018[80]). The challenge of remoteness could, for instance, be mitigated by moving some of the training requirements for apprentices to a digital platform and providing public funding to support students' transport costs where in-person training is needed, as is the case in rural Nordland in Norway (OECD/ILO, 2017[81]).

More broadly, local education and training provision needs to meet the skill demand of the local economy and establish a close link to employment if it is to have a positive impact on economic growth and job creation (EC, 2008[82]). To address staff and skills shortages in the agricultural sector, vocational training in this area should be made attractive for young people and middle-aged workers alike. At the same time, the work in this sector itself can be upgraded. In Northern Ireland (United Kingdom) for instance, an EU-funded ICT training programme was provided to farmers through a combination of computer training, face-to-face mentoring and financial support (Soldi et al., 2016, p. 72[83]). The ten-week programme allowed farmers and their families to enhance their ICT skills and make better day-to-day use of the technological tools in their work, with reported efficiency gains for their business.

Improving skill levels and the match of skills in rural regions with local employers' evolving needs by those different avenues can help render rural economies more performant and resilient.

Key policies to strengthening skills in the rural economy include:

- Fostering collaboration between public authorities, local businesses and not-for-profit organisations to ensure local education and training in a way that matches the skill needs of rural employers.
- Providing comprehensive support to rural apprentices and firms, providing training to ensure relevant learning opportunities in low-density and remote areas.
- Harnessing digital technologies to support lifelong learning for rural youth and experienced workers as automation, market trends and structural economic change reshape skill demand and job profiles.

Policies to enhance social well-being in rural places

Social well-being refers to the arrangements through families, networks, associations, institutions and economies that influence our quality of life. Much of this well-being is based on hard attributes including affordable and accessible services including healthcare, education as well as affordable housing and well-connected transportation systems. Yet, these are not sufficient to build vibrant, inclusive communities. Soft attributes including a sense of belonging and mutual trust, founded in positive social relationships and networks build through religious and educational institutions or cultural and family connections are equally important for social well-being.

In the light of demographic change, rural places have to manage a range of challenges related to social well-being. For instance, as people become more mobile and conduct more of their lives online, relationships and sense of community suffer, detracting from social well-being. In rural communities, this is especially prevalent, where demographic change, remoteness and low population density limit the availability of community centres or public transit to rural dwellers. As a result, policies seeking to improve social well-being must take a place-based approach.

Ensuring inclusive rural places for all

Inclusive policies aim to empower citizens to live happy, healthy and meaningful lives. Structural changes relating to demography require policy makers to pay special attention to the social well-being of different groups present in rural communities to ensure inclusivity. Apart from ensuring individual well-being though delivering on specific needs, inclusive policy making can also help to reduce regional inequalities, strengthen resilience and contribute to delivering on the 2030 Agenda for Sustainable Development, promising to leave no one behind.

Liveable ageing

Elderly people make up a large part of the rural population. By 2050, nearly 30% of the population in European regions outside of metropolitan areas is expected to be 65 years old or older (OECD, 2019[8]). Current elderly dependency ratios in rural regions – the share of the population aged 65 and over as a percentage of the population aged 20-64 – stands at 28.6% on average (Chapter 2). Remote regions and regions with access to a small/medium city have the highest elderly dependency rates. Four OECD TL3 regions are already above 60% in elderly dependency ratios and its ratio is over 50% in 53 TL3 regions.

This shift strains economic development as retired people are not involved in productive activities (OECD, 2019[8]).

A growing elderly population increases the need for age-related goods and services in rural places. Rural dwellers face greater difficulties in accessing health and social care services. Geographical distances and less developed transportation services amplify these challenges as people's mobility or cognitive function decreases with age. This increases the demand for adequate transportation, assistance with daily chores and activities and more frequent medial support. As rural remote regions have a higher share of elderly males, services in these regions need to specifically consider male-related factors of ageing, for instance in terms of male prone diseases or habits such as avoidance to seek medical help or social support. In addition, the rural elderly are also at risk of social isolation and feeling of loneliness, in particular, when their mobility is reduced and they often have difficulties maintaining social networks (UNECE, 2002[84]).

Ensuring the social well-being of elderly people offers opportunities for economic development. While rural regions face a shrinking labour force, developing and testing "silver" services in rural economies is an opportunity for developing the economic inclusion of the older population and can attract investment to rural economies. The consumer spending power of elderly people is significant. By 2020, it is estimated to total USD 15 trillion for the population aged 60 and over (OECD, 2014[85]). Technological innovations that are focused on finding a solution for ways to live well as we age are at the heart of this market. Broadband can help the elderly population to better participate in community life as the elderly are adopting social media to keep up family connections.

Older people are a valuable resource for making contributions to rural communities and economies. Many people do not want to stop being productive and contributing to society just because they have reached a certain age. Well-being often also means continuing to work or being productively engaged, this needs to be recognised by governments and employers alike. Older workers can contribute by bringing institutional knowledge, social maturity and stability and can pass on business relationship to younger workers (Jenkins, 2019[86]). At the same time, retirees, who have free time, can be vital in contributing to voluntary work and help mitigate gaps in regional support structures including childcare.

Increasing attractiveness for youth and newcomers

Demographic trends in OECD rural regions outline a similar pattern of outmigration of youth. While OECD remote rural regions experience the highest fertility rates among all type of regions (Chapter 2), the young population tend to leave in search of higher education levels. In Europe, 57% of regions are expected to lose population by 2050 (OECD, 2019[8]). The analysis in Chapter 2 shows that half of EU countries will have to manage population decline in remote regions and one-third of countries will need to manage population decline in regions with access to a small/medium city. This will shrink tax bases and make it more difficult to provide public services.

Gender shares in the workforce are geographically dependent. In more than half the OECD countries considered (18 out of 30), rural remote regions had larger shares of male workforce in 2017, in contrast with metropolitan regions with larger shares of females across all categories and most OECD countries considered (27 out of 30). These results suggest that rural economies offer fewer jobs to females, with many jobs happening in resource-related industries with low shares of the female workforce. Yet, this trend might be changing as the employment rate of females in rural regions has increased since the crisis. This trend, explained in part by raising service activities, can lead to an increase in female workforce participation in rural regions. The COVID-19 pandemic will likely have a significant impact on the gender participation rate, as the sectors that were heavily impacted, such as tourism, employ a relatively large share of female workers.

Rural communities that face labour market shortages and seek to stabilise service provision need to become more attractive and retain a diverse workforce. Attractiveness can be broadly defined as the factors that people generally value about their local neighbourhood, town or city, such as accessible and reliable public transport, high-quality open space, good schools as well as vibrant community life. These factors are generally immobile or place-based, thus important to regional growth and competitiveness. Enhancing regional attractiveness requires an integrated approach to improving services, local infrastructure and amenities, housing choices and opportunities for social participation.

People only come and stay in places if these offer the potential for personal and professional development. Attracting young people and especially women to rural communities requires a strategic, group sensitive approach. This fundamentally involves improvement in three key areas:

- First, ICT availability, which can facilitate a new form of economic activities and jobs including tourism, services (marketing, design), niche manufacturing and food production, and can provide alternative employment pathways for young people (OECD, 2017[87]).

- Second, the developing services related to maternal health and childcare, enabling young parents and especially women to remain active in the workforce.

- Third, communicating rural amenities, such as lower cost of living and closeness to nature, and working towards building brands that highlight progressive and modern aspects of rural economies.

Furthermore, governments and education systems need to provide specialist teaching and leadership to young rural populations and support co-business and development of networks.

Ensuring service availability and accessibility for rural well-being

The availability of quality public services is a necessary component in ensuring a high level of well-being in rural communities. Investments in public services can require economies of scale that are difficult to achieve in low-density areas, so communities must identify other arrangements to ensure adequate service provision (OECD, 2014[88]). With growing pressures on public spending due to an ageing population, regions are beginning to adopt new approaches to continue providing for rural dwellers.

Remote rural regions are much more likely to face challenges accessing services than rural places close to cities. In Denmark, for example, rural places close to cities, especially those located along regional rail lines, show the strongest performance in terms of service accessibility, household income and employment (OECD, 2016[89]). However, in remote rural regions, migration trends are increasing pressure to provide public services in conditions of stagnating or declining population and productivity. Rural places face higher costs of service delivery due to lower population density, thereby precluding any economies of scale and increasing distances that service users and providers must travel. Policy makers need to address how to ensure services reach all rural communities, particularly those less connected to large cities.

The attractiveness of rural regions can be improved through the availability of high-quality public services. Investments in public services can require economies of scale that are difficult to achieve in low-density areas, so communities must identify other arrangements to ensure adequate service provision. Integrated service delivery is one approach frequently implemented to improve services delivery by providing improved cost, quality and access. Furthermore, the COVID-19 pandemic further demonstrated the importance of access to digital health and education services. Different forms of integration include colocation, collaboration, co-operation and co-production.

Colocation is one form of integration that locates many services or agencies in one building. For example, "wraparound schools" in the US do this by providing academic support, health and mental healthcare, and enrichment opportunities for students within the school (García and Weiss, 2017[90]). Schools have implemented similar models in rural parts of the UK, where "often the only community facility locally is the school and it is usually seen as a positive resource" (Dyson, Kerr and Jones, 2016[91]). The benefits of colocation include reduced administrative and capital costs, a collaboration between professionals in different sectors and the ability to continue operating in regions with population decline. Table 3.6 provides examples of colocation strategies in four OECD countries.

Table 3.6. One-stop shops for rural service delivery

OECD country	Colocation strategies	Description
Japan	Small stations	Small stations initiatives aim to ensure effective and efficient service delivery in the wake of ageing and depopulation threats. These hubs concentrate basic service delivery, including administrative services, healthcare and shopping, among other essential functions.
France	Maisons de service au public	The purpose of the Maisons initiative is to guarantee public service delivery in low-density or isolated territories by sharing costs and employees as far as possible among communities. There are currently over 1 000 Maisons across France.
Australia	Rural Transaction Centres (RTCs)	RTCs provide economic and community benefits from the colocation of government, private sector and community services. Intended to develop into sustainable community-managed small businesses, RTCs provide locally determined needs from financial services to insurance and tourism services.
Finland	Citizen Service Offices	The Citizen Service Office system offers citizens a single outlet for services ranging from district court needs to tax and work administration. The aim is to ensure a sufficient and high-quality service network, increase productivity and reduce costs.

Source: OECD (2016[92]), Territorial Reviews: Japan 2016, https://doi.org/10.1787/9789264250543-en.

Another form of integration is *collaboration*, whereby agencies work together as part of a network to share information and training. Collaboration helps reduce gaps in service provision by providing opportunities for horizontal and vertical service integration. In rural communities, collaboration is naturally easier due to the small number of individuals and organisations involved in public service provision. By sharing knowledge, institutions and agencies can ensure rural dwellers have knowledge of and access to services.

Co-operation, a third type of integration, entails different levels of government communicating and working together on multi-agency teams. This form of horizontal co-ordination strives to lower the costs of delivering services and reduce duplication. For example, Italy created the National Strategy for Inner Areas to involve national, regional and local tiers in implementing its strategic approach to support its rural communities (ENRD, 2018[93]). Integrating national and local activities is helping to remove obstacles to service provision and local development in rural Italy. Rural-urban partnerships, discussed in a later section, are another form of co-operation connecting a territory with functional linkages.

Table 3.7. Overview of strategies to improve rural service delivery

Placing providers at the community level	Better connecting providers with users increases the odds of providing services that are useful to the community and in a cost-effective way.
Consolidation and colocation	Concentrating customers on a smaller number of service locations reduces basic overhead costs such as energy, security and administrative expenses. Pooling these costs can help generate economies of scale.
Merging similar services	Merging similar or substitute services and combining them into a single entity can ensure different organisations are not replicating work.
Alternative delivery options	Where the demand for services is widely dispersed, it may be more efficient to bring the service to the user. Some examples include mobile libraries, dental clinics and doctors.
Community-based solutions	Community-driven provision may work for some services, such as through volunteer fire departments or community-owned shops.
Geolocation	Technology can help facilities locate by matching the supply and demand of services.

Source: OECD (2010[94]), Strategies to Improve Rural Service Delivery, https://doi.org/10.1787/9789264083967-en.

Finally, *co-production* is a type of integration that involves community and non-profit groups, also known as the third sector, in providing services. By partnering with citizens and local organisations, public service providers can ensure products and programmes reflect the needs of the community as identified by the people receiving the services. Engaging citizens and citizen organisations in the design, production and delivery of services leads to higher satisfaction and cost reductions. In France, rural communities are co-producing solutions for housing and care service through "villa housing" (OECD, 2011[95]). This scheme enhancing life for the elderly through neighbourhood engagement, providing better services and quality of life for the same cost. Many existing public services already have elements of co-production but the growing imperative in rural economies to drive innovation and cut costs opens the door for greater engagement with this strategy.

Taking advantage of technology and innovation

Technological change can improve the quality and decrease the cost of delivering services in areas outside cities (see Chapter 5). This was particularly important in the COVID-19 pandemic. Education can find support in technology to overcome some challenges in areas outside cities such as distance, classroom size or teacher attraction/retention. Long-distance education, for example, can be effective in terms of student-content and peer-to-peer interactions. Likewise, health already relies on technology to modify the provision of healthcare and medical research. Drones delivering blood, t-shirts that monitor health or medical 3D printing are health solutions that are currently in use.

Box 3.6. Improving rural service provision

In light of dwindling numbers of inhabitants, villages and small towns in rural and remote areas often are often faced with difficult choices with regard to the provision of public and private services. With smaller economies of scale, there is a risk of being forced to either compromise quality or affordability of services when trying to avoid closure. However, the examples of a digitally connected school network in Québec (Canada) and a social logistics enterprise in the provinces of Burgos and Soria (Spain) show that technological and process innovations can allow improving quality of services in isolated areas in a cost-conscious way.

Harnessing digital tools to improve education quality in small schools in Québec, Canada

The Network School (*L'École en réseau*) project in Québec (Canada) seeks to provide an alternative approach to ensuring the delivery of quality education in low-density areas by other means than school consolidation. It has been introduced in around half of the province's school boards, involving more than 1 000 teachers. It stands out in seeking to use ICT to foster social innovation in a broad sense, rather than only digitalising existing practices. Since 2002, the Québec Ministry of Education has been supporting the project to create new solutions for supporting small primary and secondary schools facing dwindling student numbers. It is funded with CAF 500 000 per year and has been included among the measures of the ministry's digital plan in 2018.

By joining the network, schools are expected to enrich the learning environment and thereby address quality concerns ahead of time that would otherwise serve as potential reasons for closing schools. The project promotes a way of classroom management that seeks to establish a community of learning and knowledge development across schools by harnessing digital technology. The network involves: new ways of work organisation, namely the collaboration of two teachers in two different schools realising joint activities with their students; the inclusion of a teacher from another school in the local teacher's implementation of specific activities for their students; project-based group work involving students from different schools; remote interventions by specialists and counsellors; and support from a university team via video-conferencing to address requests and training needs. The project encourages the

---

co-operation with scientists, museum staff, experts and other partners to enhance learning activities even in remote regions.

Pedagogical and technical support plays a key role in developing the capacity of teachers to harness the new tools in their work, for instance, to participate in web conferences or participate in the forum for joint knowledge development. Students in the project were found to benefit from new opportunities to extend their skills in: using new technologies; problem-solving; reading comprehension; reasoning and argumentation in different domains; as well as oral expression in person and via video-conferencing, with an extended vocabulary. However, the project's experience also highlights that the take-up of new ICT-based teaching and evaluation practices is a gradual process and cannot be expected to take place from one day to another. For example, available analysis tools for tracking students' use of new vocabulary in the project are still underutilised by teachers.

Ensuring access to basic goods and services in rural places: A social logistics enterprise in Spain

The social enterprise La Exclusiva, based in central Spain, provides logistical support to the population of rural villages in the provinces of Burgos and Soria in view of raising the quality and attractiveness of life in sparsely populated or isolated rural communities where local shops are no longer operating. It delivers to people's homes basic goods such as: food items, meals or medication; larger items like appliances; as well as services ranging from gardening to help with submitting administrative documents. Via 5 different routes, La Exclusiva is reaching 15 000 households across 600 villages every week and plans to increase coverage over time. Orders can be placed through handwritten forms, phone, email, WhatsApp or the project website. Due to its regular face-to-face interactions, the service is valuable for elderly people, who may be isolated and not able to travel themselves, over and beyond access to goods and services.

Rather than competing with them, the delivery is financed by existing suppliers opting to sell their goods via La Exclusiva without passing on the transport costs to customers. While the social enterprise is not requesting public funding, it engages with the public administration to improve the administrative services offered to households and overcome hurdles. For instance, currently, the service is not allowed to distribute prescription medicine. This pilot project has succeeded in sustaining itself financially and there are reports that it is associated with improved eating habits, socialisation, and health and safety among the households concerned.

Source: CEFRIO (2011[96]), *L'École éloignée en réseau (ÉÉR), un modèle*, http://www.cefrio.qc.ca/fr/documents/projets/46-Ecole-eloignee-en-reseau.html (accessed on 27 January 2020); (CEFRIO, 2015[97]) CEFRIO (2015), *Usages du numérique dans les écoles québécoises*, CEFRIO, https://cefrio.qc.ca/media/1893/rapport-synthese_usages_du_numerique_dans_les_ecoles.pdf (accessed on 25 February 2020); (Québec Ministry of Educaton, 2018[98])Québec Ministry of Educaton (2018), Plan d'action numérique [Digital Action Plan], http://www.education.gouv.qc.ca/fileadmin/site_web/documents/ministere/PAN_Plan_action_VF.pdf (accessed on 5 April 2020); Boudain, J. (2020[99]), "Presentation of Josée Boudain, Director of "École en Réseau", OECD Webinar on Rural Education Delivery, 2 April 2020; Hernández, M. (2018[100]), "La Exclusiva: una segunda oportunidad para la vida rural [La Exclusiva: A second chance for the rural life]]", https://forbes.es/empresas/41955/la-exclusiva-una-segunda-oportunidad-para-la-vida-rural/ (accessed on 25 February 2020); Diario de Valladolid (2019[101]), "Soria exporta la logística social como franquicia [Soria exports social logistics as franchise]", https://diariodevalladolid.elmundo.es/articulo/las-caras-del-exito/soria-exporta-logistica-social-franquicia/20191014121700351968.html (accessed on 25 February 2020). Kohllechner-Autto, M., S. Nisula and K. Skantz (2019[102]), *Good Practice Guide: Strategies Supporting Social Enterprises, and Concrete Examples of Social Innovation and Social Enterprises from Sparsely Populated European Regions*, https://issuu.com/lapinamk/docs/d_7_2019_kohllechner-autto_nisula_s (accessed on 25 February 2020).

Innovation can also create new services for rural dwellers. Too often rural service providers seek to exploit a local monopoly situation and pay little attention to improving the quality of service. When their customers are "captive" – limited in choice – the decline in service quality did not impact the demand for it. However, with increased mobility, many users are better able to identify alternative service providers. Innovation and the willingness to consider a new methodology or approach – instead of simply rescaling the way the service is provided – is a key factor to expand the offer of services and thus improve well-being. Tailoring the service delivery to better fit the circumstances of the rural area may involve: finding a different type of service provider, a different technology for delivering the service, or even developing a new service that results in a similar outcome.

In order to benefit from ICT deployments, a multi-dimensional response is needed (as will be argued in Chapter 5). Deployment of ICT infrastructure by itself is a necessary but not sufficient condition to reap the potential benefits of new technologies. These range from attracting new economic activity and skills, improving the productivity of firms, raising the quality and reducing costs of service delivery, connecting to a new market and overcoming isolation.

Reinforcing the rural education offer

Besides healthcare, education lies at the core of public service provision the state needs to ensure in rural regions and has a key role to play for social mobility. Starting from children's early years, high-quality education and care can help raise outcomes in education and the labour market (Shuey and Kankaraš, 2018[103]; Chetty et al., 2018[104]). At the same time, for young families, the traditional gap in early childhood education and care provision between rural regions and cities can be particularly challenging (EC, 2008[82]). Children and students in pre-primary, primary and most of secondary education are limited in their geographic mobility, especially in remote areas where the school they attend will largely be determined by the location of the home of their parents or guardians. Given the lack of alternatives, rural and remote schools, therefore, have a unique responsibility for the educational opportunities of children and youth in their catchment areas.

Financial pressures and quality concerns have long forced national education policy makers to formulate a variety of responses to rural and remote education provision. Approaches like the ones discussed above, to integrate services and harness digital technologies, as also discussed in Box 3.6; providing education and other services in low-density contexts is often still at the pilot stage or limited in scope. Thus, the focus of many established policy measures lies in increasing school size. School size influences the costs per student as larger schools can more easily fill up classes to the legal maximum, whereas smaller schools risk operating under capacity given the human and physical resources that are in place (OECD, 2018[105]). This means that when student numbers dwindle, it becomes less and less financially viable to provide quality education services in proximity. In response, policy makers often seek to re-establish scale through mandated or incentivised changes to the organisation of the school network.

The consolidation of schools implies that one or more schools are being closed and that students are transferred to other providers in the vicinity. This approach of merging and closing schools is widespread and, according to the European Commission (EC), two-thirds of countries and regions in the EU enacted such measures between 2010 and 2012 (EC/EACEA/Eurydice, 2013, p. 60[106]). In Poland, for instance, the number of rural primary schools has dropped by 9.3% since 2003-04 (EC/EACEA/Eurydice, 2013, p. 61[106]). There are different mechanisms to achieve such results. If a per-student allocation determines the financial means local authorities or school leaders receive for their institutions, the operation of small schools becomes less viable and local authorities might be given temporary grants to transition to larger units (OECD, 2018[105]). When school funding is devolved to the local level, local financial constraints or priorities in favour of other expenditures can drive school consolidation without direct national influence (Ares Abalde, 2014[107]). The levels of education provided by each institution can also be adjusted to cushion the impact of consolidation on younger students. This was the case in Estonia where upper secondary education was further separated from lower secondary to allow for the consolidation of the former (Santiago et al., 2016[108]).

Another approach to fostering economies of scale is the formation of clusters or federations, i.e. structures in which schools formally co-operate under a single leadership to allocate resources, such as staff, more flexibly and efficiently (OECD, 2018[105]). Clusters can involve both horizontal (i.e. integrating schools with a similar educational offer) and vertical integration (i.e. integrating schools at different levels of education). School clusters in countries covered by a recent OECD review were of different sizes but typically comprised up to 15 geographically close schools (OECD, 2018, pp. 143-144[105]). Similar to consolidation, clusters may be established through in the context of a Ministry of Education strategy or as a locally initiated approach to foster information exchange and more efficient resource use (Giordano, 2008[109]). Co-operation can also be initiated without formal clusters, for instance through schools' or local authorities' initiatives to bundle resources and exploit synergies (OECD, 2018[105]). In Spain, for instance, so-called "grouped rural schools" (*Colegios Rurales Agrupados*) allow providers across municipalities to share resources such as peripatetic teachers and instruction materials, jointly offer extracurricular activities and support the professional community of teachers through regular co-ordination meetings (Ares Abalde, 2014[107]). Such initiatives are shaped by multiple factors, including local capacity, potential incentives as well as the presence of pre-existing co-operation structures and traditions.

The provision of school transportation is key to avoid conflicts with parents' work schedules and ensure a safe commute for students when schools are not available nearby (OECD, 2018[105]; Gottfried, 2017[110]). In Chile, for example, the central government provides transportation services for students attending municipal schools located in remote areas free of charge from pre-primary to secondary education (Santiago et al., 2017[111]). While school transportation can mitigate some of the challenges of longer travel distances, there is also a risk that increased time of travel and transportation costs affect the net benefits of school consolidations, both financially and in terms of students' learning experience (Ares Abalde, 2014[107]). As the evidence on the association between school size and educational quality is patchy, it is important to carefully weigh the educational opportunities of larger schools against potential downsides outside of the classroom for students and their families.

Making the most of social innovation

Building a vibrant community life can improve attractiveness and help tackle societal challenges specific to rural communities. Social capital, civic engagement and other softer, more intangible attributes, such as social support networks, trust and co-operative norms, often do not rank high on policy agendas. This presents a missed opportunity for rural areas. These attributes do not only support higher individual and community well-being but also influence the effective functioning of both the economy and governments. Positive impact ranges from the mental health advantages of having good social support to improved institutional performance through greater civic engagement and benefits to businesses, which can trust interactions will run smoothly (Scrivens and Smith, 2013[112]; OECD, 2019[8]).

Box 3.7. Combatting loneliness in the UK

The Jo Cox Commission on Loneliness

Launched in January 2017, the Jo Cox Commission on Loneliness has sought ways to reduce loneliness and social isolation in the UK (Loneliness, 2017[113]). The commission is supporting work to tackle loneliness, which research has linked to an increased risk of coronary heart disease and stroke, depression, cognitive decline and Alzheimer's (Department for Digital, Culture, Media and Sport, 2018[114]). The adopted strategy highlights the importance of social relationships to health and well-being. The commission's work focuses on how policies can support the social dimension of well-being through organisations and services, community infrastructure and culture.

Rural Coffee Caravan

The Rural Coffee Caravan was launched in 2003 to tackle rural isolation and promote community spirit. Recognising the difficulty of limited transport for rural dwellers in regions without any remaining shops, pubs or post offices, community leaders wanted to provide the opportunity for people to meet others and learn about services provided in their towns. A locally-driven effort, volunteers made cakes and began visiting rural communities in Suffolk during the summer but soon expanded to visit village halls year-round. In addition to fostering community and bringing people together in a relaxed social atmosphere, the Coffee Caravan works with local agencies to provide information for people to access benefits, services and information.

The ACRE Network of Rural Community Councils

The Action with Communities in Rural England (ACRE) network is a national body for 38 charitable local development agencies that seeks to influence national policy on housing, health, transport, broadband, services and fuel poverty in rural England. The network has begun prioritising work on social well-being in rural communities, recently receiving an award to fund projects tackling loneliness. ACRE supports projects like LACEUP, a pilot programme that promotes healthy lifestyles, specifically targeting participants from lower socio-economic groups, women, people over 55 and people with disabilities.

GovTech Catalyst Fund

Launched in 2017, the GovTech Catalyst Fund provides support to SMEs to address public sector problems through innovation and emerging technologies. Five companies were awarded funding to develop technology to tackle rural isolation and loneliness in Monmouthshire. The companies are developing technology platforms to manage transport in rural communities and minimise the risk of digital exclusion in more isolated areas. One company, Zipabout, is seeking ways to optimise transport capacity and resources to develop a "mobility ecosystem", delivering rural mobility as a service.

Source: Department for Digital, Culture, Media and Sport (2018[114]), *A Connected Society: A Strategy for Tackling Lloneliness - Laying the Foundations for Change*, https://www.gov.uk/government/publications/a-connected-society-a-strategy-for-tackling-loneliness (accessed on 8 August 2019); Rural Coffee Caravan (n.d.[115]), Homepage, http://ruralcoffeecaravan.org.uk/; ACRE (n.d.[116]), *Lace Up*, http://acre.org.uk/our-work/laceup; https://www.monmouthshire.gov.uk/govtech_challenge/; SIMRA (SIMRA, n.d.[117]) (n.d.[117]), *Social Innovation is a Driver of Local Development in Marginalised Rural Areas*, http://www.simra-h2020.eu/wp-content/uploads/2019/02/BROCHURE-EN-compressed.pdf; Nordregio (2019[118]), "Social service innovation in rural areas – A user involvement guide", http://norden.diva-portal.org/smash/get/diva2:1300805/FULLTEXT01.pdf., Jo Cox Commission on Loneliness (2017[113]), *Combatting loneliness one conversation at a time*, https://www.ageuk.org.uk/globalassets/age-uk/documents/reports-and-publications/reports-and-briefings/active-communities/rb_dec17_jocox_commission_finalreport.pdf

Social innovation is a tool to find new solutions to societal challenges with the goal of enhancing societal well-being. Social innovation concerns regarding conceptual, process and product change as well as changes in financing and organisation entail new relationships with stakeholders in order to identify and deliver new services that improve the quality of life of individuals and communities.

Companies today are increasingly focused on corporate social and environmental responsibility. Many companies face new constraints in decision-making processes, including the impact of activities on the climate and local communities. Companies are trying new models to strengthen community sustainability. Co-creation and mutual co-operation and consultation imply involving different actors that work together to tackling a challenge openly. Partnerships with local actors (non-governmental organisations [NGOs], co-operatives and social leaders) help the companies get a better grasp of its market and future opportunities (e.g. expand knowledge about low-income groups) and gain social and environmental value-added through this socially innovative dynamic. For example, Danone, a major foods company, has been harnessing genuine co-creation strategies with certain NGOs and social entrepreneurs throughout the world to strengthen the local "ecosystems" and thereby the sustainability of its suppliers.

Environmental dimension

The environment is an essential component of well-being. This includes environmental quality such as the cleanliness of air and water, but also biodiversity and the availability of green spaces that impact individual health status as well as subjective life satisfaction (OECD, 2011[119]; OECD, 2014[120]). Further, the environment not only contributes to our current state of well-being but also has indispensable value for future well-being, which can be described as natural capital. This includes basic aspects such as the supply of food and freshwater, balanced ecosystems for pollution breakdown, climate stability and recovery from natural disasters.

The weakening of natural capital, poses a risk to regional well-being and development. Rising sea levels and the increased frequency of extreme weather events, the depletion of stocks like water and land make certain places increasingly inhabitable and threaten people's livelihoods forcing them to migrate or move. The latest OECD *How's Life?* publication raises concerns for the state of natural capital largely due to biodiversity loss and global greenhouse gas (GHG) emissions (OECD, 2020[121]). To ensure that future generations have the resources they need natural capital needs to be preserved.

Falsely, some policy makers view the environment as a trade-off with issues of economic growth. In fact, environmental well-being is inherently linked to other dimensions of well-being. First, the well-being of future generations is largely determined by our use of natural resources today, so long-term well-being and continued economic growth will require a more concerted effort to preserve our stock of natural capital. Any economic growth is unlikely to compensate for the effects of displacement and loss of livelihoods caused by climate change. As a result, rural policies need to recognise the interconnections between rural economic activities and environmental well-being, not only for rural populations but also for society as a whole.

The relevance of rural regions in the transition to a low-carbon economy

Rural economies are pivotal in the transition to a low-carbon economy because of their natural endowments and specialisation in resource-based industries. Climate change is already affecting these economic sectors (agriculture, forestry, fisheries, mining and energy) for example, due to dislocation and costs associated with the increasing frequency and intensity of extreme weather events. Without sufficient climate action and reduction of GHG emissions, global temperatures are likely to increase by more than 4°C by 2100. The list of consequences, already at an increase of 2°C, is long and devastating, ranging from mass extinction to extreme droughts and natural disasters that are "severe, pervasive and irreversible" and significantly impact human well-being including global food shortages (Masson-Delmotte et al., 2018[122]; Field et al., 2014[123]). To adhere to the goal of the Paris Agreement – limiting global average temperature rise to only 1.5 degrees compared to pre-industrial times – the reduction of GHG emissions in all sectors, especially energy and transport, need to go hand in hand with safeguarding the world's carbon sinks and biodiversity, and creating and investing in new ways for emission removal. These efforts can result in important well-being and development opportunities for rural regions.

Safeguarding natural capital – The importance of ecosystem services and biodiversity

Ecosystems and biodiversity are key for current and future human well-being and they help mitigate environmental pressures and natural threats. Rural paces can be home to ecosystems that provide food, freshwater, purify the air, decompose and detoxify waste, or help with pest control (IPCC, 2019[124]; OECD, 2011[125]). Further, many rural regions provide flora and fauna habitat varieties. Increasing losses in biological diversity, due to unsustainable activities, pose risks to food security and undermines the resilience of agricultural systems (IPBES, 2019[126]). In order to continue to use these natural benefits and provide services vital for the well-being of society as a whole, this natural capital needs to be preserved and restored where possible. Rural policies have an important role to play in protecting biodiversity and reversing negative trends.

Land present in rural regions is fundamental to absorbing carbon from the atmosphere. Forests and wetlands function as natural carbon sinks – trees and other vegetation absorb large amounts of carbon dioxide from the atmosphere and thereby sequester an amount equivalent to roughly one-third of global emissions (IPCC, 2019[124]). To contribute to combatting climate change carbon sinks need to be maintained and enhanced in order to remove greater quantities of carbon from the atmosphere. Drained peatlands and wetlands are concentrated sources of GHG emissions and need to be restored to halt the constant high levels of emissions (Mrotzek et al., 2020[127]). Possible ways to increase sequestration include reforestation (converting land back into forests) and biodiversity-sound afforestation (planting forests where they did not previously grow), organic carbon in croplands and grasslands. Bioenergy use with carbon capture and storage can also withdraw CO_2 (IPCC, 2019[124]). These offer development opportunities for rural regions that require more sustainable use of land. They also bring local challenges including competition for land use competition and sustainability concerns that will need to be carefully managed and governed.

Rural communities and land-users are often forced to make trade-offs between the environment and economic development. Services are often only recognised as provisioning services (production of food, wood and energy) rather than the full range of supporting, regulating and cultural ecosystem services (such as nutrient cycles, pollination, water filtration, biodiversity services, disaster prevention such as for floods, or recreation) (Natural Capital Germany, 2016[128]). One reason this happens is because – unlike food or other raw materials – these public goods do not have a clearly identified market value. Alongside exchange values linked to price and markets, which primarily reflect the values of provisioning services, policy makers must give due consideration to ensuring that the providers of regulating, cultural and supporting ecosystem services are rewarded for their services to society.

Emitting and wasting less – Realising a "just transition" while reducing carbon emissions and increasing efficiency

Rural economies are disproportionately affected by policy efforts to decarbonise the economy. Carbon-intensive rural industries like agriculture, mining and energy often are important employers in regions with low economic diversity. Measures to decarbonise the economy, by phasing out certain industries for instance, threaten local livelihoods and prosperity. While the need for mineral and metal extraction as well as food production will remain and indeed increase, the type of minerals quarried and the transformation of agricultural production systems for the transition to a low-carbon economy will present significant challenges for those working in the sector. Similarly, putting a price on carbon can increase transport costs for rural households and firms reliant on car and truck transportation. This can result in discontent about transformation measures that are geographically blind. The "*gilet jaunes*" demonstrations in France, for instance, were triggered by increasing the tax on diesel and petrol to facilitate the transition to a green economy. The policy was perceived as yet another measure favouring the needs of objectives of the well-off metropolitan parts of society and sparked greater discussions about regional inequalities and a tax system de-favouring the lower and middle class (Christophe Guilluy, 2018[129]; The Guardian, 2018[130]).

Striving for a just transition, policy makers need to consider environmental sustainability in coherence with decent work and social inclusion. The concept of "just transition" defines the understanding that developments towards an environmentally sustainable economy need to be managed in a way that contributes to job creation, job upgrading, social justice and poverty eradication (ILO, 2015[131]). The international community has acknowledged the importance of promoting a just transition for instance through the Paris Agreement, the ILO's Guidelines for a Just Transition and the EU's Coal Regions in Transition initiative. Just Transition requires social consensus on an appropriate enabling environment for transition which does not further disadvantage marginalised communities.

Well-managed transitions can also result in new opportunities for workers in rural places. The ILO estimates that a transition to more sustainable economies could generate up to 60 million new jobs worldwide over the next 2 decades. In the EU, between 2000 and 2014, 1.4 million jobs were added to the green economy (ILO, 2017[132]). Yet, without intentional policy efforts, new "green" energy jobs may not arise in the same places where employment in carbon-intensive industries declines. In Germany, a new Commission on Growth, Structural Change and Employment is taking steps to address the impact of the energy transition on mining communities (Steinberg, 2018[133]). The commission is preparing a roadmap for the phase-out of coal, with a special focus on strengthening growth and employment for the people living and working in affected regions.

Opportunities arising for rural regions from the transition to a low-carbon economy

Facilitating the development of renewable energy

In 2018, electricity and heat generation accounted for 42% of global emissions. At the same time, the share of renewables in meeting global energy demand is expected to grow by one-fifth in the next 5 years to reach 12.4% in 2023 (IEA, 2018[134]). In this context, renewable energy production is expected to deliver threefold: secure the increasing demand for energy (especially from cities); add to climate change mitigation; and enable economic development through economic diversification and job creation in rural economies.

Yet, renewable energy is not a silver bullet to create employment in rural places but requires careful consideration of local conditions (OECD, 2012[135]). For instance, while large biomass plants can generate new employment opportunities in rural communities, they require sustainable biomass production. Similarly, local employment opportunities can be limited as the energy sector is more capital- than labour-intensive and installations might source labour and equipment from outside the region, instead of drawing on local labour (OECD, 2012[135]). Hence, policy makers need to develop coherent sustainable strategies that ensure local populations receive adequate benefits for the cost they bear.

If local conditions are considered, renewable energy (RE) can be an opportunity for rural areas to capitalise on assets including space and resources. Benefits from RE for rural communities can include: i) new revenue sources that can be used to support service provision and diversity the economy; ii) new job and business opportunities, especially along the RE supply chain; iii) exposure to new technologies that create innovations in product, practices and policies as they are locally adapted; iv) capacity building and community empowerment through acquiring new skills and enhancing capacity to innovate; and v) opportunities to become energy independent (OECD, 2012[135]).

In order for RE development to have positive outcomes on the climate and rural economies, important policy consideration need to be taken into account. Energy strategies should be included in the local economic development strategy so that they reflect local potentials and needs. Further, alternative energy should not be considered as a standalone sector within regional rural economies. Potential backward and forward linkages with rural industries such as forestry or manufacturing should be developed through an integrated approach to RE deployment. Collective action should be stimulated through intermediate institutions active in rural communities and policy makers should aim at involving a larger number of stakeholders in policy interventions to stimulate sustainable development and improve local support (OECD, 2012[135]).

Rethinking transportation for rural dwellers

Globally transport accounts for one-quarter of total CO_2 emissions, largely driven by road transport (IEA, 2018[134]). While reducing transport emission is crucial for rural and urban areas alike, the solutions to each will vary greatly depending on the spatial configuration. In France, for instance, transport in areas of medium density close to cities accounts for about 17% of the country's total CO_2 emissions (The Shift Project, 2017[136]). Especially, medium- and low-density areas are heavily reliant on individual transportation including cars. Measures to punish high CO_2 emissions, for instance by increasing tax on fuel to disincentive car use, are likely to disproportionally affect rural dwellers. The analysis of on-road transportation in the US shows much higher per capita emissions in rural than in urban areas. This highlights the need to investigate low-carbon transportation alternatives in these areas that are place-specific (Muratore, 2017[137]).

Reducing travel demand in rural places can save emissions and has the potential to (re)vitalise local business and services. Business and service availability play a role in reducing transport-related CO_2 emissions in rural regions. The decline in local service provision in areas outside cities often results in the need for longer transport ways. Research shows that rural people like to use local services and that temporary subsidising local services can result in long term financial viability, while at the same time reducing emissions (Kamruzzaman, Hine and Yigitcanlar, 2015[138]). Further, innovations such as the collective distribution of e-commerce purchases to reduce individual travel can be used to support local business, as they function as order and receipt points (The Shift Project, 2017[136]). Other possible interventions involve aspects like increasing scope for teleworking or innovations in car-pooling possibilities. These can reduce travel and induce local interaction, for instance, if teleworking is located in rural co-working places. Germany's first and most well-known rural co-working space is situated in Bad Belzig, in Brandenburg. The Community and Concentrated Work in Nature (Coconat) is a temporary work station in a remodelled estate. Since 2017, it has become a meeting place for digital nomads, urban working tourist and regional dwellers working for the digital and knowledge industry (Coconat, 2020[139]).

Incentivising and supporting low-carbon transportation need to consider population density. In places close to cities, improved bicycle infrastructure and service offers as well as improvement in public transports (express lanes and optimisation of train-lines) are important to offer alternatives to car use (The Shift Project, 2017[136]). In remote places, that have greater distances to overcome, solutions need to focus on alternative engines and technological innovations to reduce emissions. As new technologies enter the market, policy makers need to make sure certain sections of society such as the elderly and unemployed, who might not be able to afford or engage in these innovations, are not left behind (Kamruzzaman, Hine and Yigitcanlar, 2015[138]).

Promoting sustainable land use and resource extraction that encourages the sustainable use of resources

Land offers large potential to reduce emissions through sustainable approaches to managing land and livestock. Today, 70% of the global, ice-free land surface is affected by human use (IPCC, 2019[124]). By

2050 alone, land will need to supply 60% more food than today. Current land use (mainly agriculture and forestry) is responsible for around 25% of global GHG emissions (OECD, 2015[140]). Agricultural food production systems will need to transition to a low-carbon model in order to satisfy the demand for food production in a sustainable manner. The potential for rural development from more sustainable land use still needs to be unlocked. There is a range of instruments policy makers use to reduce emissions from land use, including standards and rules for land management, increasing investments in technologies and research, and targeting environmental outcomes or production practices. Improving the status of the natural environment contributes to the well-being of rural residents and can bring economic benefits through enhancing the potential for tourism or the value of food production. However, more remains to be done to maximise the benefits of such policy approaches for rural development, rural economies and well-being.

Resource extraction is needed for RE technologies. An increased need and growing market for certain metals (e.g. cobalt, copper, lithium, nickel and zinc) offers development potential for rural economies. At the same time, extractive industries generate a number of environmental impacts that influence local well-being. There is strong evidence that mining and extractive industries generate localised environmental impacts and externalities ranging from effects on land, water and air quality to noise, vibrations, wildlife extinction and aesthetic impediments (Noronha and Nairy, 2005[141]; Hendryx, 2015[142]; World Economic Forum, 2016[143]). This needs to be carefully managed to ensure long-term quality of life and well-being for local residents. Most common well-being effects of environmental degradation caused by mining operations relate to health impediments, disturbance of residence as well as to other livelihood activities dependent on natural resources. For instance, significant use of water in mining activities, such as copper and gold, can create conflicts with agricultural businesses, particularly in remote areas which may lack the necessary infrastructure.

Across OECD countries, mining and extractive activities are closely regulated to reduce environmental risks and impacts (OECD, 2019[8]). An essential aspect of this is environmental impact assessments (EIA) that aim to identify potential effects and damages caused by developments and help to foresee costs, losses and consequences. Despite this, some mining regions past mining and extractive activities have left legacy costs, which are costly to ameliorate. For instance, the remediation in Saxony in Germany amounts to EUR 65 billion and a project to relocate and confine uranium mining waste in Colorado is budgeted at around USD 1 billion (NEA/OECD, 2014[144]). If these costs are not defined in agreements with companies, then the cost burden can fall to public authorities or be resolved through costly litigation.

Resulting from increased public concerns for environmental preservation and sustainable practices mining companies and governments aim to make mining more sustainable. Local measures include a greater focus on more efficient use of resources (using less water, power and land) as well as a greater focus on starting remediation processes alongside mining operations and reusing and recycling commodities and metals. This offers opportunities for rural economic development, such as local universities and firms that support the development of technologies that can increase resource efficiency in mining operations and the value chain, and the potential to use decommissioned mine sites for RE production or other businesses.

The transition to a low-carbon economy needs to reduce waste and enable more sustainable use of resources. The circular economy concept aims to improve economic and resource efficiency by linking production processes so that a side or waste product of one production process is used as an input to another production process. This way, the value of products, materials and resources is maintained for as long as possible and waste is significantly reduced or even eliminated (OECD, 2019[8]).

The concept of the circular economy is not only a way to potentially achieve better environmental quality and increased resource efficiency, it is also a means for greater well-being and new job opportunities. In Romania, for instance, a modern dairy farm makes full use of all its products and by-products. The dairy farm includes an onsite biogas station that is fed by slurry and milk-processing waste from the farm and a wastewater treatment facility that provides drinking water. The upgrade of the farm has resulted in the creation of additional jobs that offer a large variety of tasks that allow the inclusion of people from different backgrounds. Success factors of the project included careful business planning, that combines profitability as all as environmental benefits with exiting regional potential (European Network for Rural Development, 2017[145]).

The full potential of the circular economy in rural communities is still largely untapped. Today, less than 10% of the global economy is circular (Circle Economy, 2019[146]). Making use of this potential requires rethinking business models to become more circular and policy makers to set the right support and incentive structures. This includes legal and financial incentives but also the stimulation of innovation and building a common knowledge base (OECD, 2019[8]).

Identify ways to capture the value of positive externalities such as ecosystem services

Land use has a unique role to play in increasing carbon removals from the atmosphere. Yet, decisions on land use including agriculture, forest and infrastructure uses, are often guided by market forces, government incentives and regulations that do not always fully consider environmental costs and benefits (OECD, 2015[140]). The ability for rural communities to benefit from this requires a shift in the conceptualisation of environmental services.

Assessing, measuring and communicating positive externalities of ecosystem services can help to promote an improved understanding of the services that are largely unpriced. International initiatives include the UN Statistical Commission, System for Environmental Accounts (SEEA) and a global partnership launched by the World Bank to help countries implement natural capital accounting. Research suggests, however, that, these methods are complex to implement and require a tailor-made approach (OECD, 2015[140]). In the UK, for instance, the National Ecosystem Assessment framework considers economic value, health value and shared social value when evaluating changes in ecosystems (UK National Ecosystem Assessment, 2011[147]).

Payment schemes are one way for governments to reward the value of the provision of ecosystem services. Payments for ecosystem services (PES) usually involve per-hectare payments for the preservation or protection of a service. In France for instance, the European Agricultural Fund for Rural Development supports framers for conserving flower species in grasslands, meadows and pastures. A key aspect of the programme is that farmers qualify for the payment on the basis of demonstrated results rather than on performing specified actions and have full autonomy in how to manage their grasslands. This autonomy is an important success factor as it provides farmers with flexibility such as when to cut the grass. As an additional benefit, farmers develop knowledge on the identification of plants and develop a positive attitude and pride towards the value of biodiversity on their land (European Network for Rural Development, 2017[145]). Alternatively, payments can be dependent on fulfilling a defined management prescription designed to deliver specific benefits (such as providing suitable breeding habitat for vulnerable birds). Greater benefits can be generated where schemes are implemented by groups of farmers/land managers rather than individuals, thus at landscape scale, and hence ways to build the scale needed to be considered by policy makers.

The OECD has developed a list of 12 key criteria essential for increasing the cost-effectiveness of PES (Box 3.8) (OECD, 2010[148]). More recent assessments, however, find that financial incentives are not yet compelling enough (OECD, 2015[140]). Other factors such as empowerment, social dynamics, availability of advice and training, respect and recognition play an important role. Further research needs to be done on how sustainable land management practices including reduced deforestation, restoring degraded land, such as drained peatland, low-carbon agricultural practices and increased carbon sequestration in soils and forests can be used to foster rural development.

> **Box 3.8. Towards cost-effective payments for ecosystem services (PES)**
>
> 1. Remove perverse incentives such as environmentally harmful subsidies.
> 2. Clearly define property rights to empower communities.
> 3. Clearly define PES goals and objectives to enhance transparency and avoid ad hoc political influence.
> 4. Develop a robust monitoring and reporting framework to assess the performance of PES.
> 5. Identify buyers and ensure sufficient and long-term sources of financing.
> 6. Identify sellers and target ecosystem service benefits.
> 7. Establish baselines and target payments for ecosystems that are at risk of loss or to enhance their provision.
> 8. Differentiate payments based on the opportunity costs of service provision.
> 9. Consider bundling multiple ecosystem services.
> 10. Address leakages.
> 11. Ensure permanence.
> 12. Deliver performance-based payments and ensure adequate enforcement
>
> Source: OECD (2010[148]), *Paying for Biodiversity: Enhancing the Cost-Effectiveness of Payments for Ecosystem Services*, http://dx.doi.org/10.1787/9789264090279-en.

Policies to create opportunities from the transition to a the low-carbon economy for rural regions

Linking policy approaches

Transition processes involve synergies and trade-offs between different policy agendas. Competing policy objectives easily create confusion, for instance when it comes to trade-offs with regard to land use. Enhancing coherence requires overcoming sectoral and segmented decision-making and the promotion of policy integration across sectors such as climate change, industry, infrastructure, food security, forestry and economic development (OECD, 2015[140]).

A number of EU countries already embed climate change objectives in the local economic development strategies and programmes (OECD, 2013[149]). An analysis of the EU's Regulation for the European Agricultural Fund for Rural Development (EAFRD) for 2014-20 which identifies "promoting resource efficiency and supporting the shift towards a low-carbon and climate-resilient economy" as one of the six priorities for rural development, features a range of examples that range from finance to investment, skills acquisition, supporting market access and enabling co-operation (EU, 2017[150]). Apart from case studies, there is no in-depth understanding to what extent regional development policies feature climate change objectives and incentives to transition to a low-carbon economy across other OECD countries. Also, more work is needed to identify how policy makers could help manage synergies and trade-offs between the different agendas to make create opportunities for environmentally sustainable rural economies.

Towards a just transition – Building trust, understanding what matters most and navigating interests

As countries make commitments to transition to a low-carbon economy, policy makers must pay special attention to the needs of rural dwellers. In terms of renewable energy, for instance, rural communities are more likely to oppose installations if they are perceived as "top-down" and do not allow for participatory decision-making or provision of local benefits. This often happens when renewable energy policies are viewed as "hard" industrial policy that offer limited possibilities for hosting the involvement of communities and hence do not feel some ownership for interventions or share in the overall vision (OECD, 2012[135]).

Box 3.9. A just transition for the Latrobe Valley

Latrobe Valley is part of the Gippsland region in the state of Victoria, Australia. This region, to the east of Melbourne, is primarily rural and includes some small cities. Lignite mining and energy generation started in the 1920s. under a state-owned company which was privatised in the 1990s. This led to significant job losses and lacked a clear transition strategy. Today, the region is still a coal-mining region that produces large amounts of electricity through burning brown coal. Yet, power stations are closing. The first of the four power stations closed in 2017 and the remaining three are to close over the next 27 years.

To secure the economic, social and environmental future of the region, in November 2016, the Victorian government established the authority to co-ordinate the transition and stimulate economic development in the area. The transition package comprises roughly AUD 300 million and aims to promote economic diversification, growth and resilience through a range of projects.

From the onset, the government pledged to "do things differently" by working with and for local communities in collaborative approaches that bring local people, industry, education providers and levels of government together. It focuses on identifying aspects that matter to local communities and empower local leadership and strength for long-term resilience. In 2019, the programme could account for its success though 1 434 workers supported through the Worker Transition Service, 865 people employed through the Back to Work Scheme, 135 community projects supported through the Community Facility Fund, as well as 962 jobs created through the Economic Facilitation Fund.

Key success factors include:

- Government creating an authorisation environment including funding for four years covering comprehensive community impacts.
- A design using elements of success from elsewhere including hiring local people working for the authority and drawing on a mixture of experiences from education, economic and human services.
- Providing core immediate-response activities – Worker Transition Service, supply chain support, economic stimulation for growth and new jobs, infrastructure to improve liveability, support for social connection.
- Engaging in recovery and strategic action – Based on continuous discovery and check in within and beyond the community – focused on gaps, strengths and opportunity.

Source: Cain, K. (2019[151]), "A just transition for the Latrobe Valley", https://www.climate-transparency.org/wp-content/uploads/2019/03/17.Karen-Cain-Latrobe-Valley-Authority-February-2019.pdf.

To improve opportunities for the active participation of rural dwellers, policy makers must create meaningful mechanisms for engagement. Case studies suggest that, operating with a low communication threshold and offering platforms to involve different voices, is crucial to building trust in transition processes. Further, early engagement with key stakeholders in goal setting and planning will also help ensure the relevance and consistency of policy objectives and expectations. Generally, governments play a key role in terms of brokering and facilitating solutions between different stakeholders. They can balance multiple interests and objectives between researchers, private companies and civil society and are crucial to opening up new networks, supporting and mobilising leaders and enabling people to identify the collective benefit.

Figure 3.4. Overview of opportunities from the low-carbon economy for rural regions

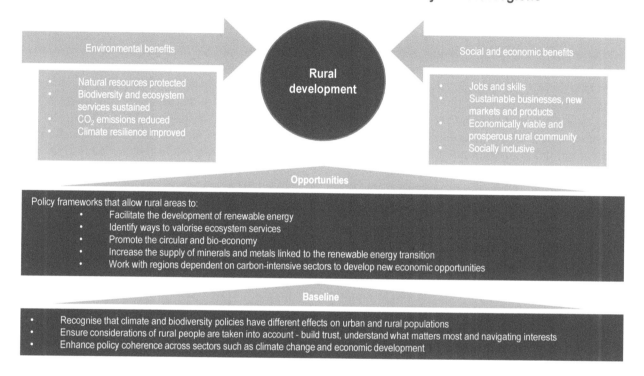

Crosscutting areas

Across these three priority objectives, a couple of crosscutting themes emerge. These are important to highlight the interconnectedness between the areas and to build an enabling environment for all three objectives.

- The first relates to human capital in rural regions. Upgrading skills and knowledge is needed to deal with upcoming changes in technology, demography and climate as well as to increase the attractiveness of rural regions to balance outmigration through improving quality of life across all three dimensions.

- The second relates to digital infrastructure and its possibility to open new frontiers of well-being in rural regions by enabling new ways to produce, work, communicate, trade, consult and manage.

- This is closely linked to the third, which deals with setting up required innovation systems to enable new opportunities, such as developing advanced automated production processes and new ways of public service delivery to remote places, as well as improving resource efficiency and smart ways to safeguard natural capital.

- Finally, the fourth suggests that all policy areas need to be sustainable. This not only means that policies should be aligned with environmental and climate change goals, they also need to consider well-being implications and outcomes for future generations and deliver on equity amongst peoples.

Demographic, economic and environmental changes require investment in human capital in rural communities, to ensure adaptability to a changing world and the uptake and creation of new ideas and technologies. Many rural places cannot draw on knowledge and skills as readily available as cities; instead, regional economies need to build human capital or attract people that have the needed skills and knowledge. Only in this way can rural communities ensure the future use of economic, social and environmental opportunities. Economically, human capital is key to build competitive economies, transition to higher-value-added activities and become more dynamic in adjusting to new market requirements and technological innovations, including expanding digital infrastructure. Similarly, upgrading skills is required to effectively deliver and maintain a new generation of educational and health services that embrace technological progress and require an understanding of software and hardware in all age groups. Environmentally, rural communities can only become resilient to climate change and drive mitigation activities if they possess the right expertise in sustainability practices and technologies, including sustainable land management and circular economy systems. The section above outlines different techniques that can be used to build human capital, ranging from improving local education offers and making use of currently underutilised knowledge such as traditional Indigenous knowledge and the internationalisation and attraction of migrants to access and build new networks and knowledge streams. In order to attract and retain people, rural places will also need well-maintained airports, roads and ports and other infrastructure to facilitate accessibility, as well as high-quality public services.

Any choice of location, be it for private or personal reasons, nowadays largely depends on available and affordable Internet connections in order to overcome distances to markets, services and knowledge. In the endeavour to attract people and businesses to rural communities, digital infrastructure including high-speed broadband as well as accompanying requirements such as stable energy, wires and computing centres is indispensable. Digital infrastructure can spur new forms of economic activities and jobs including tourism, services (marketing, design), niche manufacturing and food production and can provide alternative employment pathways for young people. It also enables contact and exchange with other sectors and markets which generates innovation. Further, it allows for the delivery of quality services at a reduced cost, for instance long-distance education. It can also be essential to overcome isolation and facilitate teleworking, as demonstrated during the COVID-19 crisis. Environmentally digital infrastructure is relevant as it can reduce the need for transportation and travel, which is an important source of emissions, but also enables a better understanding of land use through live tracking to inform policy making. Without the right incentives and policy interventions, rural communities could miss out on the benefits of the ongoing technological revolution further widening inequalities. Box 3.10 summarises good practices of rural broadband development.

Box 3.10. Good practices in broadband deployment

Building and expanding broadband networks and services can be challenging to different degrees for governments. The mechanisms used and resources available for expansion vary between countries and within regions. Nevertheless, there a few examples of initiatives that governments can take that can encourage private investment and redirect public resources to ensure the expansion of networks and, importantly, high quality Internet access for rural regions. Government initiatives to encourage high-quality broadband deployment in rural regions can be summarised in three broad types of initiatives: those that reduce financial costs to providers; those that reduce administrative costs to providers and those that encourage competitive markets to benefit consumers.

Investing in broadband infrastructure calls for heavy capital investments and long-term commitments both from governments and the private sector. In addition to ensuring that broadband infrastructure expenditure has a geospatial lens, governments can also work with the private sector to spur deployment by reducing costs to firms offering provision in rural regions. Where possible governments

---

can look for ways to subsidise, promote a reduction or a sharing of costs for new providers of broadband networks or services when they satisfy rural access requirements. This can include reducing or subsidising deployment costs related to constructing new networks or upgrading old ones, encouraging the use of existing networks from older technologies (such as telephony) for new purposes, or limiting financial barriers for the entry of new innovative technologies for broadband service deployment. In New Zealand, the US and the EU for example, public subsidies also serve the purpose of reducing financial (and physical barrier) costs for multiple service providers, as governments often tie requirements for "open access" in "last mile" or "middle mile" services. In Spain, a mandated "open access" regulation for the use of shared ducts in mobile networks fostered the deployment of fibre-to-the-home (FTTH) solutions (OECD, 2018[22]).

Second, municipalities and private sector stakeholders face a variety of administrative barriers and regulatory uncertainty when making investment decisions to expand broadband deployment. Ensuring that regulations are transparent, evidence-based and stable reduces the risks in undertaking long-term investment but helping co-ordinate between bodies to ensure that administrative barriers for municipalities and firms are reduced is an important initiative to encourage further broadband deployment. For example, in Spain, the General Telecommunications Law of 2014 set up a co-ordinating body whose purpose was to study and facilitate urban planning needs with municipalities and their applications procedures with the government authority in charge of issuing reports preceding broadband deployment (OECD, 2018[22]).

A critical aspect of broadband deployment in rural regions is public procurement practices that are fair, transparent and competitive. Competitive bidding and tender processes ensure higher quality standards and can encourage the geographical expansion of services depending on the conditionalities in the bidding process. Furthermore, in addition to better governance practices, governments can use competitive bidding processes to incorporate obligations that ensure access and quality of service to rural regions. Good practices in competitive bidding and tender processes for broadband deployment in rural regions include technologically neutral terminology, universal frameworks that reach geographical regions and minimum access and speed requirements. For example, in Portugal, the 2012 800 MHz Multiband Auction (4G) required mobile operators to extend coverage to 480 parishes which "tended to lack mobile broadband coverage" at speeds between 7.2 Mbps and 43.2 Mbps. In 2017, the renewal of contracts required extending mobile coverage to an extra 588 parishes (OECD, 2018[22]).

In addition, bottom-up approaches in broadband deployment can ensure that broadband deployment benefits rural communities. Municipal networks such as those in Sweden ("village fibre") directly involve the community in the planning, building and operation of the local fibre networks in co-operation with municipalities. Alternatively, government-backed reduced loans can specifically target deployment and development of rural municipalities as is observed in Germany by the KfW Development Bank (OECD, 2018[22]).

Source: OECD (2018[22]), "Bridging the rural digital divide", https://doi.org/10.1787/852bd3b9-en (accessed on 13 May 2020).

Rural communities can offer a quality of life and amenities attractive to people with skills and capital through innovation. While (product and service) innovations are important in the economic context to increase competitiveness and open up new market possibilities, they are also vital in solving societal and environmental challenges. Social innovations can be used as a tool to enhance social well-being and add to building vibrant community lives through advancing social support networks and trust amongst different population groups by reconfiguring societal practices in response to societal challenges. To integrate and retain migrants for instance, actions might include connecting migrants to the local labour market, learning about different traditions through communal social activities. Similarly, innovations are crucial to move away from unsustainable climate-damaging actions and seek solutions to improve aspects like energy efficiency, closing waste cycles and protecting biodiversity. Supporting the emergence of new practices can benefit rural regions across all three objectives. Innovation strategies should support a wide-ranging collaboration and partnership among public, private, not-for-profit and educational organisations to promote relationships and build trust, while also equipping local actors with leadership and networking skills, complementing know-how and assuring access to finance.

Overall, the policy focus must evolve away from short-term and sectoral support towards helping to build conditions favourable for the long-term sustainability of rural economies. Investments in human capital, digital infrastructure and innovation are important to enable the development of sustainable long-term goals rather than coming up with short-term responses. To secure well-being for future generations, sustainability – in terms of aligning economic, social and environmental objectives – is required. It is not enough to just deliver on one objective as all are interconnected. This means that policies to increase productivity cannot fall short of environmental or social considerations. Similarly, environmental considerations such as transitioning out of carbon-intensive industries must be economically and socially just. Hence all rural policies should make sure they are sustainability-proof.

Concluding remarks

Rural Well-being: Geographies of Opportunities is a policy framework aimed at helping national governments support rural development across different types of rural regions, encompasses economic, social and environmental objectives and is inclusive of different stakeholders. Earlier frameworks in OECD countries on rural development focused on sectoral support and subsidies to promote rural development. The rural well-being approach is a progression and a refinement of the New Rural Paradigm from 2006 and represents a people-centred approach, focusing on how to improve the well-being of rural dwellers, making rural regions places of opportunities.

In essence, the OECD's new rural development framework, *Rural Well-being: Geography of Opportunities*, is built on:

- **Three types of rural regions** – Those near a large city, those with a small or medium city and remote regions.
- **Three objectives** – Encompassing not only economic but also social and environmental objectives.
- **Three different stakeholders** – Including the government as well as the private sector and civil society.

The framework is based on what OECD countries have learned facing numerous structural changes that have had strong implications for rural region, many of which have been amplified by the recent COVID-19 pandemic. Structural changes include global megatrends like demographic change, increased digitalisation and environmental change that play out differently in rural regions: the population has grown slower in rural regions compared to metropolitan regions; shrinking shares of younger populations create labour market shortages; technology will have the ability to improve living standards but also carries the risk of job relocations; and rural regions are crucial but also vulnerable during the transition to a low-carbon economy. The chapter further explains how the shift to a service-driven economy bundled with GVCs has disadvantaged OECD rural regions that have limited economic diversity and rely on tradeable goods. Growing regional inequalities have further shown that GDP is not good enough to understand what constitutes a good life for people as well as what assets regions might have. In line with that, the chapter argues for a more comprehensive framework to cope with current and forthcoming changes in rural places. It highlights the need for rural policy makers to find ways to succeed in a dynamic environment and address a number of interconnected challenges and opportunities at once.

The analysis of contemporary rural trends suggests three priority dimensions of action for OECD countries to increase well-being. The first, the economic dimension, is focusing on how to increase productivity and foster competitiveness in the context of GVCs and digitalisation. This includes implementing incentives and mechanisms that support rural economies in identifying unique assets, enhancing innovation investments in enabling factors such as developing skills and fostering internationalisation. The second, the social dimension, is how to adapt to an ageing population and address demographic pressures. Focus areas include making rural places more attractive through the provision of high-quality services and leveraging economic opportunities associated with an ageing population. Further, it highlights opportunities resulting from social innovation and reinforcing rural education systems. The third, environmental dimension is supporting rural economies in the shift to a low-carbon economy and ensuring the protection of natural capital. Priorities will include facilitating shifts to more sustainable forms of land use, investment in renewable energy, devising new systems of rural transportation and proactive support for regions affected by economic restructuring. Across all of these dimensions, four crosscutting areas are identified. They include: investments in human capital; digital infrastructure; innovation; and sustainable thinking. These areas are important to build and create an enabling environment for all three objectives illustrating their interconnectedness.

References

ACRE (n.d.), *Lace Up*, Action with Communities in Rural England, http://acre.org.uk/our-work/laceup. [116]

Aiyar, S. and C. Ebeke (2019), "Inequality of opportunity, inequality of income and economic growth", *IMF Working Paper*, International Monetary Fund, https://www.imf.org/en/Publications/WP/Issues/2019/02/15/Inequality-of-Opportunity-Inequality-of-Income-and-Economic-Growth-46566 (accessed on 10 July 2019). [43]

Ares Abalde, M. (2014), "School Size Policies: A Literature Review", *OECD Education Working Papers*, No. 106, OECD Publishing, Paris, https://dx.doi.org/10.1787/5jxt472ddkjl-en. [107]

Autor, D. (2019), "Work of the past, work of the future", *AEA Papers and Proceedings*, Vol. 109, pp. 1-32, http://dx.doi.org/10.1257/pandp.20191110. [23]

Barrientos, S. (2014), *Gender and Global Value Chains: Challenges of Economic and Social Upgrading in Agri-Food*, European University Institute, https://cadmus.eui.eu/bitstream/handle/1814/32897/RSCAS_2014_96.pdf?sequence=1&isAllowed=y (accessed on 25 July 2019). [57]

Bernanke, B. (2005), "Federal Reserve Board speech", https://www.federalreserve.gov/BoardDocs/speeches/2005/20050119/default.htm (accessed on 6 June 2019). [44]

BHP Billiton Chile (2013), *Sustainability Report 2014 - BHP Billiton Pampa Norte Minera Escondida*, https://www.bhp.com/-/media/documents/community/2014/csr-eng150518sustainabilityreport2014bhpbillitonchileoperations.pdf. [75]

Bosworth, G. and V. Venhorst (2017), "Economic linkages between urban and rural regions - What's in it for the rural?", http://dx.doi.org/10.1080/00343404.2017.1339868. [16]

Botta, E. (2018), "A review of "Transition Management" strategies: Lessons for advancing the green low-carbon transition", OECD, Paris, https://www.oecd.org/greengrowth/GGSD_2018_IssuePaper_Transition_Management.pdf (accessed on 2 August 2019). [39]

Boudain, J. (2020), *Presentation of Josée Boudain, Director of "École en réseau"*, OECD Webinar on Rural Education Delivery, 2 April 2020. [99]

Brummitt, C. et al. (2018), *Machine-learned patterns suggest that diversification drives economic development*, https://arxiv.org/pdf/1812.03534.pdf (accessed on 22 July 2019). [59]

Bulderberga, Z. (2011), "Rural-urban partnership for regional development", *Social Research*, Vol. 1/22, pp. 14-24, http://www.su.lt/bylos/mokslo_leidiniai/soc_tyrimai/2011_22/bulderberga.pdf (accessed on 30 July 2019). [20]

Cain, K. (2019), "A just transition for the Latrobe Valley", https://www.climate-transparency.org/wp-content/uploads/2019/03/17.Karen-Cain-Latrobe-Valley-Authority-February-2019.pdf. [151]

Canuto, O. and M. Cavallari (2012), "Natural Capital and the Resource Curse", *World Bank - Economic Premise* 83. [50]

CEFRIO (2015), *Usages du numérique dans les écoles québécoises*, CEFRIO, https://cefrio.qc.ca/media/1893/rapport-synthese_usages_du_numerique_dans_les_ecoles.pdf (accessed on 25 February 2020). [97]

CEFRIO (2011), *L'École éloignée en réseau (ÉÉR), un modèle*, http://www.cefrio.qc.ca/fr/documents/projets/46-Ecole-eloignee-en-reseau.html (accessed on 27 January 2020). [96]

Chetty, R. et al. (2018), *The Opportunity Atlas: Mapping the Childhood Roots of Social Mobility*, National Bureau of Economic Research, Cambridge, MA, http://dx.doi.org/10.3386/w25147. [104]

Christophe Guilluy (2018), "France is deeply fractured. Gilets jaunes are just a symptom", The Guardian, https://www.theguardian.com/commentisfree/2018/dec/02/france-is-deeply-fractured-gilets-jeunes-just-a-symptom (accessed on 5 August 2019). [129]

Circle Economy (2019), *Circularity Gap Report 2019*. [146]

Coconat (2020), *Coconat - A Workation Retreat*, https://coconat-space.com/ (accessed on 23 July 2020). [139]

Committee on Climate Change (2019), *Net Zero - The UK's Contribution to Stopping Global Warming*, https://www.theccc.org.uk/publication/net-zero-the-uks-contribution-to-stopping-global-warming/ (accessed on 27 April 2020). [36]

Cornia, G. et al. (2017), "Economic inequality and social progress", https://comment.ipsp.org/chapter/chapter-3-inequality-and-social-progress#-chapter-3-inequality-and-social-progress- (accessed on 29 May 2019). [10]

Darby, M. (2019), "Which countries have a net zero carbon goal?", *2019*, https://www.climatechangenews.com/2019/06/14/countries-net-zero-climate-goal/ (accessed on 18 July 2019). [37]

De Muro, P., U. Degli Studi and R. Tre (2010), "Rethinking rural well-being and poverty", [13] http://www.fao.org/fileadmin/templates/ess/pages/rural/wye_city_group/2010/May/WYE_2010 .1.1_De_Muro.pdf (accessed on 11 June 2019).

Department for Digital, Culture, Media and Sport (2018), *A Connected Society: A Strategy for* [114] *Tackling Lloneliness - Laying the Foundations for Change*, https://www.gov.uk/government/publications/a-connected-society-a-strategy-for-tackling-loneliness (accessed on 8 August 2019).

Diario de Valladolid (2019), "Soria exporta la logística social como franquicia [Soria exports [101] social logistics as franchise]", Diario de Valladolid, https://diariodevalladolid.elmundo.es/articulo/las-caras-del-exito/soria-exporta-logistica-social-franquicia/20191014121700351968.html (accessed on 25 February 2020).

Dyson, A., K. Kerr and I. Jones (2016), *Increasing the Use of School Facilities - Part A: UK and* [91] *International Evidence - Part B: Evidence from Wales Ian Bottrill (Learning for Leadership Cymru) and Pam Boyd (ShawBoyd Associates)*, http://ppiw.org.uk/files/2016/04/Increasing-the-Use-of-School-Facilities-Report.pdf (accessed on 5 June 2019).

EBRD (2018), *Transition Report 2018-19*, European Bank for Reconstruction and Development, [28] https://www.ebrd.com/transition-report (accessed on 4 July 2019).

EC (2015), *Territorial Agenda 2020 Put In Practice - Enhancing the Efficiency and Effectiveness* [42] *of Cohesion Policy by a Place-Based Approach - Volume I – Synthesis Report*, European Commission, https://ec.europa.eu/regional_policy/sources/policy/what/territorial-cohesion/territorial_agenda_2020_practice_report.pdf (accessed on 6 June 2019).

EC (2008), "Poverty and social exclusion in rural areas", European Commission, Brussels, [82] https://ec.europa.eu/social/BlobServlet?docId=3032&langId=en.

EC/EACEA/Eurydice (2013), *Funding of Education in Europe 2000-2012: The Impact of the* [106] *Economic Crisis*, http://dx.doi.org/10.2797/50340.

Echazarra, A. and T. Radinger (2019), "Learning in rural schools: Insights from PISA, TALIS and [32] the literature", *OECD Education Working Papers*, No. 196, OECD Publishing, Paris, https://doi.org/10.1787/8b1a5cb9-en (accessed on 3 July 2019).

ENRD (2018), "Strategy for Inner Areas Italy - A new laboratory for integrated rural development [93] and service innovation", Working Document, https://enrd.ec.europa.eu/sites/enrd/files/tg_smart-villages_case-study_it_0.pdf (accessed on 5 June 2019).

EU (2017), *Green Economy Opportunities for Rural Europe*, European Union, [150] http://ec.europa.eu/ecolabel/ (accessed on 22 August 2019).

European Network for Rural Development (2017), *Transition to Greener Rural Economies*, [145] Projects Brochure, http://dx.doi.org/10.2762/824841.

Exton, C. and M. Shinwell (2018), "Policy use of well-being metrics: Describing countries' [12] experiences", *OECD Statistics Working Papers*, No. 2018/07, OECD Publishing, Paris, https://doi.org/10.1787/d98eb8ed-en (accessed on 22 July 2019).

Field, C. et al. (2014), "Part A: Global and sectoral aspects: Working group II contribution to the fifth assessment report of the intergovernmental panel on climate change", in *Climate Change 2014 Impacts, Adaptation and Vulnerability*, Cambridge University Press, http://dx.doi.org/10.1017/CBO9781107415379. [123]

Freshwater, D. et al. (2019), "Business development and the growth of rural SMEs", *OECD Regional Development Working Papers*, No. 2019/07, OECD Publishing, Paris, https://dx.doi.org/10.1787/74256611-en. [51]

Freshwater, D. and T. Wojan (2014), *User Entrepreneurship: Defining and Identifying an Explicit Type of Innovation*, https://ideas.repec.org/p/ags/ukysps/229301.html (accessed on 12 June 2019). [21]

Frocrain, P. and P. Giraud (2017), "The evolution of tradable and non-tradable employment: Evidence from France", http://www.i-3.fr/ (accessed on 18 June 2019). [52]

García, E. and E. Weiss (2017), *Reducing and Averting Achievement Gaps: Key Findings from the Report 'Education Inequalities at the School Starting Gate' and Comprehensive Strategies to Mitigate Early Skills Gaps*, https://www.epi.org/files/pdf/130888.pdf (accessed on 5 June 2019). [90]

Giordano, E. (2008), "School clusters and teacher resource centres", International Institute for Educational Planning, UNESCO. [109]

Glaeser, E. and J. Gottlieb (2008), "The economics of place-making policies", https://www.brookings.edu/wp-content/uploads/2008/03/2008a_bpea_glaeser.pdf (accessed on 4 July 2019). [29]

Gottfried, M. (2017), "Linking getting to school with going to school", *Educational Evaluation and Policy Analysis*, Vol. 39/4, pp. 571-592, http://dx.doi.org/10.3102/0162373717699472. [110]

Graham, C. (2018), "Subjective well-being in economics", *The Oxford Handbook of Well-Being and Public Policy*, http://dx.doi.org/10.1093/oxfordhb/9780199325818.013.14. [11]

Gungor, R. and E. Prins (2011), *Distance Learning in Adult Basic Education: A Review of the Literature*, Institute for the Study of Adult Literacy, The Pennsylvania State University, https://ed.psu.edu/goodling-institute/research/abe-lit-review-for-rural-pa-8-4-11 (accessed on 25 March 2020). [78]

Halseth, G. and L. Ryser (2006), "Trends in service delivery: Examples from rural and small town canada, 1998 to 2005", *Journal of Rural and Community Development*, https://journals.brandonu.ca/jrcd/article/view/40 (accessed on 11 July 2019). [26]

Hendryx, M. (2015), "The public health impacts of surface coal mining", *The Extractive Industries and Society*, Vol. 2/4, pp. 820-826, http://dx.doi.org/10.1016/J.EXIS.2015.08.006. [142]

Hernández, M. (2018), "La Exclusiva: una segunda oportunidad para la vida rural [La Exclusiva: A second chance for the rural life]]", Forbes España, https://forbes.es/empresas/41955/la-exclusiva-una-segunda-oportunidad-para-la-vida-rural/ (accessed on 25 February 2020). [100]

Hojem, P. (2015), *Mining in the Nordic Countries: A Comparative Review of Legislation and Taxation*, http://www.norden.org (accessed on 31 March 2020). [73]

IEA (2018), *CO2 Emissions from Fuel Combustion 2018*, International Energy Agency. [134]

ILO (2017), *A Just Transition to a Sustainable Future - Next steps for Europe*, International Labour Organization, https://www.ilo.org/wcmsp5/groups/public/---europe/---ro-geneva/---ilo-brussels/documents/publication/wcms_614024.pdf (accessed on 19 August 2019).   [132]

ILO (2015), *Guidelines for a Just Transition Towards Environmentally Sustainable Economies and Societies for All*, International Labour Organization, http://www.ilo.org/publns (accessed on 2 August 2019).   [131]

IPBES (2019), *Report of the Plenary of the Intergovernmental Science-Policy Platform on Biodiversity and Ecosystem Services on the Work of Its Seventh Session*, Intergovernmental Science-Policy Platform on Biodiversity and Ecosystem Services, https://www.ipbes.net/system/tdf/ipbes_7_10_add-1-_advance_0.pdf?file=1&type=node&id=35245 (accessed on 19 August 2019).   [126]

IPCC (2019), *Climate Change and Land*, Intergovernmental Panel on Climate Change, https://www.ipcc.ch/site/assets/uploads/2019/08/4.-SPM_Approved_Microsite_FINAL.pdf (accessed on 14 August 2019).   [124]

IPCC (2018), "Summary for policymakers - Global warming of 1.5 °C", in *An IPCC Special Report on the Impacts of Global Warming of 1.5°C Above Pre-Industrial Levels and Related Global Greenhouse Gas Emission Pathways*.   [122]

Jenkins, J. (2019), "An ageing workforce isn't a burden. It's an opportunity", World Economic Forum, https://www.weforum.org/agenda/2019/01/an-aging-workforce-isnt-a-burden-its-an-opportunity/ (accessed on 2 September 2019).   [86]

Kamruzzaman, M., J. Hine and T. Yigitcanlar (2015), "Investigating the link between carbon dioxide emissions and transport-related social exclusion in rural Northern Ireland", *International Journal of Environmental Science and Technology*, Vol. 12, http://dx.doi.org/10.1007/s13762-015-0771-8.   [138]

Kline, P. and E. Moretti (2014), "People, places, and public policy: Some simple welfare economics of local economic development programs", http://dx.doi.org/10.1146/annurev-economics-080213-041024.   [34]

Kline, P. et al. (2013), "Local economic development, agglomeration economies and the big push: 100 years of evidence from the Tennessee Valley Authority", https://eml.berkeley.edu//~pkline/papers/TVA_web.pdf (accessed on 6 June 2019).   [41]

Kohllechner-Autto, M., S. Nisula and K. Skantz (2019), *Good Practice Guide: Strategies Supporting Social Enterprises, and Concrete Examples of Social Innovation and Social Enterprises from Sparsely Populated European Regions*, Publications of Lapland UAS, Rovaniemi, https://issuu.com/lapinamk/docs/d_7_2019_kohllechner-autto_nisula_s (accessed on 25 February 2020).   [102]

Loneliness, J. (2017), *Combatting loneliness one conversation at a time*.   [113]

Malamud, O. and A. Wozniak (2012), *The Impact of College on Migration Evidence from the Vietnam Generation*, http://jhr.uwpress.org.ezproxy.princeton.edu/content/47/4/913.full.pdf (accessed on 2 July 2019).   [31]

Meijers, E. and M. Burger (2017), "Stretching the concept of 'borrowed size'", *Urban Studies Journal Limited*, Vol. 54/1, pp. 269-291, http://dx.doi.org/10.1177/0042098015597642.   [19]

Mitchell, C. and K. O'Neill (2015), "Tracing economic transition in the mine towns of northern Ontario: An application of the "resource-dependency model"", *The Canadian Geographer / Le Géographe canadien*, Vol. 60/1, pp. 91-106, http://dx.doi.org/10.1111/cag.12238. [69]

Mrotzek, A. et al. (2020), "Mass balances of a drained and a rewetted peatland: On former losses and recent gains", *Soil Systems*, Vol. 4/1, p. 16, http://dx.doi.org/10.3390/soilsystems4010016. [127]

Mudambi, R. (2008), "Location, control and innovation in knowledge-intensive industries", *Journal of Economic Geography*, Vol. 8, pp. 699-725, http://dx.doi.org/10.1093/jeg/lbn024. [58]

Muratore, P. (2017), *Driving Transportation Emission: A Spatial Analysis of On-Road CO2*, Tufts Univeriisty, https://sites.tufts.edu/gis/files/2018/03/Muratore_Paulina_UEP232_2017.pdf (accessed on 21 August 2019). [137]

NAKANO (2014), "The "sixth industrialization" for Japanese agricultural development", *The Ritsumeikan Economic Review*, Vol. LXIII/3. [47]

National Endowment for the Arts (2017), *Rural Arts, Design, and Innovation in America - Research Findings from the Rural Establishment Innovation Survey*, https://www.arts.gov/artistic-fields/research-analysis/arts-data-profiles/arts-data-profile-15. [65]

Natural Capital Germany (2016), *Ecosystem Services in Rural Areas – Basis for Human Wellbeing and Sustainable Economic Development - Summary for Decision-Makers*, Leibniz University Hanover, Hanover, Helmholtz Centre for Environmental Research – UFZ, Leipzig, https://www.ufz.de/export/data/global/190551_TEEB_DE_Landbericht_Kurzfassung_engl_web_bf.pdf (accessed on 19 August 2019). [128]

NEA/OECD (2014), *Managing Environmental and Health Impacts of Uranium Mining*, OECD, Paris, https://www.oecd-nea.org/ndd/pubs/2014/7062-mehium.pdf (accessed on 8 May 2019). [144]

Nordregio (2019), "Social service innovation in rural areas – A user involvement guide", *Policy Brief no. 2*. [118]

Noronha, L. and S. Nairy (2005), *Assessing Quality of Life in a Mining Region*, https://www.jstor.org/stable/pdf/4416014.pdf (accessed on 6 March 2019). [141]

OECD (2020), *How's Life? 2020: Measuring Well-being*, OECD Publishing, Paris, https://dx.doi.org/10.1787/9870c393-en. [121]

OECD (2019), *Agricultural Policy Monitoring and Evaluation 2019*, OECD Publishing, Paris, https://doi.org/10.1787/39bfe6f3-en (accessed on 4 July 2019). [6]

OECD (2019), *Climate: Reclaiming our Common Future*, OECD, Paris, http://www.oecd.org/environment/cc/climate-lecture-reclaiming-our-common-future.pdf (accessed on 18 July 2019). [35]

OECD (2019), *Linking Indigenous Communities with Regional Development*, OECD Rural Policy Reviews, OECD Publishing, Paris, https://dx.doi.org/10.1787/3203c082-en. [49]

OECD (2019), *Linking the Indigenous Sami People with Regional Development in Sweden*, OECD Rural Policy Reviews, OECD Publishing, Paris, https://dx.doi.org/10.1787/9789264310544-en. [40]

OECD (2019), *OECD Mining Regions Case Study: Outokumpu and North Karelia, Finland*, OECD Rural Policy Reviews, OECD Publishing, Paris, https://doi.org/10.1787/cd72611b-en. [53]

OECD (2019), *OECD Regional Outlook 2019: Leveraging Megatrends for Cities and Rural Areas*, OECD Publishing, Paris, https://dx.doi.org/10.1787/9789264312838-en. [8]

OECD (2019), *OECD SME and Entrepreneurship Outlook 2019*, OECD Publishing, Paris, https://doi.org/10.1787/34907e9c-en (accessed on 13 June 2019). [4]

OECD (2019), *OECD Territorial Reviews: Hidalgo, Mexico*, OECD Territorial Reviews, OECD Publishing, Paris, https://dx.doi.org/10.1787/9789264310391-en. [71]

OECD (2018), "Bridging the rural digital divide", *OECD Digital Economy Papers*, No. 265, OECD Publishing, Paris, https://doi.org/10.1787/852bd3b9-en (accessed on 13 May 2020). [22]

OECD (2018), "Enhancing Rural Innovation - 11th OECD Rural Development Conference", OECD, Paris, http://www.oecd.org/regional/Proceedings.pdf (accessed on 21 June 2019). [62]

OECD (2018), *Job Creation and Local Economic Development 2018: Preparing for the Future of Work*, OECD Publishing, Paris, https://dx.doi.org/10.1787/9789264305342-en. [76]

OECD (2018), *OECD Regions and Cities at a Glance 2018*, OECD Publishing, Paris, https://dx.doi.org/10.1787/reg_cit_glance-2018-en. [61]

OECD (2018), *OECD Rural Policy Reviews: Poland 2018*, OECD Rural Policy Reviews, OECD Publishing, Paris, https://dx.doi.org/10.1787/9789264289925-en. [3]

OECD (2018), *Productivity and Jobs in a Globalised World: (How) Can all Regions Benefit?*, OECD Publishing, Paris, https://doi.org/10.1787/9789264293137-en (accessed on 18 June 2019). [18]

OECD (2018), *Responsive School Systems: Connecting Facilities, Sectors and Programmes for Student Success*, OECD Reviews of School Resources, OECD Publishing, Paris, https://dx.doi.org/10.1787/9789264306707-en. [105]

OECD (2018), "Rural 3.0. Policy note - A framework for rural development", OECD, Paris, https://www.oecd.org/cfe/regional-policy/Rural-3.0-Policy-Note.pdf (accessed on 19 August 2019). [48]

OECD (2018), *Seven Questions about Apprenticeships: Answers from International Experience*, OECD Reviews of Vocational Education and Training, OECD Publishing, Paris, https://dx.doi.org/10.1787/9789264306486-en. [80]

OECD (2018), *The Productivity-Inclusiveness Nexus*, OECD Publishing, Paris, https://dx.doi.org/10.1787/9789264292932-en. [45]

OECD (2018), *Working Together for Local Integration of Migrants and Refugees*, OECD Publishing, Paris, https://dx.doi.org/10.1787/9789264085350-en. [25]

OECD (2017), *How's Life? 2017 Measuring Well-being*, OECD Publishing, Paris, https://doi.org/10.1787/how_life-2017-en (accessed on 13 August 2019). [15]

OECD (2017), *Investing in innovation and skills: Thriving in global value chains*, OECD Publishing, Paris, https://doi.org/10.1787/9e296b43-en (accessed on 19 June 2019). [68]

OECD (2017), "Mining regions and their cities - Scoping paper", OECD, Paris. [72]

OECD (2017), *OECD Territorial Reviews: Northern Sparsely Populated Areas*, OECD Territorial Reviews, OECD Publishing, Paris, https://doi.org/10.1787/9789264268234-en (accessed on 3 September 2019). [87]

OECD (2016), "Global Value Chains and Trade in Value-Added: An Initial Assessment of the Impact on Jobs and Productivity", *OECD Trade Policy Papers*, No. 190, OECD Publishing, Paris, https://doi.org/10.1787/5jlvc7sb5s8w-en (accessed on 26 July 2019). [77]

OECD (2016), *Job Creation and Local Economic Development 2016*, OECD Publishing, Paris, https://dx.doi.org/10.1787/9789264261976-en. [70]

OECD (2016), *OECD Regional Outlook 2016: Productive Regions for Inclusive Societies*, OECD Publishing, Paris, https://dx.doi.org/10.1787/9789264260245-en. [7]

OECD (2016), *OECD Territorial Reviews: Japan 2016*, OECD Territorial Reviews, OECD Publishing, Paris, https://dx.doi.org/10.1787/9789264250543-en. [92]

OECD (2016), *Well-being in Danish Cities*, OECD Publishing, Paris, https://dx.doi.org/10.1787/9789264265240-en. [89]

OECD (2015), "Aligning policies for the transition to a low-carbon economy", OECD, Paris. [140]

OECD (2015), *The Innovation Imperative: Contributing to Productivity, Growth and Well-Being*, OECD Publishing, Paris, http://dx.doi.org/10.1787/9789264239814-en. [64]

OECD (2015), *The Metropolitan Century: Understanding Urbanisation and its Consequences*, OECD Publishing, Paris, https://dx.doi.org/10.1787/9789264228733-en. [46]

OECD (2014), *How's Life in Your Region?: Measuring Regional and Local Well-being for Policy Making*, OECD Publishing, Paris, https://dx.doi.org/10.1787/9789264217416-en. [120]

OECD (2014), *Recommendation of the Council on Effective Public Investment Across Levels of Government*, OECD, Paris, http://www.oecd.org/regional-policy (accessed on 6 June 2019). [88]

OECD (2014), "The Silver Economy as a Pathway for Growth Insights from the OECD-GCOA Expert Consultation", OECD, Paris, https://www.oecd.org/sti/the-silver-economy-as-a-pathway-to-growth.pdf (accessed on 2 September 2019). [85]

OECD (2013), *Interconnected Economies: Benefiting from Global Value Chains*, OECD Publishing, Paris, https://doi.org/10.1787/9789264189560-en (accessed on 25 July 2019). [55]

OECD (2013), *Policy Instruments to Support Green Growth in Agriculture*, OECD Green Growth Studies, OECD Publishing, Paris, https://dx.doi.org/10.1787/9789264203525-en. [149]

OECD (2012), *Linking Renewable Energy to Rural Development*, OECD Green Growth Studies, OECD Publishing, Paris, https://dx.doi.org/10.1787/9789264180444-en. [135]

OECD (2012), *Promoting Growth in All Regions*, OECD Publishing, Paris, https://doi.org/10.1787/9789264174634-en (accessed on 29 July 2019). [5]

OECD (2011), *Compendium of OECD Well-being Indicators*, OECD Better Life Initiative, OECD, Paris, http://www.oecd.org/sdd/47917288.pdf (accessed on 29 May 2019). [14]

OECD (2011), *Help Wanted?: Providing and Paying for Long-Term Care*, OECD Publishing, Paris, https://doi.org/10.1787/9789264097759-en. [24]

OECD (2011), *Regions and Innovation Policy*, OECD Reviews of Regional Innovation, OECD Publishing, Paris, http://dx.doi.org/10.1787/9789264097803-en. [63]

OECD (2011), *The Economic Significance of Natural Resources: Key Points for Reformers in Eastern Europe, Caucasus and Central Asia*, OECD, Paris, http://www.oecd.org/env/outreach/2011_AB_Economic%20significance%20of%20NR%20in%20EECCA_ENG.pdf (accessed on 20 June 2019). [125]

OECD (2011), *Together for Better Public Services: Partnering with Citizens and Civil Society*, OECD Public Governance Reviews, OECD Publishing, Paris, https://doi.org/10.1787/9789264118843-en (accessed on 24 July 2019). [95]

OECD (2011), *Well-being Topics and Indicators*, OECD, Paris, http://www.oecd.org/regional/regional-policy/website-topics-indicators-overview.pdf (accessed on 18 May 2019). [119]

OECD (2010), *Paying for Biodiversity: Enhancing the Cost-Effectiveness of Payments for Ecosystem Services*, OECD Publishing, Paris, https://dx.doi.org/10.1787/9789264090279-en. [148]

OECD (2010), *Strategies to Improve Rural Service Delivery*, OECD Rural Policy Reviews, OECD Publishing, Paris, https://dx.doi.org/10.1787/9789264083967-en. [94]

OECD (forthcoming), *OECD Mining Case Study of Upper Norrland*, OECD Publishing, Paris. [1]

OECD (forthcoming), *The Mining Global Value Chain and the Impact of Embodied Services*, OECD Publishing, Paris. [54]

OECD/ILO (2017), *Engaging Employers in Apprenticeship Opportunities: Making It Happen Locally*, OECD Publishing, Paris, https://dx.doi.org/10.1787/9789264266681-en. [81]

Québec Ministry of Educaton (2018), *Plan d'action numérique [Digital Action Plan]*, Québec Ministry of Educaton, Québec, http://www.education.gouv.qc.ca/fileadmin/site_web/documents/ministere/PAN_Plan_action_VF.pdf (accessed on 5 April 2020). [98]

Ranasinghe, J. (2014), *Research into Drivers of Service Costs in Rural Areas*, http://www.lgfutures.co.uk|T.01908410811 (accessed on 11 July 2019). [27]

Rodríguez-Pose, A. (2018), "The revenge of the places that don't matter (and what to do about it)", *Cambridge Journal of Regions, Economy and Society*, Vol. 11/1, pp. 189-209, http://dx.doi.org/10.1093/cjres/rsx024. [30]

Runco, M. (ed.) (2018), "Design, innovation, and rural creative places: Are the arts the cherry on top, or the secret sauce?", *PLOS ONE*, Vol. 13/2, p. e0192962, http://dx.doi.org/10.1371/journal.pone.0192962. [66]

Rural Coffee Caravan (n.d.), *Homepage*, http://ruralcoffeecaravan.org.uk/. [115]

Santiago, P. et al. (2017), *OECD Reviews of School Resources: Chile 2017*, OECD Reviews of School Resources, OECD Publishing, Paris, https://dx.doi.org/10.1787/9789264285637-en. [111]

Santiago, P. et al. (2016), *OECD Reviews of School Resources: Estonia 2016*, OECD Reviews of School Resources, OECD Publishing, Paris, https://dx.doi.org/10.1787/9789264251731-en. [108]

Scrivens, K. and C. Smith (2013), "Four Interpretations of Social Capital: An Agenda for Measurement", *OECD Statistics Working Papers*, No. 2013/6, OECD Publishing, Paris, https://dx.doi.org/10.1787/5jzbcx010wmt-en. [112]

Shih, S. (1992), *Empowering technology—making your life easier*, Acer's Report, Acer's, New Taipei. [56]

Shuey, E. and M. Kankaraš (2018), "The Power and Promise of Early Learning", *OECD Education Working Papers*, No. 186, OECD Publishing, Paris, https://dx.doi.org/10.1787/f9b2e53f-en. [103]

SIMRA (n.d.), *Social Innovation Is a Driver of Local Development in Marginalised Rural Areas (brochure)*, Social Innovation in Marginalised Rural Areas. [117]

Söderholm, P. (2014), "Mining, regional development and benefit-sharing", Luleå University of Technology. [74]

Soldi, R. et al. (2016), *A New Skills Agenda for Europe*, Committee of the Regions, Brussels, http://dx.doi.org/10.2863/708323. [83]

Soubbotina, T. and K. Sheram (2000), *Beyond Economic Growth: Meeting the Challenges of Global Development*, World Bank, http://www.worldbank.org/html/schools (accessed on 29 July 2019). [152]

Steinberg, P. (2018), "Role and perspectives for German coal regions", German Commission on Growth, Structural Change and Employment, https://ec.europa.eu/energy/sites/ener/files/documents/5_german_commission_on_growth_structural_change_and_employment-_role_and_perspectives_for_german_coal_regions_dr._philipp_steinberg_director_gener.pdf (accessed on 18 July 2019). [133]

Stiglitz, J., A. Sen and J. Fitoussi (2009), *Report by the Commission on the Measurement of Economic Performance and Social Progress*, https://ec.europa.eu/eurostat/documents/118025/118123/Fitoussi+Commission+report (accessed on 29 May 2019). [9]

Stimson, R., R. Stough and B. Roberts (2006), *Regional Economic Development: Analysis and Planning Strategy*, Springer. [60]

The Guardian (2018), "Who are the gilets jaunes and what do they want?", https://www.theguardian.com/world/2018/dec/03/who-are-the-gilets-jaunes-and-what-do-they-want (accessed on 27 April 2020). [130]

The Shift Project (2017), "Décarboner la mobilité dans les zones de moyenne densité", https://theshiftproject.org/wp-content/uploads/2018/03/resume_aux_decideurs_rapport_decarboner_la_mobilite_dans_les_zdm_the_shift_project_web_v2.pdf (accessed on 21 August 2019). [136]

U.S. Global Change Research Program (2014), *National Climate Assessment*, https://nca2014.globalchange.gov/downloads (accessed on 18 July 2019). [38]

UK National Ecosystem Assessment (2011), "UK National Ecosystem Assessment: Synthesis of the Key Findings", http://dx.doi.org/10.1007/s10640-010-9418-x. [147]

UNECE (2002), "Older persons in rural and remote areas - Policy brief", http://www.unece.org/pau/welcome.html (accessed on 2 September 2019). [84]

Veneri, P. (2017), "Urban spatial structure in OECD cities: Is urban population decentralising or clustering?", *Papers in Regional Science*, Vol. 97/4, pp. 1355-1374, http://dx.doi.org/10.1111/pirs.12300. [17]

Watson, S. (2013), "New digital technologies: Educational opportunities for Australian Indigenous learners", *Australian Journal of Indigenous Education*, Vol. 42/1, pp. 58-67, http://dx.doi.org/10.1017/jie.2013.8. [79]

Wojan, T., D. Lambert and D. Mcgranahan (2017), *The Emergence of Rural Artistic Havens: A First Look*, http://www.uwplatt.edu/cont_ed/artsbuild/welcome.html. [67]

World Bank Group (2017), *Growing the Rural Nonfarm Economy to Alleviate Poverty*, http://www.worldbank.org (accessed on 19 July 2019). [2]

World Economic Forum (2016), *Responsible Mineral Development Initiative*, http://www3.weforum.org/docs/Responsible_Mineral_Development_Initiative.pdf (accessed on 14 May 2019). [143]

Yagan, D. et al. (2014), "Moving to opportunity? Migratory insurance over the Great Recession", https://eml.berkeley.edu/~yagan/MigratoryInsurance.pdf (accessed on 27 June 2019). [33]

4 Implementing the Rural Well-being Policy Framework: Guidelines and the institutional picture of OECD countries

This chapter covers the third dimension of the Rural Well-being Policy Framework, the engagement of governments, businesses and people to implement rural polices. The chapter starts with an overview of the multi-level governance approach for a coherent and co-ordinated implementation of rural policy. It analyses horizontal and vertical co-ordination strategies as well as urban-rural partnerships to attain policy complementarities and effective policy implementation. The second and final section of the chapter outlines the mechanisms for multi-stakeholder engagement, including civil society, private sector and third sector.

Key messages

Achieving the three policy objectives (economic, social and environment) of the Rural Well-being Policy Framework requires implementation mechanisms that effectively engage different levels of governments, people and business.

Policy interventions that target administrative boundaries or economic sectors in silos miss opportunities to unlock synergies and meet broad policy objectives for rural regions and countries. Recovery from external shocks, such as the 2008 Global Financial Crisis or the 2020 COVID-19 crisis, will require effective multi-level governance and stakeholder co-ordination as identified in the OECD Principles on Rural Policy adopted in 2019 by the Regional Development Policy Committee.

To effectively deliver rural well-being, horizontal co-ordination is needed between traditional ministries in charge of rural development (e.g. agriculture) with other ministries responsible for enablers of development (innovation, services, roads). Horizontal co-ordination across levels of government involves an approach in which policy makers mainstream rural issues across all policies (also called *rural proofing*) to ensure rural needs are taking into account. While a sound rural proofing is a necessary approach to reviewing new policy initiatives through a rural lens, it is not sufficient for efficient co-ordination. Thus, governments also need to ensure policy complementarities among different policy strategies. Other important aspects to take into account for successful co-ordination among governments include:

- Identifying the right scale of intervention by adapting policies and governance to functional geographies. According to the 2018-19 OECD institutional survey, for most OECD countries (80% of surveyed countries), the rural definition for policy making recognises the heterogeneity of rural regions. About 51% of surveyed OECD countries consider at least 3 types of "rural" areas (mixed rural/urban areas, rural regions close to cities and remote rural regions).

- Setting a clear leadership role for policy co-ordination on rural issues to better integrate national rural policies, promoting synergies and upgrading the concept of rural development within the country. The 2018-19 OECD institutional survey on rural policy outlines how OECD countries are improving co-ordination and setting leadership on rural policy:

  o To overcome a sectoral bias and siloed policy making, many OECD countries have established an inter-ministerial committee or body to define rural development policies. Most OECD countries (85% or 29 out of 34 surveyed countries) have established an inter-ministerial committee in the form of advisory councils, platforms, networks or presidential committees.

  o While OECD countries tend to have more than 1 ministry in charge of rural development, in most cases (62% or 21 out of the 34 surveyed countries), the lead ministry on rural policy is explicitly related to agriculture.

- Strengthening inter-municipal co-operation arrangements between regions or municipalities. For this, a number of OECD countries have established institutionalised municipal co-ordinating bodies at the regional level or voluntary inter-municipal co-operation mechanisms. Other countries have developed inter-municipal development agencies to support municipal governments in improving the business environment and well-being locally.

- Promoting rural-urban partnerships to take advantage of functional links. These links include economic and demographic linkages, delivery of public services, exchange of amenities and environmental interactions. Some strategies to overcome challenges for this regional collaboration include:

- ○ Focus on integrated territorial strategies that address the outcomes and actual needs of residents rather than simply focusing on outputs.
- ○ Ensure objectives are clearly defined.
- ○ Improve understanding of interdependencies and leadership.
- Improving vertical coordination between higher and lower levels of government, including their institutional, financial and informational aspects. In many OECD countries, a first step of co-ordination is through the development of the national development plans. Other mechanisms can include contracts between levels of government (even at international level), national level regional development agencies, national representatives in regions, co-funding agreements and consultation or regional forums.

Multi-stakeholder engagement and a "bottom-up" approach is a key ingredient to ensure sustainability and local ownership of rural policies. As globalisation deepens and the gaps between rural and other regions expand, rural regions increasingly feel that their needs are being overlooked by national policy making. New technologies, fiscal consolidation efforts, socio-political changes, declining levels of trust and the COVID-19 crisis have increased the demand for government transparency, accountability, and attention to the mechanisms through which governments can move beyond a "provider role" towards a "partnering relationship" with citizens and the private sector.

Involving local actors in policy design and implementation requires recognising a different vision of development from rural regions and in turn adapting the strategies to include citizens, the private sector and civil society in the policy making process. It involves supporting community-led initiatives and strengthening rural leadership to build capacity for effective involvement of local communities as partners in the multi-level governance process.

Countries and regions have adopted different approaches to engaging local actors varying from basic communication, full-co-production and co-delivery of policies. These engagement strategies include:

- Citizen's engagement: Participative and open budgeting, co-production of social service delivery, fora or policy summits.
- Private sector engagement: Public-private partnerships and platforms for dialogue.
- Collaboration with high education institutions: Partnerships to co-produce regional and local plans, programmes to support skills of public staff and support the local innovation strategy.

Introduction

Achieving the three policy objectives (economic, social and environment) of the Rural Well-being Policy Framework requires implementation mechanisms that effectively engage different levels of governments, people and business in order to increase the well-being across all types of rural regions. Rural development extends across a wide range of policy areas and involves a variety of actors, which makes it impossible for a complete separation of policy responsibilities and outcomes across levels of government. Policy interventions that target administrative boundaries or an economic sector in silos miss opportunities to unlock synergies and meet broad policy objectives for rural regions and countries. Thus, promoting a better co-ordination across levels of government, different types of regions and stakeholders is fundamental to attain sustainable and effective policy outcomes.

The active engagement of citizens, businesses and third sector (education institutions and non-profit organisations) within policy making is a key ingredient to ensure sustainability and local ownership of rural policies. Greater involvement of local actors in policy design and implementation leads to a more transparent, inclusive, legitimate and accountable policy making process, which in turn strengthens trust in government and in the policy interventions. Such multi-stakeholder engagement has increasingly gained relevance since new technologies, fiscal consolidation efforts and socio-political changes are pressing governments to become partners rather than providers in policy implementation.

This chapter covers the third dimension of the Rural Well-being Policy Framework: the implementation of rural policies through the engagement of different levels of government and local actors. The chapter finds that an effective policy implementation requires a coherent and co-ordinated approach that promotes multi-level governance co-operation and engagement between different types of regions and local actors. Integrating different sectoral policies across all levels of government with a bottom-up approach is recognised as a cornerstone to unlock policy complementarities and attain sustainable outcomes in policy implementation.

Based on the 2018-19 OECD institutional survey on rural policy, the chapter outlines that most OECD countries have in fact embraced an integrated and complementary policy approach for rural development by relying on national rural policies and co-ordination mechanisms across ministries or inter-ministerial bodies. Likewise, OECD countries have adopted implementation instruments beyond subsidies, including contracts and agreements with local communities. The chapter also finds that a large majority of OECD countries have made efforts to identify the right scale for rural policy intervention by recognising the diversity of rural areas for policy purposes.

The chapter starts with an overview of the multi-level governance approach for a coherent and co-ordinated implementation of rural policy. It analyses horizontal and vertical co-ordination strategies as well as urban-rural partnerships to attain policy complementarities and effective policy implementation. The second and final section of the chapter outlines the mechanisms for multi-stakeholder engagement, including civil society, the private sector and the third sector.

Multi-level governance co-ordination to deliver better rural policies

As many policy areas, rural policy is cross-cutting by nature and involves a variety of governmental and non-governmental actors. According to the OECD Principles on Rural Policy, rural policy is defined as "all policy initiatives designed to promote opportunities and deliver integrated solutions to economic, social and environmental problems in rural places through the valorisation of resources, promotion of their recreational, ecological and cultural heritage, as well as through improving manufacturing activities and public service delivery in close co-operation with subnational authorities, while actively involving civil society and the private sector" (OECD, 2019[1]).

Addressing the interdependencies of rural policy and attaining the sustainability of policy outcomes require the adoption of multi-level governance mechanisms with strong multi-stakeholder engagement. This approach draws from OECD experience on rural and regional policy and the guidelines set by the Principles on Rural Policy (OECD, 2019[1]).

Multi-level governance involves co-ordination among national, regional and local institutions. A multi-level governance framework encourages different levels of government to engage in vertical (across different levels of government), horizontal (among the same levels of government) or networked co-operation in order to design and implement better policies (OECD, 2010[2]). It acknowledges that regions and localities are in many cases the ones responsible for much of the service delivery and public investment, which determines economic growth and people's well-being. Furthermore, since rural communities tend to have a smaller population than their urban peers, rural regions are less likely to have significant levels of representation at the national level (OECD, 2016[3]). The multi-level governance approach thus aims to address the former challenges and leverage on the relevance of local governments to ensure a sound policy implementation by translating national policy design and implementation at the local level, promoting bottom-up solutions and increasing national policy effectiveness.

Multi-level governance mechanisms need to take into account the institutional differences across countries. OECD country experiences show that there is no universal consensus on the optimal structure of multi-level governance. OECD countries have a diverse institutional landscape and structure of subnational governance. It is therefore key to understand and manage the relationships and the mutual dependence across levels of governments efficiently in each country, by identifying and properly addressing the different multi-level governance challenges and gaps (Box 4.1).

With 37 countries in May 2020, the OECD gathers 9 federal and quasi-federal countries and 27 unitary countries. The majority of countries (19) have 2 administrative levels of subnational government (state/regions and municipalities), 10 countries have only 1 administrative subnational level (municipalities), while 8 countries have 3 administrative levels (state/regions, intermediary governments and municipalities). Instruments used to promote regional development in different regions should thus reflect country specificities and adapt to different contexts. A number of institutional characteristics, including the degree of decentralisation and autonomy, would influence the decision of how rural policy will be delivered. Sweden's highly decentralised approach is one example of a multi-level governance system that accounts for rural policy needs by providing room for dialogue and compromise (OECD, 2017[4]).

Box 4.1. The OECD approach to multi-level governance challenges

Complete separation of policy responsibilities and outcomes across levels of government is impossible to reach. The relationships among levels of government are characterised by a mutual dependence: vertical (across different levels of government), horizontal (among the same level of government) and networked. Governments must therefore bridge a series of vertical and horizontal "gaps".

These gaps include, in particular, the fiscal capacity of governments to meet obligations and information asymmetries between levels of government. Other major challenges include gaps in administrative responsibility (when administrative borders do not correspond to functional economic and social areas), gaps in policy design (when line ministries take purely vertical approaches to cross-sectoral regulation that can require co-design of implementation at the local level) and finally a lack of human or infrastructure resources to deliver services and design strategies. Countries may experience these gaps to a greater or lesser degree but given the mutual dependence that arises from decentralisation and the network-like dynamics of multi-level governance, countries are likely to face them simultaneously.

OECD member and partner countries are increasingly developing and using a wide variety of mechanisms to help bridge these gaps and improve the coherence of multi-level policy making. These mechanisms may be either "binding" (such as legal mechanisms) or "soft" (such as platforms for discussion), and must be sufficiently flexible to allow for territorially specific policies. Involvement of subnational governments in policy making takes time but medium- to long-term benefits should outweigh the costs of co-ordination

Source: OECD (2017[5]), *Multi-level Governance Reforms: Overview of OECD Country Experiences*, https://dx.doi.org/10.1787/9789264272866-en.

Horizontal co-ordination

Horizontal co-ordination across levels of government involves an approach in which policy makers review all policies to ensure people across the country, including those in rural regions, receive equitable treatment (Shortall and Alston, 2016[6]). It means applying a rural mainstreaming to all policies (also known as rural proofing) by deliberately reviewing new policy initiatives through a rural lens. The overall goal of rural proofing is to ensure and monitor that all domestic policies and the different institutions and sectors take into account rural circumstances and particularities. Rural proofing arrangements are normally based on *ex ante* ministerial assessment and review of rural development coherence done by each government body or on *ex post* regional assessment evaluation of different ministries' policy decisions on rural regions.

For example, the United Kingdom (UK) has adopted a policy of rural mainstreaming and rural proofing to keep the needs of rural regions at the forefront (Box 4.2). Other countries, including Canada, Finland and New Zealand, have implemented their own forms of rural proofing. In 2016, the European Union (EU) also committed to rural proofing its policies.

Rural proofing as a policy strategy is not without challenges. Taking a rural lens to sectoral or national policies may be challenging due to the difficulties in the ability of any single department to influence the behaviour of another department. Furthermore, this approach is not fully effective if there is no co-ordination and integration among the sectoral policies that were rural proofed. Conducting separately rural proofing, for instance, on transport and housing policies, without integration among them, will create inefficiencies on policy implementation and even undesirable outcomes (e.g. housing developments without transport connections). A lack of policy co-ordination leads to missing opportunities on investment and policy complementarities.

Box 4.2. Rural proofing in the United Kingdom

In the UK, rural proofing is integral to the policy making cycle. In England, 9.8 million people (19% of the population) live in rural areas. Virtually all policies impact upon rural communities. Rural proofing helps achieve good economic, environmental and social solutions that contribute to growth. Rural proofing is a commitment by the government to ensure that domestic policies take account of rural circumstances and needs. It is a mandatory part of the policy process, which means as policies are developed, policy makers should:

- Consider whether their policy is likely to have a different impact in rural areas, because of particular circumstances or needs.
- Make a proper assessment of those impacts, if they are likely to be significant.
- Adjust the policy where appropriate, with solutions to meet rural needs and circumstances.

The point of encouraging early assessments of expected, or likely, impacts in rural areas is a critical factor for rural mainstreaming. This type of prior assessment of policy goes well beyond a mere audit. It is about making the right evidence on rural dynamics available to the key decision-makers in a timely fashion so as to enable the introduction of corrective measures. Rural proofing applies to all policies, programmes and initiatives and it applies to both the design and delivery stage. The Department for Environment, Food & Rural Affairs (DEFRA) Rural Communities Policy Unit (RCPU) has been established as the centre of rural expertise within government and is able to advise policy makers on the likelihood and possible scale of rural impacts and suggest actions that might be taken to mitigate these. The RCPU can provide up-to-date information on rural areas and key rural stakeholders. At the same time, DEFRA has developed a suite of local-level rural proofing materials, to guide and help local decision-makers to "rural proof" local policies and practices.

Source: OECD (2011[7]), *OECD Rural Policy Reviews: England, United Kingdom 2011*, http://dx.doi.org/10.1787/9789264094444-en.

Such an approach to policy complementarities among different levels of government is set to bring a more efficient and sustainable result to the implementation. It involves co-ordinating different sectoral and political interests towards a single goal for rural development (Box 4.3). A cornerstone of these complementarities is the focus on integrated investments and delivering services and programmes that are adapted to and meet the needs of rural communities. Integrated investments have the potential to reap the benefits of complementarities when they are adapted to the different types of rural regions (Table 4.1).

Table 4.1. Policy complementarities for different types of rural regions

Type of rural region	Land use	Infrastructure/ accessibility	Resource use	Public services
Close to cities	Manage land conversion to limit urban sprawl.	Control expansion of sewer and water systems to slow land conversation. Plan road and public transit to manage development.	Maintain environmental quality and restrict activity that is not sustainable. Work to valorise rural amenities used by urban residents.	Provide local high-quality services that are integrated into adjacent urban capacity.
Remote	Restrict land use practices that create environmental externalities. Preserve high-value land that provides natural or cultural benefits.	Improve connectivity to urban regions through broadband, roads and rail.	Maintain environmental quality and restrict activity that is not sustainable. Work to valorise rural amenities used by urban residents.	Develop innovative ways to deliver high-quality public services in health, education, business support and workforce training. Local countercyclical revenue stabilisation plan/support.

Box 4.3. Policy complementarities

The concept of policy complementarity refers to the mutually reinforcing impact of different actions on a given policy outcome. Policies can be complementary because they support the achievement of a given target from different angles. This has been an important idea in terms of how to integrate and sequence structural reforms. This concept can be applied to regional development issues, for example:

- Increased broadband Internet access in rural regions should proceed along with policies that focus on the accessibility and diffusion of these services to the population.

- Changes in land use zoning in cities induce shifts in mobility patterns, which requires co-ordination with transport planning and infrastructure improvements.

- Investments in innovation and business ecosystems increase demand for skills within local labour markets and, therefore, complementary local initiatives to attract talent and develop human capital are needed.

In effect, governments should frame interventions in infrastructure, human capital and innovation capacity within common policy packages that are complementary to sectoral approaches as well. This is particularly important when dealing with complexities associated with Indigenous economic development at the local and regional levels. Policies need to be integrated horizontally, through management arrangements and development plans amongst different sectors, services and agencies within a given level of government. It also requires that policies are vertically integrated, from the national to the local level of government, and that interventions are territorially integrated and consider the interrelationships and interdependencies between different territories.

Source: OECD (2016[8]), *OECD Regional Outlook 2016: Productive Regions for Inclusive Societies*, https://dx.doi.org/10.1787/9789264260245-en.

Implementing at the right scale

A first step to implement rural policy is identifying the right scale of intervention by adapting policies and governance to functional geographies (OECD, 2019[11]). In line with the Principles on Rural Policy 1 and 2

(Box 4.4), sound implementation of rural policy involves developing a clear definition of rural areas to effectively target rural people and businesses as well as unlock complementarities with other regions. As Chapter 3 outlined, rural or low-density economies are different from urban economies, across various dimensions including the physical distance from markets, the costs in terms of connectivity to transport people and goods and the prominence of specific natural endowments for the local economy. The implementation of rural policies thus needs to match the scale of rural economies (e.g. local labour markets, food chains, environmental services and amenities), based on current and future needs of the areas, and ensure effective government mechanisms at the relevant scale to realise rural policy objectives.

Box 4.4. Principles on Rural Policy 1 and 2

Principle 1. Maximise the potential of all rural places, by:

- Leveraging the unique assets of each rural area to adapt and respond to emerging megatrends (digitalisation, globalisation and trade, climate change, population ageing, and urbanisation).
- Adapting policy responses to different types of rural regions including those close to cities and rural remote regions.

Principle 2. Organise policies and governance at the relevant geographic scale by:

- Implementing rural policies at different scales that match with functional relationships (e.g. local labour markets, food chains, environmental services and amenities) based on current and future needs.
- Ensuring that there are effective government mechanisms at the relevant scale to realise rural policy objectives.
- Encouraging the efficient and effective provision of public services and infrastructure (e.g. shared services, integrated service delivery, e-services) in order to maintain quality and accessibility, address market failures and respond to emerging needs, especially in underserved rural communities.

Source: OECD (2019[1]), *OECD Principles on Rural Policy,* http://www.oecd.org/cfe/regional--policy/Principles%20on%20Rural%20Policy%20Brochure%202019_Final.pdf.

In most OECD countries, the rural definition for policy making purposes has recognised the heterogeneity of rural areas. According to the 2018-19 OECD institutional survey (Annex 4.A), 51% of OECD countries consider at least 3 types of rural areas for policy design and delivery: mixed rural/urban (i.e. rural inside functional urban areas), rural close to cities and remote rural. A second group of countries consider 2 types of rural (23%), often mixed rural/urban and remote rural, while 20% consider only 1 type of rural, mainly mixed rural/urban (Figure 4.1). The standardisation of criteria when defining the rural dimension is of vital importance in order to be able to benchmark policy outcomes in rural places. While many countries have defined rural based on population density and accessibility, in line with the OECD rural definition (see Box 2.3 in Chapter 2), many countries have included particular criteria in their definitions, including economic activity or distance to services (i.e. Australia, Israel and Italy).

Figure 4.1. Number of categories of rural areas considered for policy making

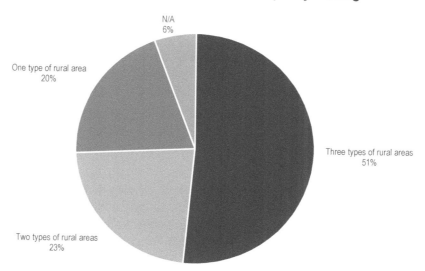

Note: The three categories refer to: mixed rural/urban areas, rural areas close to cities or remote rural areas. Self-reported answers to the question: "Please mark with an "X" if the rural definition for policy making considers the following rural area: mixed rural/urban areas, rural areas close to cities and remote rural areas". Selection of multiple categories was allowed.

National coherence and leadership on rural policy needs to avoid a sectoral approach

National rural policies are an instrumental tool to attain such co-ordination among actors and pool resources and capabilities across entities to collectively accomplish what no individual actor can achieve independently. Effective rural policies involve the engagement of a broad array of actors and multi-level governance mechanisms.

Given the cross-cutting nature of rural development, most OECD countries (89%) have put in place a national rural policy. OECD countries have this national policy defined by law or in a strategic policy document. The timeframe to renew this policy varies from every year to four or more years. The competent bodies for defining national rural policy are distributed differently across countries. This body in charge of rural development tends to be the same and often follows a concerted effort. For example, in Chile, the National Rural Development Policy is set by the Ministry of Agriculture, while in Sweden, the body in charge is the Swedish Agency for Economic and Regional Growth. Finland offers a long tradition of policy coherence through a National Rural Programme (Box 4.5).

Box 4.5. The National Rural Policy Programme in Finland

The National Rural Policy Programme is the main instrument to provide coherence to the different sectoral policies oriented towards rural areas in Finland. It is drawn up by the Rural Policy Committee, an institution that brings together nine ministries, other public organisations and federations, as well as research centres and private stakeholders. The National Rural Policy Programme includes strategic guidelines and specific practical measures for different sectors and for different entities of the government. Under the leadership of the Rural Policy Committee, which also promotes the implementation of the measures, the programme has been shaped by many different stakeholder organisations.

The National Rural Policy Programme is divided into two parts: the Plan of Action of the Rural Policy Committee and the Special Programme or the Report of the Government. The Plan of Action of the

---

Rural Policy Committee contains proposals to be undertaken by a wide number of actors. The separate Special Rural Policy Programme is drawn up on the basis of the Plan of Action, and only contains decisions and proposals within the competency of the government. For example, the Fourth Rural Policy Programme (2005-08) entitled "Viable Countryside – Our Joint Responsibility" included 133 proposals. Based on it, a Special Rural Policy Programme was prepared for its political support for 2005-06 consisting of 52 government decisions. This system has contributed to the allocation of responsibilities, information sharing and linking the planning and implementation stages.

The programme is revised about every four years and contains both a strategic perspective and concrete proposals with explicit references to those responsible for implementing them. The Rural Policy Committee carries forward the proposals of the programme through negotiations, projects, theme group work and by influencing various processes.

These documents have been central in providing rural policy with a policy framework. Ministries need to report twice a year the actions undertaken in line with the proposals/decisions contained in the Rural Policy Programme/Special Programme. Additionally, the continuation of these programmes over a time frame of more than two decades (there have been five National Rural Policy Programmes, 1991-96, 1996-2000, 2001-04, 2005-08 and 2009-13) has contributed to providing a long-term vision to rural policy. Finally, the distinction of two programmes, one within the government domain (the Special Rural Policy Programme) and one broader where a number of other organisations are involved, contributes to the allocation of responsibilities, decision-making, information sharing and linking the planning and implementation stages.

Key strengths of the process are: i) the involvement of civil society and academia in the preparation as providers of local and technical knowledge, reducing a critical knowledge gap that many central governments have in targeting the priorities of rural policy; ii) the ownership of the programme by the different government and non-government actors involved, resulting from a long process of multi-arena negotiation and aligning the actions of all key stakeholders; iii) clarity in the allocation roles and responsibilities within the government; and iv) the annual or biannual monitoring and evaluation process on how the proposals/decisions have been put forward.

Source: OECD (2014[9]), *OECD Rural Policy Reviews: Chile 2014*, https://doi.org/10.1787/9789264222892-en.

A clear leadership role on rural issues is key to better integrate national rural policies, promote synergies and upgrade the concept of rural development within the country. The appropriate place that rural policy should occupy within the "government" is an open and long-standing debate in OECD countries (OECD, 2014[9]). As the Ministry of Agriculture is traditionally the body interacting with rural regions in OECD countries, countries have often created a department in charge of rural development within this ministry. Yet, the solution where the Ministry of Agriculture is the only one in charge of rural development is often second best as the inter-sectoral aspect of rural development is significantly limited when only within one sectoral ministry. Further, this ministry tends to have strong incentives to revert to traditional methods given that agricultural interests are generally better organised than rural development interest. In EU countries, the institutional arrangements of EU funds often play a determining role in the lead selection of the lead ministry (Box 4.6).

While OECD countries tend to have more than one ministry in charge of rural development, in most cases (62%; 21 out of the 34 surveyed countries), the lead ministry on rural policy is related explicitly to agriculture. Yet, in an increasing number of countries (24%), the lead ministry on rural policy is not directly associated with agriculture or rural development (Figure 4.2). It includes the Ministry of Enterprise and Innovation (Sweden) or the Ministry of Industry, Business and Financial Affairs (Denmark). In the remaining countries (18%), the lead ministry deals with regional development or rural affairs.

Figure 4.2. Name of lead ministry/body on rural policy development in OECD countries

According to the main reference in the name of lead ministry/body

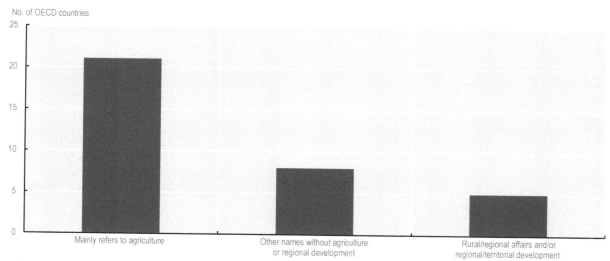

Note: Others refer to Federal Ministry for Sustainability and Tourism (Austria), Ministry of Industry, Business and Financial Affairs (Denmark), Ministry of Transport and Local Government (Iceland), Ministry of Local Government and Modernisation (Norway), Ministry of Enterprise and Innovation (Sweden), State Secretariat for Economic Affairs (Switzerland) and Presidency of Strategy and Budget (Turkey).
Self-reported answers to the question: "What are the lead ministry(ies) and other co-ordination bodies in charge of rural development" mention most important first.

Box 4.6. External factors in the place occupied by rural policy within EU governments

The place that rural policy should occupy within the "government" is an open debate. In many OECD countries, the Ministry of Agriculture has traditionally been the lead ministry in charge of rural development. In some cases, this leadership happened naturally as the ministry had the first contact with rural actors. However, there are also external factors that play a determining role in defining the lead ministry.

This is the case of EU member countries which have to cope with external funding streams and rules that influence the decision of where to locate rural development policies. The two main streams of EU funds are the Common Agricultural Policy (CAP) and (Regional) Structural Funds. Since rural development funds have emerged from the CAP (the so-called "second pillar") and not from regional funds (although many countries, including Finland, have used structural funds for rural development), the most obvious place for rural development policies within EU countries' government structures has tended to be the Ministry of Agriculture, in charge of administering CAP funds.

Nevertheless, several countries have sought to break the inertia by creating a new body with expanded scope and explicit jurisdiction over rural development policies or by assigning this jurisdiction to another ministry. An example of the first case is the UK, where the same central authority, DEFRA, embodies wider responsibilities over a broader set of areas, including the environment, food and rural affairs. A number of EU countries have also created a broad-based inter-ministerial committee to deal with rural development. It brings together nine ministries, other public organisations and federations, as well as research centres and private stakeholders.

Source: OECD (2014[9]), *OECD Rural Policy Reviews: Chile 2014*, https://doi.org/10.1787/9789264222892-en.

To overcome a sectoral bias and a silo policy making approach, many OECD countries have established an inter-ministerial committee or body to define rural development policies. Most OECD countries (85% - 29 out of 34 surveyed countries) have established an inter-ministerial committee in the form of advisory councils, platforms, networks or presidential committees. An inter-ministerial committee of rural development has the advantage of being able to gather a broad set of actors, including the relevant ministries, public agencies, representatives from the territories and the regions. It could also have a flexible and adaptable organisation, working in different commissions. In the OECD, many countries (20 out of the 29 countries) have more than one inter-ministerial body dealing with themes that involve rural issues. For example, South Korea created in 2003 the Presidential Committee on National Balanced Development which gathers different ministries representatives to establish and co-ordinate regional development policies.

Likewise, not all OECD countries target a single policy objective for rural development. On average, 53% of OECD countries prioritise economy over other matters for rural development policies, while 13% define environmental matters as the main priority for rural policies. A smaller proportion of countries (7%) place social matter as the main priority (Figure 4.3). A number of countries apply the same degree of priority to economy and social matter (13%).

Figure 4.3. Degree of priority in OECD rural development policies among economic, social and environmental areas

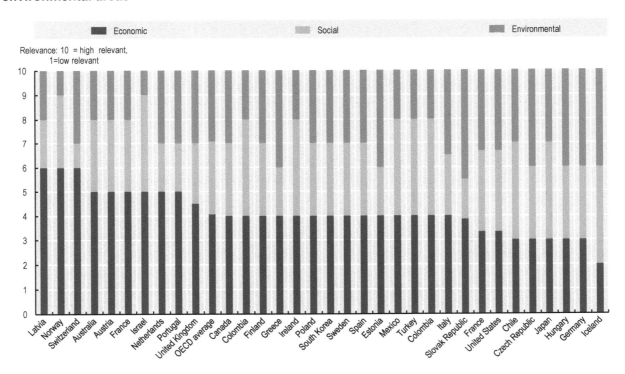

Note: Self-reported responses from country delegates to the question: "Please grade from 1 to 10 the importance rural development policies in your country assign to economic, social and environmental areas". The sum of the 3 areas must be equal to 10.

While the rural policy approach has moved beyond a sectoral focus, most OECD countries still classify agriculture as the most important strategic sector for rural policy. According to the 2018-19 OECD institutional survey on rural policy, agriculture was ranked as an extremely/very relevant strategic sector by a majority of countries, 27 out of the 34 countries that answered this question. Yet, strategic areas such as innovation and quality of life are also highly relevant for OECD countries. Innovation support was ranked as extremely important by 22 out of the 34 countries, while quality of life by 20 countries. Other strategic themes that were ranked as highly relevant are service delivery (19), land use (18) and support to the private sector (18) (Figure 4.4).

Figure 4.4. Relevance of objectives in rural development policy in OECD countries

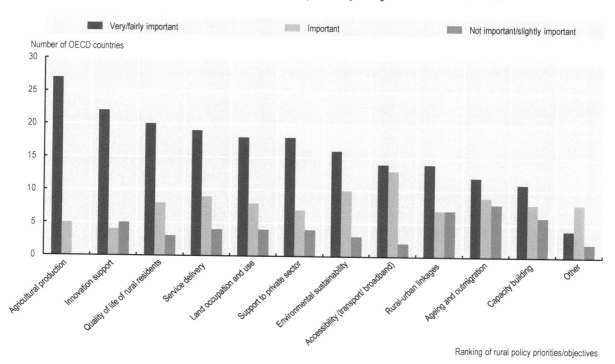

Note: Self-reported responses from country delegate to the question: "How important are the following objectives in your country's rural development policy? Grade from 1 to 5, where 1 is not important and 5 is very important". Other objectives include cultural and rural identity, rural tourism and access to credit. Countries could grade a number of sectors with the same value.

Boosting co-ordination among regions and municipalities

Horizontal co-ordination also refers to co-operation arrangements between regions or between municipalities. These agreements are increasingly common as a means by which to improve the effectiveness of local public service delivery and implementation of development strategies. Co-ordination across jurisdictions, both at the municipal and regional levels, is crucial to being in the right position to take advantage of spill-overs and to increasing efficiency through economies of scale. The small scale of public investment projects that regions or municipalities can often undertake can result in low returns and, as a result, prevent the local definition of infrastructure projects (OECD, 2014[10]). To bridge this gap, formal mechanisms of collaboration allow municipalities and regions to identify the relevant functional scale of infrastructure investments. Overcoming jurisdictional barriers requires the capacity to see and execute opportunities while gathering the necessary political support.

A better co-ordination among municipalities can contribute to addressing some of the structural challenges rural regions face (Chapter 3). Rural governments, particularly in remote rural regions, tend to lack staff capacity and have fragmented access to information on business needs and labour skills. It can pose challenges for municipalities to become strong partners to support the development of the local market. Furthermore, a larger co-ordination among municipalities to expand the local offer of products and services can help attain economies of scale and retain locally the benefits of economic operations. To strengthen inter-municipal co-ordination, OECD countries have established institutionalised municipal co-ordinating bodies at the regional level or voluntary inter-municipal co-operation mechanisms (i.e. voluntary federations of local authorities to work together on particular services or municipal associations) (Box 4.7).

Box 4.7. Municipal associations in Chile

In Chile, municipal associations have existed since 1993 with the creation of the Chilean Municipal Association (*Asociación Chilena de Municipalidades*, AChM), which at that time grouped together 96% of Chilean municipalities. Its mission was the political and technical representation of municipalities at the national level. The AChM also has regional representations including all municipalities within each region. Thanks to the stimulus provided by the AChM and SUBDERE, other associations emerged for specific activities such as the co-management of services. The associations that have emerged group municipalities with similar issues and with clear and specific objectives. As of today, it is possible to identify four types of municipal associations:

- *National associations*: They represent municipalities politically at the national level. The main association is the AChM, grouping the vast majority of Chilean municipalities; it is the most important and widely recognised association in the country. The Association of Chilean Municipalities (*Asociación de Municipalidades de Chile*, AMUCH), created in 2013, is also a national association, grouping around 40 municipalities with similar political affiliation.
- *Regional associations*: The AChM has regional representations which correspond to the associations of all municipalities within the region. The degree of development and autonomy of each of these regional associations varies among regions.
- *Territorial associations*: These associations group neighbouring municipalities with a common project. The vast majority of these associations form out of a common political will. In general, municipalities that form an association share a common identity in terms of culture or economic activities.
- *Thematic associations*: They bring together municipalities to address a specific, common issue (tourism, mining activities and productive development) or solve common problems such as waste management or the purchase of health material.

Source: OECD (2017[11]), *Gaps and Governance Standards of Public Infrastructure in Chile: Infrastructure Governance Review*, https://dx.doi.org/10.1787/9789264278875-en.

Other countries have developed inter-municipal development agencies to support municipal governments in attracting business environment and well-being locally. Many OECD rural municipalities have developed their own type of development agencies to provide services to businesses and promote investment in the local market. However, stand-alone municipal agencies, especially in remote rural regions, tend to face staff shortage and in some cases create competitive business environments among neighbouring municipalities due to a lack of co-ordination in conducting development policies (skill and business attraction). Against this backdrop, some OECD regions have developed inter-municipal agencies or centralise the co-ordination within the regional government with the aim of integrating common strategic municipal tasks under a single body with the capacity to hire skilled staff, find synergies among municipal strategies and support local businesses with advice. Finland is an example where inter-municipal development agencies, such as Business Joensuu Ltd. in North Karelia, help implement strategic policies across municipalities (Box 4.8).

Box 4.8. Business Joensuu

At the beginning of the 21st century, smaller municipalities in North Karelia decided to set up a joint development agency to address some pressing challenges in the local market, including scarcity of resources, lack of special knowledge to handle business advisory services and competition between neighbouring municipalities.

The municipalities negotiated, on the city board level and with all municipalities around the capital of the region (Joensuu), the creation a functional body, called Josek, organised on the level of the region around Joensuu.

In 2018, two municipalities decided to reduce the number of services acquired from Josek and developed inhouse business advisory services (retaining access to project development and facilitation services). This led to a reform in the development agency and the creation of Business Joensuu.

Business Joensuu provides services to start-ups and foreign investors interested in the region and supports the internationalisation of local companies. In addition, Business Joensuu produces an operating environment for different industries by creating the best conditions for companies to operate in the Joensuu region.

The company is governed by a board of directors that is selected by the following institutions:

- Joensuu City Council.
- The University of Eastern Finland.
- Joensuu University Support Foundation.
- The North Karelia Educational Council Group Riveria.

In 2019, representatives from the above-mentioned institutions plus representatives from the National Coalition Party and private companies (*Outokummun Metalli Oy, Blancco Oy*) formed the board of directors.

Business Joensuu services include:

- Business growth and development.
- New businesses, businesses and internationalisation.
- Placement and attraction, marketing.
- Space, community and event services for the science park.

Overall, the company managed 25 programmes focused on different sectors including export capacity in the region (ExportGrowth), the bioeconomy sector (Digital Forest Vitality), business digitalisation (Joensuu Smartcity, digital training) and entrepreneurship (women entrepreneurship). It is also involved in two active EU programmes to support the mining sector (REMIX and MIREU).

The services are typically 1-3 year-long customer-oriented development projects. They are initiated by designated industry-responsible experts who are responsible for promoting the business environment of their businesses, starting with the business needs of their companies.

Source: OECD (2019[12]), *OECD Mining Regions and Cities Case Study: Outokumpu and North Karelia, Finland,* https://dx.doi.org/10.1787/cd72611b-en.

Vertical co-ordination among the national and subnational government levels

Vertical co-ordination refers to the linkages between the higher and lower levels of government, including their institutional, financial and informational aspects. Local capacity building and incentives for the effectiveness of subnational levels of government are crucial issues for improving the quality and coherence of public policy (OECD, 2017[5]). In countries where the national government plays a prominent role in the delivery of public policy and services, the states need to reach the central government with a unified voice.

Mechanisms to support vertical co-ordination

Institutional mechanisms to ensure better co-ordination among national and local policies vary among countries. While the instrument can vary among countries, a common goal should ultimately be influencing stakeholders in the multi-level governance relationship towards more effective sharing of information and objectives. In many OECD countries, a first step of co-ordination is through the development of national development plans or national plans for regional development. Other instruments can include contracts between levels of government, national-level regional development agencies, national representatives in regions, co-funding agreements or consultation fora (Charbit and Romano, 2017[13]).

- National platforms or regional fora at the national level where subnational government representatives meet are useful to strengthen co-ordination and propose a common project to national government (Box 4.9).

Box 4.9. Fora for dialogue and co-ordination platforms for regional development

In order to ensure that various levels of government take a more co-ordinated approach to regional development and public investment, many OECD countries use vertical and horizontal co-ordination platforms. These can include institutional mechanisms, co-financing arrangements, formalised consultation of subnational governments and platforms for regular intergovernmental dialogue. Practices in Australia, the Netherlands, New Zealand, Portugal and the UK provide relevant examples.

Infrastructure **Australia** (IA) was established in 2008 by Australia's federal government to co-ordinate investments of national importance with Australian states and territories. IA advises the national government on investment priorities in the transport, communication, energy and water sectors, and helps states identify infrastructure projects that align with national priorities. IA assesses individual state or territory applications for funding under the Building Australia Fund, which is the country's main mechanism for financing critical infrastructure projects.

In the **Netherlands**, the various levels of government establish their own vision documents: the SVIR at the national level, the Provincial Structural Vision (provincial level) and zoning plans (municipal level). These documents serve as input to "area agendas", which help all levels of government discuss and align their questions and projects in the physical domain (i.e. housing, industry, public transport, environment). Within the multi-year investment programme (MIRT), each region has its own, collective area agenda, containing the co-ordinated vision, goals and projects of the various government levels in the specific MIRT region. Aligning the visions of each level of government in an MIRT area leads to better solutions and ultimately greater effectiveness. While formal discussions take place multiple times per year, decision-making on the content of area agendas occurs at an annual meeting at the political level (BO MIRT), with the outcome discussed in parliament. Likewise, a new National Strategy on Spatial Planning and the Environment provides a sustainable perspective for the living environment with an approach of consultation with local stakeholders and with the shared responsibility of all levels of government.

New Zealand's Government Policy Statement establishes high-level priorities for transport investment, which are then implemented through the New Zealand Transport Agency (NZTA) in collaboration with subnational governments. NZTA officials work with each local authority to determine co-funding arrangements for the maintenance and renewal of the country's regional and local roads (approximately 90% of all roads). Vertical co-ordination is largely confined to investment in Auckland. Auckland Council's special plan sets out long-term priorities for public investment and is designed to guide the investment decisions of central and local government, particularly in transport and also in social infrastructure (e.g. schools and hospitals).

Portugal's Comissão de Coordenação e Desenvolvimiento Regional (CCDR) was created in 1979 for planning. Currently, CCDR activities cover: spatial planning; promoting strategic and integrated regional development planning; monitoring the design and implementation of deconcentrated policies; and providing an opinion on the national government's public investment expenditure programme (PIDDAC) at the regional level. Under the EU Cohesion Policy, each region was requested to draft its own Regional Strategy 2020 under the direction of the CCDR in order to improve collaboration among the CCDR, municipalities and the regional directorates of various ministries operating in the regions.

Source: Adapted from OECD (2016[8]), OECD Regional Outlook 2016: Productive Regions for Inclusive Societies, http://dx.doi.org/10.1787/9789264260245-en.

- Financial incentives for co-ordination, including co-financing arrangements, can also mobilise municipalities to collaborate around concrete projects. For example, in France, the central government provides a basic grant plus an "inter-municipality grant" to encourage municipalities to constitute "public establishment for inter-municipal co-operation" (EPCI), a body that assumes limited, specialised and exclusive powers transferred to them by member communes (OECD, 2014[14]).

- Contracts are also frequently used for regional development policy in OECD countries (Box 4.10). Contracts can potentially ensure that national-level policy decisions and regional priorities contribute coherently to common development targets. Contracts, referred to as arrangements, reorganise the rights and duties of governments, beyond those established in the constitution (Charbit and Romano, 2017[13]). Previous OECD surveys show that 23 out of 30 OECD surveyed countries use contracts as tools for vertical co-ordination (Charbit and Romano, 2017[13]). Contracts are especially effective in rural communities where they can be established without requiring formal restructuring or changes to the constitution and as short-term agreements, such as to run a new development project, whereby a small municipality may become more involved in national processes.

Box 4.10. Regional deals

Barkly Regional Deal, Australia

The Australian Government delivered the country's first Regional Deal in the Barkly region, Northern Territory. The region's main town is Tennant Creek and is ranked as the second-largest local government area in Australia. Signed on 13 April 2019, the Barkly Regional Deal is a AUD 78.4 million, a 10-year commitment between the Australian government, the Northern Territory Government and the Barkly Regional Council to support productivity and liveability in the Barkly region.

The Barkly Regional Deal comprises 28 initiatives identified through an extensive 6-month consultation process which included close engagement with local Aboriginal stakeholders and representatives across the Barkly region, and other key industry stakeholders. Taken together, the initiatives are inter-dependent and respond to 3 community priority areas – economic development, social development, and culture and place-making, with the Australian government contributing AUD 45.4 million towards a range of these measures.

The Barkly Regional Deal will target investment decisions to accelerate regional economic development and strengthen the resilience of the region to respond to future shifts in the economy. This will include diversifying the industry and employment composition of the region and building the knowledge, skills and capability of the local workforce. The Barkly Regional Deal has set high the need for improving outcomes for Aboriginal people, helping to build sustainable, intergenerational wealth in Aboriginal communities. These initiatives will strengthen the Barkly region as a great place to live, work, invest and visit. The effectiveness of the Barkly Regional Deal will be measured as of the 10-year life of the deal, with a series of reviews scheduled throughout its implementation phase and an independent evaluation.

Contracts in France

State-region planning contracts (*Contrat de plan État-région* – CPER) have been in operation since 1982 and are important tools in regional policy in terms of planning, governance and co-ordination. They are characterised by their broad thematic coverage and cross-sectoral nature, with a territorial approach being applied across diverse policy fields including industrial, environmental and rural issues. The President of the Regional Council and Prefect, as the representative of the central government and different ministries, draft the contract. The co-financing of interventions is seen as an important co-ordination mechanism.

Planning Contracts 2007-13 and 2014-20: A New Generation of State-Region Contracts was introduced in 2007 alongside the EU Structural Funds programmes, in order to increase the links between French and EU regional policies. For the first period 2007-13, there are three priorities: i) the promotion of territorial competitiveness and attractiveness; ii) the environmental dimension of sustainable development; and iii) social and territorial cohesion. For the second period 2014-20, the priorities include: i) higher education; ii) research and innovation; iii) national coverage with high-speed broadband and development of the uses of digital technologies; iv) innovation, promising niches and the factory of the future; v) multimodal mobility; (vi) environmental and energy transition. Moreover, as employment, as a priority for the government, will be treated as a cross-cutting issue in the contracts.

The new contracts have demonstrated an emphasis on sustainable development. To reinforce the joint France-EU alignment, they have the same duration as the EU operational programmes and are based on joint territorial analysis and integrated systems for monitoring. As with the Structural Funds, regions can decide to release funding 18 months after project approval if no commitment has been made.

Contracts in Chile

Programming agreements (*Convenios de Programación*, CPs) in Chile are formal binding agreements between one or more regional governments and one or more national ministries, detailing measures and procedures to be undertaken in projects of common interest over a specified period of time. These agreements can also include other public or private national, regional or local institutions. The subscription of an agreement implies an allocation of their already approved budget to be spent through these agreements.

Formally, the steps for signing a CP include: i) identification of projects; ii) signing of a protocol of purpose that initiates negotiations between the parties and defines the objectives, areas of intervention and resources that each institution will contribute; iii) deciding on investments that will be included in the agreement with the technical recommendation; iv) drafting the programming agreement and negotiation (technical); and v) presentation of the agreement to the Regional Council for approval and signature. After the approval and execution of the agreement, there is a formal monitoring and evaluation stage in which a technical team made up of representatives from all parties involved is supposed to monitor its execution. Projects are carried out using the resources of both line ministries and regional governments (grants from the National Fund for Regional Development).

These agreements offer a useful legal framework for co-ordinating regional and national priorities and responsibilities. So far, they have mostly been used for shared planning and financing of large infrastructure projects.

Source: OECD (2017[5]), *Multi-level Governance Reforms: Overview of OECD Country Experiences*, https://dx.doi.org/10.1787/9789264272866-en.

There is no one mechanism better than another, while co-ordination between levels of government remains the most important feature to implement sound rural policies. In the OECD, a majority of countries (42%) use both deconcentrated national agencies[1] and autonomous regional agencies[2] to deliver rural policy at the regional level (Figure 4.5). Some OECD countries (29%) deliver rural policy solely through deconcentrated national agencies (e.g. Finland, Germany, Ireland), while a smaller number of countries (15%) rely on autonomous regional agencies (e.g. Australia, France, South Korea). A small group of countries (14%) use other types of structure including a whole-of-government approach (Canada), devolution of implementation to regions and municipalities (e.g. Mexico) or implementation directly from the national level (e.g. Latvia, Luxembourg).

Figure 4.5. Type of institution in charge of rural policy at the regional level

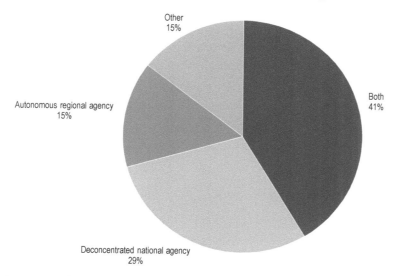

Note: Self-reported answers to the question: "Please mark with an "X" the type of institution (s) in charge of rural development policy at the regional and/or local level. Options available: Deconcentrated national agency, Autonomous regional agency or other". Multiple choices were allowed.

Investing in rural policy under a fiscal consolidation context

The recovery process from the 2020 COVID-19 crisis adds increased pressure to improve co-ordination among different levels of governments to implement the rural policy. During the crisis, governments have raised public spending in order to strengthen the health system and support people and businesses with grants and subsidies. As a result, governments might face further pressure to enhance the management of public investments in a context of tight public budgets, which will make the efficiency of the public investment a cornerstone of the recovery from the crisis.

Fiscal consolidation efforts to come out from the crisis will require governments to improve the management of regional development policies and particularly public investment, to efficiently deliver services in rural regions, and attain substantial savings and enhanced productivity. Improving management of public investments will be also important to attract and mobilise private investment into rural regions. Evidence suggests that institutional quality and governance processes affect the expected returns on public investment and the capacity to leverage private investment (OECD, 2016[3]). To this end, the OECD principles on public investment provide guidance to boost the efficiency of subnational public investments and overcome major challenges linked to investments across levels of governments (Box 4.11).

Financial tools to deliver rural policy in OECD countries varies largely depending on the type of country and government structure. Different mechanisms can serve multiple and complementary objectives, which ultimately requires countries to adopt a suitable combination of different mechanisms to improve how the public budget is spent and invested. Tools to finance rural policy include grants and financial instruments such as loans or co-funding methods (Box 4.12). When it comes to grants, governments leverage contracts and conditions attached to aid transfers that enable the alignment of priorities and encourage parties to co-operate (OECD, 2018[15]). Grants or subsidies are normally provided by supranational or national-level to subnational governments without obligation of repayment. Financial incentives include loans, public equity and venture capital, and credit guarantees (OECD, 2018[15]). They can involve challenges in contract design to ensure adaptation to contextual characteristics.

While countries traditionally relied on direct subsidies as the main mechanism to implement rural policies, an increasing number deliver rural policy through dedicated grant programmes or loans on specific matters. All OECD countries surveyed in the 2018-19 OECD institutional survey reported the use of grant programmes to implement rural development policy. Some countries (10) complement such grant programmes with contracts and agreements with local communities. EU countries highlighted EU-specific instruments including CAP and LEADER as mechanisms of rural policy implementation. Frame conditions such as legislation and regulations are also relevant tools to implement policies.

Box 4.11. OECD Principles on Public Investment

The OECD instrument groups 12 principles under 3 pillars: co-ordination, capacities and framework conditions.

Pillar 1: Co-ordinate across governments and policy areas

1. Invest using an integrated strategy tailored to different places.
2. Adopt effective co-ordination instruments across levels of government.
3. Co-ordinate across subnational governments to invest at the relevant scale.

Pillar 2: Strengthen capacities and promote policy learning across levels of government

4. Assess upfront long-term impacts and risks.
5. Encourage stakeholder involvement throughout the investment cycle.
6. Mobilise private actors and financing institutions.
7. Reinforce the expertise of public officials and institutions.
8. Focus on results and promote learning.

Pillar 3: Ensure sound framework conditions at all levels of government

9. Develop a fiscal framework adapted to the objectives pursued.

10. Require sound, transparent financial management.

11. Promote transparency and strategic use of procurement.

12. Strive for quality and consistency in regulatory systems across levels of government.

Source: OECD (2014[16]), *Effective Public Investment Across Levels of Government Toolkit*, www.oecd.org/effective-public-investment-toolkit.

Box 4.12. Between financial instruments and grants for policy delivery

From a policy design perspective, financial instruments are an alternative and complementary delivery mechanism to grants. Both instruments can be used to address gaps in access to finance. When deciding over grants or financial instruments to finance projects, it is key to answer which delivery mechanism will be most effective and efficient to achieve policy objectives.

In practical terms, financial instruments can be used to finance investments that generate income or save costs, enabling the initial support to be repaid. This means that where public intervention is justified by the need for public goods, repayable support is unlikely to be well suited. There is some consensus in the advantages of financial instruments over grants in three dimensions:

- *Sustainability*: Financial instruments appear to be more sustainable than grants because funds need to be repaid, creating a legacy to invest.

- *Project quality*: Projects financed through financial instruments seem to have greater quality as private sector appraisals enhances due diligence and repayment obligation encourages project managers to focus on results. There might be also a psychological dimension as both investee and investor share the risk.

- *Cost-effectiveness*: Financial instruments can make more cost-effective use of public funds partly because funds may be recycled, but also because of their potential to attract private funds.

Other important benefits of financial instruments are the decrease in grant dependency, the promotion of an "entrepreneurial culture" and stronger support towards market development (niche). Yet, to encourage and make their use more efficient is important to articulate policies linked to grants and financial instruments.

In general, financial instruments are not attractive when grants are available for the same purposes. Financial instruments play an important role in limiting grant dependency, provided that financial instruments and grants are appropriately dovetailed. To optimise their use, it is crucial a comprehensive strategy that complements the use of financial instruments and grants and ensures advice and support through technical assistance, training, audits.

Source: OECD (2018[15]), *Rethinking Regional Development Policy-making*, https://doi.org/10.1787/9789264293014-en; Wishlade, F. and R. Michie (2017[17]), "Financial instruments in practice: uptake and limitations", Background paper prepared for the seminar "When to use financial instruments" held 28 June 2017, OECD Headquarters, Paris.

Rural-urban partnerships

Cities and rural regions are highly interconnected through systems of governance, infrastructure, economic transactions and other linkages. Rural-urban partnerships take advantage of functional links by connecting a territory which shares value chains, labour markets or natural resources. Although economic linkages are often the basis of these partnerships, demographic linkages, delivery of public services, exchange of amenities, environmental goods, and other governance interactions also drive the need for rural-urban interaction (Table 4.2). Linkages allow regions to collaborate on territorial branding, service delivery, environmental protection and other issues (OECD, 2014[10]). Such partnerships acknowledge the interdependency and mutual interests of rural regions and cities. Furthermore, as mentioned in Chapter 2, rural-urban interactions are not encompassed within administrative boundaries but occurred throughout a rural-urban continuum. Environmental, demographic and economic interactions, for instance, go beyond administrative boundaries.

Table 4.2. Goals and challenges of rural-urban partnerships by type of interaction

Type of rural-urban linkage	Subtype	Possible purposes of a rural-urban partnership	Challenges
Demographic linkages	Urbanisation	Relocating public services in rural regions; helping capacity building	Dealing with the demographic decline of remote areas
	Counter-urbanisation and enlargement of commuting space	Improving transport connection within labour market areas	Coping with the decline of old urban centres Developing better connections
Economic transactions and innovation activity	Productive relations	Fostering supply chains (e.g. agro-industry)	Boosting activities with a high territorial multiplier
	Knowledge diffusion and innovation links	Fostering links between small- and medium-sized enterprises (SMEs) and universities/research centres	Boosting competitiveness in remote areas
Delivery of public services	Public service (education, health, waste, etc.)	Developing information and communication technology (ICT) infrastructure for service provision	Ensuring access to basic services and combatting depopulation in remote areas
	Public transport	Co-ordination investments in transport within functional areas	Ensuring access to both urban and rural resources
Exchange in amenities and environmental goods	Consumption links of urban amenities	Improving accessibility (transport) Better spatial planning and landscape preservation	Ensuring complex consumption for rural residents/quality of life
	Rural amenities and ecosystem services	Co-ordination utility providers and local authorities (e.g. Water)	Ensuring regional environmental sustainability and quality of life
Other "governance" interactions	Joint planning	Setting a common development plan	Improving the efficiency of public policy
	Co-ordination among local authorities	Building a common voice in dealing with higher government	Increasing political relevance and access to funds

Source: OECD (2013[18]), *Rural-Urban Partnerships: An Integrated Approach to Economic Development,* https://dx.doi.org/10.1787/9789264204812-en.

Developing rural-urban partnerships can take on varying degrees of formality and openness. Most urban-rural interactions are shaped by physical proximity. Yet, despite the importance of physical proximity, other types of urban-rural interactions have ubiquitous rather than contiguous impacts. This type of relationship has been referred to as "organised proximity" and may include economic relationships between firms, tourism and other flows related to exchange in amenities (e.g. recreation), as well as some specific forms of institutional collaboration. Formal policy strategies to promote rural-urban partnerships can also use contracts among regions. This is the case of France where "reciprocity contracts" allow cities and surrounding rural regions partner on common areas of concern such as employment, the environment and local services (European Network for Rural Development, 2018[19]). Despite the type of co-operation, as stated in the third Principle on Rural Policy, governments should support interdependencies and co-operation between urban and rural areas by leveraging their spatial continuity and functional relationships, carrying out joint strategies and fostering win-win rural-urban partnerships (2019[1]).

Just as the types of territory are recognised by common characteristics (large cities are focal points of economic innovation and growth while remote communities are sector-specific areas) so are the linkages established across them (Table 4.3). Regional linkages are not always predictable but can be defined according to a spatial and functional dimension. Policies and funds supporting rural-urban partnerships tend to focus on metropolitan regions and sub-regional centres, excluding partnerships and resources for strengthening linkages of small- and medium-sized cities and their linkages to rural surroundings (Carriazo et al., 2015[20]). The OECD has differentiated the spatial dimension of these links following three different categories of regions (OECD, 2013[18]):

- **Linkages around metropolitan regions**. As Chapter 2 depicted, (large) metropolitan regions are composed of urban cores that gather diverse and dynamic economic activity pulling in increasingly firms and workers. The influence of the urban engine often extends across the region and beyond the labour commuting distance. Rural regions close to these urban poles may house those who commute to the central core. Rural dwellers in these regions can access a range of services and economic opportunities provided in cities. At the same time, rural regions provide larger living spaces and good quality environment. The interaction, in this case, include co-ordination on mass transport systems or placed-based housing and environmental policies that take into account the negative externalities of proximity to a large urban region (increased housing prices and pollution). One of the most frequently noted factors driving co-operation was the improvement of the transport network, which allows urban boundaries to expand functionally and offers greater accessibility to both metropolitan and rural regions (OECD, 2013[18]).

- **Linkages around small and medium-sized cities**. These cities are still producing the bulk of services for surrounding rural communities, yet the economy is spatially diffused. Cities and rural regions are less clearly separated, and often strongly linked with one another in terms of food production, transport and environmental ecosystems. Rural regions close or with small/medium cities act as semi-autonomous growth poles but depend on urban centres for specialised services or for accessing larger markets. The development potential and attractiveness of these networks has been associated with their accessibility to urban cores, their capacity to provide skilled labour for specialised industrial clusters, and their cultural dynamism (especially small cities with university campuses). A frequent issue inspiring co-operation is a desire to operate at a larger scale, to attract business and investment, but also to enhance administrative capacity and political relevance (OECD, 2013[18]).

- **Linkages in remote rural regions.** These areas have a lower population density and are far away from urban centres. As their regional economy tends to rely on natural resource actives, small-size cities act as market and logistic points (i.e. access to input, airport, ports) and sources of labour or specialised services. Rural-urban co-operation also helps rural communities retain the benefits of the exploitation of resources and improve the capacity of administration. Since the ownership of resources, main competencies and strategic management are often located in urban areas, the co-operation around shared benefit arrangement in extractive activities is a potential for rural-urban co-operation.

Table 4.3. Different interactions in different territorial contexts

Type of linkage by territory	Metropolitan functional regions	Polycentric networks of medium-sized cities	Rural regions where small towns depend on the rural economy
Typical demographic challenges	Urbanisation processes. Difficulties to maintain governance, service delivery, infrastructure and other policies. This is often associated with intense pressure on surrounding rural regions.	Constant population growth at a slow pace. There is a gradual urbanisation of the countryside.	Ageing and depopulation (except in high amenity areas).
	Urbanisation has given way in some industrialised economies to **counter-urbanisation**. Rural regions in peripheral zones show population growth, while the central area is losing population. This can lead to gentrification.		
	Integration and assimilation of migrants.		
Economic linkages	The core city acts as a source of services for a large peri-urban and rural region, which specialises in goods production (e.g. primary resources and manufacturing).	Urban centres act as gateways for larger markets.	Urban centres are market towns. Most of the regional services are produced directly in rural regions.
	Fringe areas can develop residential economies.	Rural regions can generate cumulative causation and agglomerate firms.	Resource-based communities exposed to international shocks.
	Fringe areas can also generate enough momentum to start a cumulative causation dynamic outside the core region.	Rural regions are home to some highly specialised services that need to be located close to their clients (firms).	Diversify or localise the service related to the production of research and development (R&D) for the dominant local rural industry
	Change in the land values in the fringe area.		
	Risk of loss of labour and traditional activities as well as the fall of economic activities of rural regions not functionally linked to the central region.		
Delivery of public services	The influx of former urban residents in rural regions may increase the demand for public services in rural regions (homogenisation of the demand for services).	Each urban centre is part of the functional region, which produces and delivers similar public services.	Service delivery is expensive, which leads to greater collaboration among surrounding areas.
	Large city primacy in public expenses for services. Availability of service in peri-urban areas can be low.	Urban centres within the functional region specialise in the production of a particular service (e.g. university, hospital, etc.).	
		Rural inhabitants piggyback urban services.	
Cultural and environmental amenities	Urban sprawl. Different sectors (housing, manufacturing, and agriculture) compete for land.	Urbanisation of the countryside can impinge upon the quality of the landscape.	Rural regions can host renewable energy production which improves the sustainability of urbanisation.

Type of linkage by territory	Metropolitan functional regions	Polycentric networks of medium-sized cities	Rural regions where small towns depend on the rural economy
	Demand for recreational areas by urban dwellers.	Competition between industry and agriculture for the land.	Rural regions might provide space for recycling infrastructure sustainable manufacturing.
	Availability of amenities affects housing prices and modes of residential development.	Rural inhabitants converge to urban areas to consume cultural amenities.	
	Preservation of the agricultural land and of the landscape		
	Rural inhabitants converge to urban areas to consume cultural amenities		
Multi-level governance	The largest local government may "obscure" the others and take over the regional leadership.	Polycentric areas may suffer from fragmented local governments and may fail to co-ordinate in the provision of services.	Within the functional region local governments may suffer from: i) an information gap; ii) a capacity gap; iii) a lack of co-ordination; and iv) and a policy gap.
	Where there is a strong local government, there is the possibility of having problems with supra-local governments.		

Co-ordination on land use governance is often a relevant matter that requires close collaboration among rural and urban areas. The OECD's work on the governance of land use has further profiled these linkages with a focus on land management including how proximate rural and urban communities work to address such issues as traffic congestion, growing suburbanisation, the loss of high-quality agricultural soil and demands for new types of infrastructure (e.g. renewable energy installations).

Partnerships can also come with potential risks. Rural-urban linkages without policy intervention do not necessarily lead to better development outcomes. While the urban-rural linages are seen as a way of reducing spatial inequality, there is no evidence to suggest that increased connections between different types of territories can lead by its own to a better distribution of resources and a more equitable outcome. Rural-urban partnerships without policy intervention can also lead to negative externalities, including rapid urbanisation, deterioration of environmental amenities (natural parks or clean air in rural regions) and increased transaction costs. An unbalanced distribution of benefits among partners can also damage the effectiveness of such partnerships.

The role of policies is thus key to shape the strength of these linkages and their effect on local well-being and spatial inequalities. The OECD (2013[18]) identified a number of factors that can facilitate and hinder rural-urban partnerships (Box 4.13). To overcome imbalances, regions should focus on integrated territorial strategies, which address the outcomes and actual needs of residents rather than simply focusing on outputs. Clearly defined objectives, a solid understanding of interdependencies and leadership can help facilitate lasting co-operation between rural and urban regional partners.

The design and support for rural-urban partnerships from different levels of governments is also crucial for the sustainability of these linkages across diverse types of territory. Achieving the balance of these interactions needs then governance mechanisms that incorporate the vision from different actors, from the national, regional and local levels. Therefore, the rural-urban linkages should materialise at three different levels of policy: i) supranational levels; ii) the national level (i.e. within national rural policy); and iii) the regional and local levels (i.e. within regional and municipal development plans).

Box 4.13. Factors that could facilitate or hinder rural-urban partnerships

When rural-urban partnerships are effective, they can extend the reach of any single organisation or agency and support the broader territorial agenda. Based on a series of cases studies, the OECD identified the main factors that can hinder or facilitate rural-urban partnerships. While these factors do not represent a comprehensive list, they can provide insight into what makes for more effective rural-urban partnerships.

Factors that facilitate rural-urban partnership

- *An understanding of the interdependence of rural and urban areas*. Acknowledging how the rural and urban areas are connected in the territory is the core ingredient of a rural-urban partnership. To co-operate effectively, mutual understanding should also be generated through common projects and goals.
- *Mutual understanding of the need to act in concert to address a critical problem*. Mutual understanding leads to a shared vision for partnership. Efforts should focus on facilitating that both urban and rural actors realise that working together is the appropriate solution.
- *Clearly defined objectives*. Rural-urban partnerships must have a clear purpose. This must be responsive to local needs and incorporate the needs of both the rural and urban areas.
- *Representational membership and democratic participation*. Effective rural-urban partnerships need to involve the right decision-makers, in order to reflect the interests of the territory.
- *Leadership*. Without strong leaders working collaboratively towards a common goal, the process of formation and advocacy can grind to a halt and piecemeal efforts can become the norm.

Factors that hinder rural-urban partnership

- *Regulatory and political barriers*. The institutional framework can sometimes constrain rural-urban partnerships. Inflexible regulatory frameworks or with no mechanism or incentives for co-operation can undermine a rural-urban partnership.
- *Lack of trust/social capital*. A lack of social capital is important but is more likely to slow rather than stall the emergence of a rural-urban partnership.
- *Space blind policies*. National policies on services delivery or economic growth with no differentiation between urban and rural economies work against integrating rural and urban.
- *Low incentive to collaborate/lack of buy-in*. Much of the work of the partnership members involves making a small financial investment or incentive to attract private and non-agency commitments and resources.

Source: OECD (2013[18]), *Rural-Urban Partnerships: An Integrated Approach to Economic Development*, https://dx.doi.org/10.1787/9789264204812-en.

Multi-stakeholder engagement for developing rural policies

Crafting effective policies requires decision-makers to listen and respond to the needs of their constituencies. With the deepening of globalisation, rural regions increasingly feel that their requirements are overlooked in policy making (Jetten, Mols and Selvanathan, 2020[21]; Cramer, 2016[22]). Protests such as those of the "gilet jaunes" in France or the causes behind the Brexit vote in the UK are prominent examples of rural people demanding more visibility in policies made at the national level (Jetten, Mols and

Selvanathan, 2020[21]; Dijkstra, Poelman and Rodríguez-Pose, 2019[23]). New technologies, fiscal consolidation efforts, socio-political changes and declining levels of trust have increased attention on the mechanisms through which governments can not only become more transparent and accountable but also move beyond a provider role towards a partnering relationship with citizens and the private sector (Box 4.14). Evidence suggests that government efforts to widening opportunities for citizen participation into policy making represent an important strategy for improving trust in public institutions and policies (OECD, 2016[3]).

Box 4.14. Stakeholder engagement as a leading paradigm of policy making

The notion of participation has evolved over recent years towards the concept of engagement. Participation typically refers to the involvement of individuals and groups in designing, implementing and evaluating a project or plan. Engagement goes beyond procedures and methods to consult, inform and partner and targets the whole set of relevant stakeholders, including the private sector. As a result, concepts, such as co-creation and co-production, have emerged to describe the systematic pursuit of continuous co-operation between government agencies and stakeholders in a manner that defines again the roles and relationship between governments and citizens.

Today, engagement with broader constituencies is identified as an important factor in determining whether institutions and policies will be effective and enduring, in particular from the point of view of bringing new forms of participatory problem-solving to address societal demands. The concept of inclusive policy making through stakeholder engagement largely overlaps with that of open government, defined as "the transparency of government actions, the accessibility of government services and information and the responsiveness of government to new ideas, demands and needs" (OECD, 2005[24]). As a result, openness and inclusion represent two pillars to deliver better policy outcomes not only for, but with, citizens. Today, inclusive policy making through stakeholder engagement is set to enhance government accountability, broaden citizens' influence on decisions and build civic capacity.

Source: OECD (2016[3]), *The Governance of Inclusive Growth*, https://dx.doi.org/10.1787/9789264257993-en.

The new philosophy of the Rural Well-being Policy Framework acknowledges that rural communities are well equipped to identify their local development opportunities and closely support and complement national policies and strategies. A "bottom-up" approach for rural policy allows rural dwellers to decide and collaborate to implement their own development future. For this, the policy making process needs to incorporate aspects of well-being that communities prioritise, following their local needs, connection to the national agenda and cultural singularity. Policy design and implementation should ultimately recognise a different vision of development from rural regions, involve the communities and support their capacity and leadership to ensure they fully participate in the multi-level governance process. This section will thus explore the mechanisms for governments to further engage citizens, the private sector and third sector (education institutions) in policy making design and process.

Engaging citizens in rural policy

Citizen engagement in policy making provides significant benefits to policy design and delivery (OECD, 2018[25]). It can improve the quality of laws and services by incorporating knowledge and feedback from the actors who will be the most impacted in rural regions. Rural dwellers not only have better knowledge of local conditions but also the capacity to adapt policies to the context. In addition, the participation and involvement of citizens are associated with higher levels of policy compliance and an important driver of legitimacy and trust in the government. Research has found that public interest groups report higher satisfaction with the policy outcome the more they participate in, which ultimately can unlock opportunities of direct and representative democratic practices (OECD, 2017[26]). In many cases, the public works with the government in designing a future vision for their place or for a specific policy/project design and implementation.

Countries and regions have adopted different approaches to public engagement. Modalities of engagement vary from basic communication – the weakest form of engagement – to full-co-production and co-delivery of policies with a balanced share of power among stakeholders (OECD, 2016[27]). Although not all policies allow for a full engagement, when strategic decisions of long-term policies are taken, citizens should be engaged at every stage of the policy process and not be considered solely as agents of implementation. Beyond the different approaches, a sound engagement process should bring legitimacy to the final plan. The approaches to engage citizens in policy design and implementation include:

- *Participative and open budgeting* where citizens can propose projects to be implemented, vote among several proposed projects or prioritise investments. One example of this mechanism occurs in Paris, where the city – since 2014 – gives its citizens the opportunity to decide on the use of 5% of its investment budget (2014-20) and propose projects that would then be voted on (OECD, 2016[3]).

- *Co-production of social service delivery.* In the water sector, for instance, many utilities rely on governance or advisory boards, where stakeholders have a say in strategic orientations or in which different actors take collective decisions. For example, the public water utility in Grenoble, France, has over the last 20 years engaged with consumer associations when deciding on water tariffs (OECD, 2016[3]).

- Many OECD regions have also *established fora or policy summits where citizens can propose and define policy priorities and strategies* (Box 4.15). Some of these platforms combine elected officials, businesses, social partners and other relevant stakeholders (universities), which contribute to promoting regional development strategies and oversee implementation.

Box 4.15. Citizen engagement summit

The Baltic Urban Laboratory is a European initiative example based on the concept of people-private-public partnerships (4P), involving a wide variety of projects in Nordic countries.

Within this framework, a project for the inclusion of citizens in deciding on climate change adaptation options, entitled "Citizens vote on climate change adaptation options in Kalundborg", was carried out in 2011. Kalundborg is a municipality located on the island of Sjælland in Denmark and home to 20 000 inhabitants. Its coastline, lowlands and sensitive areas with delta characteristics are threatened by the impacts of climate change. Sea level rise and changes in rainfall, as well as infrastructure and water quality, are the main risks associated with climate change. The municipality of Kalundborg, together with the Danish Board of Technology (DBT), organised a citizens' summit where 350 local citizens discussed how Kalundborg should adapt to a future with a warmer climate.

Before the summit, citizens were given relevant information material and presented with the pros and cons of the different adaptation options obtained through a scenario workshop. The methodology used for the workshop was to present to local stakeholders the implications of the possible flooding of the Kalundborg area. On this basis, they developed different solutions to the challenges in a scenario workshop. Finally, citizens debated and voted on these options.

As a result, two-thirds voted in favour of phasing out the current land use – mostly farmland – to become wetlands, rather than building dykes. In terms of the period for action, the vast majority of citizens (90%) requested that the municipality act now and develop long-term plans based on climate change

---

scenarios. Thanks to the participatory nature of the decision-making process, local politicians were able to make broader decisions taking into account a broader view of local interests.

Source: Interreg Central Baltic (2012[28]), "Citizens vote on climate change adaptation options in Kalundborg", https://www.balticurbanlab.eu/goodpractices/citizens-vote-climate-change-adaptation-options-kalundborg.

Local governments in rural regions can benefit from a closer relationship with their citizens to implement public policy. Local governments in rural regions might find greater opportunities to engage with the population as rural communities tend to have stronger social ties than in large metropolitan areas. At the local scale, the tools to engage citizens may for example involve methods with greater face-to-face interaction or be focused on very specific policy concerns (OECD, 2016[3]). Citizen engagement in a rural area should account for how people perceive and interact with the world. In some OECD rural regions, close interaction with Indigenous Peoples is crucial to improve legitimacy and trust in the strategic projects (Box 4.16). Overall, rural dwellers are an important source of information about their region, including how space should be used, how to better design public services or even economic opportunities for development.

Box 4.16. Engagement with Indigenous Peoples

There are approximately 38 million Indigenous People across OECD member countries. Indigenous Peoples are concentrated mainly in rural regions as compared to non-Indigenous populations. Significant challenges still exist in how Indigenous Peoples participate in decision-making, leading to mismatches between the needs of Indigenous communities and the services and programmes they receive.

An integral element of countries' moving towards a people-centred rural approach is making greater use of local knowledge through partnerships and engagement with Indigenous Peoples. This also supports the United Nations Declaration on the Rights of Indigenous Peoples, which includes a statement that states shall co-operate in good faith with Indigenous Peoples before adopting and implementing measures that may affect them.

Processes with low degrees of participation, such as information or consultation, bear the danger of trust erosion and consultation fatigue as there is no obligation to consider views in the final outcome. High levels of engagement, such as providing Indigenous Peoples with the opportunity to make decisions in the policy making process, including the definition of the problem, the development of policies, as well as implementation and evaluation of outcomes, have been assessed as successful.

New Zealand, for instance, has introduced laws that require engagement. The Resource Management Act of 1991 (No. 69) and the Local Government Act (2002) set out obligations for councils to ensure Māori are included in local government decision-making and have processes for participation in place. While processes remain uneven between councils and the level of engagement remains subject to political discretion, good practice examples have been observed regarding co-management and joint-entities.

Overall, governments can create opportunities for meaningful participation in government decision-making for Indigenous Peoples by:

- Establishing protocols and obligations for engagement of Indigenous Peoples across the policy cycle (definition of the problem, the development of policies as well as the implementation and evaluation of outcomes).

- Addressing the asymmetries of power in engagement processes and strengthening the capacity of Indigenous leaders and organisations to participate in decision-making about development.
- Developing cross-cultural competencies within public institutions at all levels.
- Supporting the recruitment and progression of Indigenous staff in public institutions.

Source: OECD (2019[29]), *Linking Indigenous Communities with Regional Development*, https://doi.org/10.1787/3203c082-en.

Supporting community-led initiatives is also a vector to strengthen and complement the implementation of rural policies. The strong community networks in rural regions offer opportunities for self-organisation that enable the adaptability and resiliency to structural changes. Local initiatives are increasingly advocated by all levels of government as one remedy to global economic restructuring and local decline. In times of crisis, as in the COVID-19 pandemic, rural communities can quickly mobilise their local networks and co-operative structures to face the effects of the economic shocks. For example, during the confinement periods of the COVID-19 pandemic, rural communities established car-sharing models and community fleets to transport medical workers and elderly population (i.e. Belgium, France and Italy). Some of the local initiatives that emerged to address specific challenges can in turn be adopted by policy makers as official policies. Policies can indeed support successful community-based development projects by enhancing the community's active participation and co-ordination.

Digitalisation is an increasingly common tool to engage public and private stakeholders in policy making and implementation. ICT and the widespread use of information technologies, social media and open data in the society provide opportunities for governments to develop new methods of co-operation and to create public value through inclusive and more informed policy making processes, fostering thus user-driven service design and delivery. For example, in the context of social discontent in France in 2019 ("gilets jaunes" strikes), the French government developed a digital platform to collect opinions and recommendations from the population. The platform collected around 1.9 million comments online, which were classified in themes and available to the citizens through open data mechanisms. In Colombia, the Ministry of Information Technology and Communications established the Centre for Digital Public Innovation, aiming to strengthen the public innovation ecosystem to solve complex problems within the public administration (OECD, 2018[25]). The innovation centre provides training courses to increase government capacity, a laboratory for solutions to public challenges, a knowledge agency for research and a collaboration platform to support community and partnerships.

Engaging the private sector and universities in rural policy

Increasing collaboration with the private sector is of great importance for policy implementation. The magnitude of the needs and the tight fiscal context for governments requires mobilisation and partnerships with private sources. Governments can leverage private sector engagement to enhance government capacity by benefitting from risk transfer, private sector incentives, know-how and innovation (OECD, 2018[30]). How private sector engagement occurs needs to be informed by clear criteria for partnership that consider responsible business conduct, due diligence procedures and consideration of economic, social and environmental impacts.

Public-private partnerships (PPPs) are relevant to meet local demand for better and sufficient infrastructure. Public sources of funding are insufficient to cover the investment needs in regions (OECD, 2018[30]). However, PPPs are not risk-free. Maximising the benefits and minimising the downsides of PPPs requires substantial public sector capacity, in particular at the subnational government level. The decision to partner with the private sector should be rooted in the analysis of whether and how the private sector is best placed to help realise specific development results (OECD, 2016[31]). Across OECD countries, most (83%) reported that between 0% and 5% of public sector infrastructure investment had been made through

PPPs (OECD, 2019[32]). Subnational level governments have pursued PPPs to develop a wide variety of infrastructure on water, roads and telecommunications (Box 4.17). The OECD has developed a number of recommendations to improve the governance and implementation of PPPs for infrastructure at the subnational level (Box 4.18).

Box 4.17. Implementation of basic services with private partnerships

In Poland, the partnership between the French company SAUR and the municipality of Gdańsk makes for a good example of a PPP. Indeed, a PPP was set up due to the high investment required both for the water supply and the collection and treatment of wastewater from the neighbouring cities of Gdańsk and Sopot (OECD, 2008[33]). By 2007, more than 1 300 km of the water supply network and almost 1 100 km of sewerage had been installed in both cities. The resulting PPP is a 30-year contract, owned 51% by Saur and 49% by the city of Gdańsk, supplying water to 500 000 people (SAUR, 2020[34]).

In 2010, the ISO:2005 certification formalised the quality of the water distributed in Gandsk. SAUR-Gdańsk has thus become a valuable key player in Poland for the management of water services.

Source: SAUR (2020[34]), "Water supply and wastewater treatment services in Poland", http://www.saur.com/en/the-group/international/saur-worldwide/poland/.

Box 4.18. Making the most of subnational infrastructure public-private partnerships

The OECD (2018[30]) identified a number of recommendations to maximise the benefits and minimise the downsides of PPPs at the subnational level:

Legal and policy framework

- Create a flexible and inclusive statutory framework that supports private sector participation.
- Create PPP-specific legal arrangements with rigorous project selection and review.
- Establish clear and transparent PPP review requirements, based on value for money, affordability, but also provisions for debt review, independent audits and official findings of public interest.
- Ensure coherence of laws and regulations across levels of government and subnational jurisdictions.
- Strengthen the sustainability and credibility of contracts so that they do not fall apart with new political pressures.

Financial and budgetary arrangements

- PPP proposals must demonstrate superior predicted outcomes compared to traditional public procurement alternatives.
- Minimise accounting incentives to move projects "off the budget".
- Use standard *ex ante* evaluation instruments.
- Adopt third-party scrutiny and approval prior to tender and/or before contract signature.
- Look to the involvement of private actors to offer more than just financing for projects, but also a way to strengthen capacities of governments at all levels.

PPP-supporting tools

- Establish subnational PPP units in line ministries or at an arm's length from government.
- Provide standardised documents and examples of contracts adapted to different sectors, to dilute preparation costs and better support subnational governments in the preparation of PPPs.
- Higher levels of government may opt for advisory rather than mandatory guidance in order to minimise the risk that standardisation constrains flexibility and innovation at the subnational level.
- Develop or strengthen performance indicator systems for PPP design and implementation.
- Create peer-to-peer knowledge exchange platforms for subnational governments as well as mechanisms for inter-municipal and regional co-ordination.
- Establish national observatories/platforms to collect data and advise cities and regions in their choices to follow PPP performance.
- Collect data on subnational PPPs more systematically to fill the data gaps.

Source: OECD (2018[30]), *Subnational Public-Private Partnerships: Meeting Infrastructure Challenges*, https://doi.org/10.1787/9789264304864-en.

Governments have involved the private sector in the phase of design and long-term strategy for regional policy. Platforms for dialogue with national and regional governments and the private and third sectors are mechanisms to materialise this collaboration. For example, Sweden's National Strategy for Sustainable Regional Growth and Attractiveness 2015-20 aims to facilitate and maintain a continuous dialogue among a wide and diverse array of public sector bodies with the third and private sectors, via the Forum on Sustainable Regional Growth and Attractiveness. The emphasis of the present policy is to give more power to the regions to stimulate regional growth, taking into account the priorities of the private sector as well as municipality realities (OECD, 2017[4]).

Collaboration with high education institutions can enhance local governance capacity and regional development. While universities' missions and operations become more outward-oriented and cosmopolitan, there is also a shift towards more local and subnational engagement, described as "service" or "third task" work. Higher education institutions in rural regions are cultural/research hubs that provide tangible and intangible services, including improved identity, place-based attachment and skills for local needs (OECD, 2020[35]). Municipal governments tend to lack the skill capacity to benefit from innovation partnerships, due to staff shortage and lack of appropriate skills. Thus, local governments can benefit from an improved partnership with higher education institutions to strengthen policy capacity and delivery. In remote rural regions, these intuitions can be effective partners to move forward local innovation strategies (Box 4.19).

Box 4.19. Co-operating with universities for rural development

The Academy for Smart Specialisation in Värmland, Sweden

The Academy for Smart Specialisation is a result of a collaboration that originated in an OECD project over ten years ago about universities' role in regional development. This initiative is a continuation of the agreement of intention that was made for the period 2010-14 when ten new professorships were instituted at Karlstad University. This project also involves research co-operation and will go on until the year 2020.

The academy aims to utilise research for the benefit of industry, the county administration, the county council and the municipalities in Värmland, and to strengthen the research environments in the region. High-quality research is expected to attract more external funding to the university.

The six areas of specialisation identified by Värmland's research and innovation strategy are the foundation of the Academy for Smart Specialisation. Karlstad University and the region of Värmland will run the academy jointly for the purpose of serving as a meeting place for researchers, companies, financiers and entrepreneurs. By linking research innovation and education, the academy will prepare Karlstad University students for employment to drive the industrial development in the six prioritised areas in Värmland.

Source: Karlstad University (2020[36]), *Academy for Smart Specialisation*, https://www.kau.se/en/external-relations/research-and-innovation-collaboration/research-collaboration/academy-smart.

Engagement of citizens and the private sector does not necessarily need to be a separate process. Both types of co-operation are expected to influence the same planning process. An integrated frame of collaboration with different types of actors can lead to positive synergies in policy outcome. Triple- and four-helix partnerships are increasingly common around OECD regions. These partnerships tend to be set up to move forward innovation policies by involving firms, governments, civil society and (in the case of the four-helix approach), higher education institutions. This type of partnership should follow a demand-led approach of projects from the private sector (involving different levels of firms). The innovation system in Brainport, the Netherlands, is an example of creating this partnership to spur innovation through collaborative work among stakeholders (Box 4.20).

Box 4.20. Triple-helix partnerships to promote innovation

The case of Brainport Development in Eindhoven (Netherlands)

The Brainport Eindhoven region is the industrial high-tech heart of the Netherlands, covering Eindhoven and 20 surrounding municipalities, and is part of the South East-Netherlands (ZON) region. Industrial activity in the region ranges from the manufacturing of complex machines and systems to semiconductor industry, embedded systems for automotive and advanced medical systems and design.

Innovation in the region was previously based on closed organisational forums and mainly driven by Philips. The company's loss of international competitiveness drove it to establish the first knowledge campus and transitioned from a closed model of innovation into an open model by stimulating strong involvement of the private sector.

The innovation system of Brainport is to a great extent "business-driven", powered by entrepreneurial leadership and strong collaboration between industry, knowledge institutes and the government in the triple-helix and ample participative involvement of civic society.

Besides collaboration in the triple helix, its governance depends on how the national, regional and local governments co-operate and interact, and how Brainport connects to and collaborates with other regions (domestically and internationally). The most important innovation policy instrument, both in funding size and in popularity, is the national WBSO scheme for corporate tax deduction of R&D expenditures.

The project management approach consists of a large number of bottom-up initiatives with external project owners. Brainport Development invites firms or knowledge institutes involved to take ownership of initiatives and projects that are being carried out.

Brainport Development was declared the Intelligent Community of the Year 2011 out of more than 400 participants and won the Eurocities Award in 2010 in the "co-operation" category, for co-operation among companies, knowledge institutions and the government.

Source: OECD (2013[37]), *Innovation-driven Growth in Regions: The Role of Smart Specialisation*, https://www.oecd.org/innovation/inno/smart-specialisation.pdf.

Concluding remarks

Achieving the three policy objectives (economy, society and environment) identified by the Rural Well-being Policy Framework requires implementation mechanisms that effectively engage all actors at the national and local levels. It requires supporting co-ordination across different levels of government, different types of regions (urban and rural) and stakeholders. The sustainability and efficiency of a policy are highly dependent on the degree of support from citizens and the private sector. While not all policies require the same level of integration with citizens and the private sector, a continuous effort to involve these actors in the policy decision-making process would enhance the legitimacy of and trust in the government.

Addressing the interdependencies of rural policy and attaining the sustainability of policy outcomes require the adoption of multi-level governance mechanisms with strong multi-stakeholder engagement. This approach draws from OECD experience on rural and regional policy and the guidelines set by the OECD Principles on Rural Policy, adopted in 2019 by the OECD Regional Development Policy Committee.

Multi-level governance co-ordination is crucial to address the cross-cutting nature of rural regions. It includes horizontal (across level of governments) and vertical (among levels of governments) co-ordination. Multi-level government mechanisms involve a number of policy approaches and strategies to attain an effective policy implementation. This includes:

- **Horizontal co-ordination to support rural proofing** (deliberately reviewing new policy initiatives through a rural lens) and ensure policy complementarities (co-ordination among sectoral policies). A sound policy implementation involves:
  - Identifying the right scale of intervention by recognising the heterogeneity of rural areas.
  - Attaining policy coherence at the national level with clear leadership on rural policies. This can be done through national rural policies and an inter-ministerial committee or body to define rural development policies.
- **Horizontal co-operation arrangements between regions or between municipalities**. This co-ordination can address local governments' challenges, including lack of staff capacity, fragmented access to information on business needs and labour skills, and difficulties to attain economies of scale on service delivery. This co-operation can be done through institutionalised municipal co-ordinating bodies or independent agencies at the regional level or voluntary inter-municipal co-operation mechanisms.
- **Promoting rural-urban partnerships that bring benefits to rural and urban regions**. This collaboration takes advantage of functional links by connecting a territory which shares, among others, value chains, labour markets and/or natural resources. While economic linkages are often the basis of these partnerships, demographic linkages, delivery of public services, exchange of amenities, environmental interactions also drive the need for rural-urban collaboration. The type of rural-urban interaction varies with the type of rural area. Some strategies to overcome challenges for this regional collaboration include:

- ○ Focus on integrated territorial strategies, which address the outcomes and actual needs of residents rather than simply focusing on outputs.
- ○ Clearly defined objectives.
- ○ A solid understanding of interdependencies and leadership.
- **Improving vertical co-ordination between higher and lower levels of government, including their institutional, financial and informational aspects**. In many OECD countries, a first step of co-ordination is through the development of the national development plans. Other mechanisms can include contracts between levels of government (even at international level), national level regional development agencies, national representatives in regions, co-funding agreements and consultation or regional forums.

Governments can rely on a number of tools to achieve policy co-ordination and involvement of local actors:

- Common mechanisms to engage citizens in policy design and implementation include participative and open budgeting, co-production of social service delivery fora and policy summits.
- When it comes to private sector engagement, public-private partnerships and platforms for dialogue are relevant tools to meet local demand for services and materialise projects.
- Collaboration with higher education institutions can be promoted to enhance local governance capacity and regional development.

References

Carriazo, F. et al. (2015), "Cities, territories, and inclusive growth: Unraveling urban-rural linkages in Chile, Colombia, and Mexico", *World Development*, Vol. 73, pp. 56-71, http://dx.doi.org/10.1016/J.WORLDDEV.2014.12.013. [20]

Charbit, C. and O. Romano (2017), "Governing together: An international review of contracts across levels of government for regional developme", *OECD Regional Development Working Papers*, No. 2017/04, OECD Publishing, Paris, https://doi.org/10.1787/ff7c8ac4-en. [13]

Cramer, K. (2016), *The Politics of Resentment: Rural Consciousness in Wisconsin and the Rise of Scott Walker*. [22]

Dijkstra, L., H. Poelman and A. Rodríguez-Pose (2019), "The geography of EU discontent", *Regional Studies*, pp. 1-17, http://dx.doi.org/10.1080/00343404.2019.1654603. [23]

European Network for Rural Development (2018), *Reciprocity Contracts France*, http://cordis.europa.eu/project/rcn/207230_fr.html. [19]

Interreg Central Baltic (2012), "Citizens vote on climate change adaptation options in Kalundborg", https://www.balticurbanlab.eu/goodpractices/citizens-vote-climate-change-adaptation-options-kalundborg. [28]

Jetten, J., F. Mols and H. Selvanathan (2020), "How economic inequality fuels the rise and persistence of the yellow vest movement", *International Review of Social Psychology*, Vol. 33/1, http://dx.doi.org/10.5334/irsp.356. [21]

Karlstad University (2020), *Academy for Smart Specialisation*, https://www.kau.se/en/external-relations/research-and-innovation-collaboration/research-collaboration/academy-smart. [36]

OECD (2020), "An ecosystem approach to knowledge exchange and collaboration", Expert workshop, France, 13-14 February 2020, OECD, Paris. [35]

OECD (2019), *Linking Indigenous Communities with Regional Development*, OECD Rural Policy Reviews, OECD Publishing, Paris, https://doi.org/10.1787/3203c082-en. [29]

OECD (2019), *OECD Mining Regions and Cities Case Study: Outokumpu and North Karelia, Finland*, OECD Rural Policy Reviews, OECD Publishing, Paris, https://dx.doi.org/10.1787/cd72611b-en. [12]

OECD (2019), *OECD Principles on Rural Policy*, OECD, Paris, http://www.oecd.org/cfe/regional-policy/Principles%20on%20Rural%20Policy%20Brochure%202019_Final.pdf. [1]

OECD (2019), *OECD Regional Outlook 2019: Leveraging Megatrends for Cities and Rural Areas*, OECD Publishing, Paris, https://dx.doi.org/10.1787/9789264312838-en. [32]

OECD (2018), *Digital Government Review of Colombia: Towards a Citizen-Driven Public Sector*, OECD Digital Government Studies, OECD Publishing, Paris, https://dx.doi.org/10.1787/9789264291867-en. [25]

OECD (2018), *Rethinking Regional Development Policy-making*, OECD Multi-level Governance Studies, OECD Publishing, Paris, https://dx.doi.org/10.1787/9789264293014-en. [15]

OECD (2018), *Subnational Public-Private Partnerships: Meeting Infrastructure Challenges*, OECD Multi-level Governance Studies, OECD Publishing, Paris, https://dx.doi.org/10.1787/9789264304864-en. [30]

OECD (2017), *Gaps and Governance Standards of Public Infrastructure in Chile: Infrastructure Governance Review*, OECD Publishing, Paris, https://dx.doi.org/10.1787/9789264278875-en. [11]

OECD (2017), *Multi-level Governance Reforms: Overview of OECD Country Experiences*, OECD Multi-level Governance Studies, OECD Publishing, Paris, https://dx.doi.org/10.1787/9789264272866-en. [5]

OECD (2017), *OECD Territorial Reviews: Sweden 2017: Monitoring Progress in Multi-level Governance and Rural Policy*, OECD Territorial Reviews, OECD Publishing, Paris, https://dx.doi.org/10.1787/9789264268883-en. [4]

OECD (2017), *Trust and Public Policy: How Better Governance Can Help Rebuild Public Trust*, OECD Public Governance Reviews, OECD Publishing, Paris, https://dx.doi.org/10.1787/9789264268920-en. [26]

OECD (2016), *OECD Regional Outlook 2016: Productive Regions for Inclusive Societies*, OECD Publishing, Paris, https://dx.doi.org/10.1787/9789264260245-en. [8]

OECD (2016), *Open Government: The Global Context and the Way Forward*, OECD Publishing, Paris, https://dx.doi.org/10.1787/9789264268104-en. [27]

OECD (2016), *Private Sector Engagement for Sustainable Development: Lessons from the DAC*, OECD Publishing, Paris, https://dx.doi.org/10.1787/9789264266889-en. [31]

OECD (2016), *The Governance of Inclusive Growth*, OECD Publishing, Paris, https://dx.doi.org/10.1787/9789264257993-en. [3]

OECD (2015), "Recommendation on Effective Public Investment Across Levels of Government", http://www.oecd.org/cfe/regional-policy/recommendation-effective-public-investment-across-levels-of-government.htm. [38]

OECD (2014), *Effective Public Investment Across Levels of Government Toolkit*, OECD, Paris, http://www.oecd.org/effective-public-investment-toolkit. [16]

OECD (2014), *OECD Rural Policy Reviews: Chile 2014*, OECD Rural Policy Reviews, OECD Publishing, Paris, https://dx.doi.org/10.1787/9789264222892-en. [9]

OECD (2014), "Recommendation of the Council on Effective Public Investment Across Levels of Government", http://dx.doi.org/www.oecd.org/regional-policy. [10]

OECD (2014), "Recommendation on Effective Public Investment Across Levels of Government – Implementation Toolkit", https://www.oecd.org/effective-public-investment-toolkit/. [14]

OECD (2013), *Innovation-driven Growth in Regions: The Role of Smart Specialisation*, OECD, Paris, https://www.oecd.org/innovation/inno/smart-specialisation.pdf. [37]

OECD (2013), *Rural-Urban Partnerships: An Integrated Approach to Economic Development*, OECD Rural Policy Reviews, OECD Publishing, Paris, https://dx.doi.org/10.1787/9789264204812-en. [18]

OECD (2011), *OECD Rural Policy Reviews: England, United Kingdom 2011*, OECD Publishing, Paris, http://dx.doi.org/10.1787/9789264094444-en. [7]

OECD (2010), "Multi-level Governance: A Conceptual Framework", in *Cities and Climate Change*, OECD Publishing, Paris, https://dx.doi.org/10.1787/9789264091375-11-en. [2]

OECD (2008), *OECD Territorial Reviews: Poland 2008*, OECD Territorial Reviews, OECD Publishing, Paris, https://dx.doi.org/10.1787/9789264049529-en. [33]

OECD (2005), *Modernising Government: The Way Forward*, OECD Publishing, Paris, https://dx.doi.org/10.1787/9789264010505-en. [24]

SAUR (2020), "Water supply and wastewater treatment services in Poland", http://www.saur.com/en/the-group/international/saur-worldwide/poland/. [34]

Shortall, S. and M. Alston (2016), "To rural proof or not to rural proof: A comparative analysis", *Politics & Policy*, Vol. 44/1, pp. 35-55, http://dx.doi.org/10.1111/polp.12144. [6]

Wishlade, F. and R. Michie (2017), "Financial instruments in practice: uptake and limitations", Background paper prepared for the seminar "When to use financial instruments" held 28 June 2017, OECD Headquarters, Paris. [17]

Notes

[1] Centrally-led agencies located in regions and able to plan their actions and collaborate amongst themselves; with the state continuing to lay down guidelines, mitigate resource inequalities and evaluate their performance.

[2] Agencies with a differentiated governance structure and independent authority for management, decision-making and policy implementation.

Annex 4.A. 2018-19 OECD survey on rural policy

The OECD conducted an institutional survey between July 2018 and August 2019 amongst delegates of the OECD Working Party on Rural Policy. It served as the basis to build the country notes on rural policy that complement this report. The survey aimed to identify the institutional structure, the delivery mechanisms and priorities on rural development policy across OECD countries. The survey was answered in full or partially by 34 countries. It acknowledged that the OECD institutional landscape is diverse in the type of government structures (federal and unitary countries), subnational governance systems and mechanisms for policy delivery. The responses also stressed the relevance of subnational governments to ensure policies are adapted to country needs and effectively reach people and businesses. The main findings of the survey are:

- Overall, rural policy in OECD countries is conducted throughout different ministries and the majority of countries have an inter-ministerial committee/body to co-ordinate this policy.

- While in most OECD countries, the Ministry of Agriculture is the lead ministry/institution for rural policy, in many OECD countries, the lead ministry for rural policy has a mandate beyond agriculture, including environmental protection, regional economy or tourism.

- Most OECD countries implement rural policy through dedicated grant programmes, which are in many cases combined with contracts with local governments.

- The definition of rural areas in most OECD countries acknowledges different types of rural areas. In some countries, the definition of rural varies among institutions and policy programmes.

- Most OECD countries have a national rural policy defined by law or a strategic policy document. National rural policies are rarely explicit and are normally updated with the change of government.

- In terms of priorities, rural development policies in most OECD countries assign greater importance to economic areas, followed by environmental and social matters.

- Agriculture, innovation and well-being are the most important objectives in rural policies across OECD countries. Yet, service delivery and support to private sector rank high in the policy agenda.

5 Rural regions of the future: Seizing technological change

This chapter outlines the importance of digitalisation for rural development and the well-being of rural citizens and policy responses needed to make the most of future opportunities that may emerge. The first section describes the trends and impacts of digitalisation in rural communities and examines the policies needed to harness the benefits brought by technological change. The second section maps a number of disruptive technologies and how governments may seize their benefits for rural regions. The last section outlines how the emerging opportunities for rural development can be used as a tool to reach countrywide and global Sustainable Development Goals in the rapidly approaching 2030 Agenda.

Key messages

The Rural Well-being Policy Framework stresses the need to be forward-looking and embrace technology to ensure rural regions can take advantage of opportunities brought by technological change and contribute to global agendas, including SDGs and climate change.

Megatrends such as digitalisation, demography and climate change are bringing new challenges and opportunities to rural communities. Innovation and technological change can bring new solutions for rural regions to overcome their remoteness to markets, higher transportation costs and lack of critical mass, and increase rural resilience.

Digitalisation can reduce the cost of moving people and goods, which in turn reduces the relevance of location for workers and businesses. These changes might lead to more distributed production structures and working methods, making rural environments more competitive internationally and attractive for people and firms. Technological progress can also improve quality and access to services, and political participation, enhance entrepreneurship and local labour markets and help regions transition to a low-carbon economy.

Nevertheless, without a forward-looking approach, technological change can negatively impact growth opportunities in rural regions and increase the urban-rural income disparity. Rural regions face a relatively high risk of job automation (with economies holding a high share of repetitive tasks), a lack of diversification and outmigration of highly skilled workers.

To ensure rural communities and businesses can fully seize the benefits of the digital age and trigger innovation, governments need to ensure and strengthen a number of enabling factors in rural regions. They include:

- Ensuring high-quality broadband in all types of rural communities. Rural communities face a lack of digital connectivity in comparison with urban areas, especially in terms of broadband quality. Low-speed networks (less than 20 Mbps) can prevent communities benefitting from many technologies, including advanced telemedicine and cloud computing. Improving broadband access in rural regions would benefit from:
  - o Greater government involvement in broadband investments either through direct investment with public-private partnerships (PPPs) or promotion of incentives for competitive tendering.
  - o A sound policy framework that reflects the need for a wider diffusion of digital networks.
  - o Support for bottom-up models in rural regions to finance and deploy high-speed networks. For example, municipal networks or high-speed networks fully or partially facilitated or financed by local governments.
- Strengthening infrastructure (e.g. telecommunications infrastructure and roads). Even in the digital age, a strong infrastructure backbone is required to provide quality information and communication technology (ICT) services. As more connections are made wirelessly, the speed and rate of download of these connections ultimately depend on the capacity of fixed networks. New technologies such as autonomous vehicles or trucks also need good quality roads to expand their service across the whole territory.
- Upskilling the labour force and preparing skills for the future. Workers with skills that complement technology and can perform non-routine tasks are the most likely to benefit from high-skilled/high-paid job opportunities in the digital age. Policies to make workers thrive in technology-rich work environments include:
  - o Investing in training in digital skills, a mix of cognitive skills (literacy, numeracy and problem solving), along with ICT and behavioural skills.

- ○ Shaping career pathways focused on skills rather than jobs makes it easier for people to make occupational transitions and enhances the life-long productive capacities of the rural labour force.
- ○ Co-ordination of education and training providers, employers and labour unions provide training options that match workers' needs for career progression and transitions.
- ○ Work with educational systems at the national and local levels to adapt the curriculum in rural schools and promote access to high-end technological devices.
- Developing forward-looking policies and regulations with greater involvement of rural communities. This includes foresight planning to ensure policies are flexible and prepared to face rapid changes in the future, improving information systems (on skills and demographics of workers) and enabling technological trials and awareness strategies about the forthcoming changes and involvement of the community.
- Improving the understanding of how innovation occurs in rural regions. Innovation in rural regions occurs differently and has a different impact than in densely populated areas. It often happens through adaptive measures that try to overcome market and policy failures, with entrepreneurs in rural regions often creating innovative products and processes through an aggregation of smaller changes, such as learning by doing.

Forward-looking rural policies need also to comply with global agendas and Sustainable Development Goals (SDGs), including climate change, poverty reduction and gender equality. Achieving the SDGs will require participation at the local level, where governments are directly responsible for delivering on SDG targets. Rural regions are crucial to the achievement of these global objectives as they provide the world's biodiversity, natural resources, food and raw materials. Leveraging innovation and working alongside local communities is key for rural regions to contribute to the global reduction of poverty and the transition to a low-carbon economy.

Introduction

A number of global shifts are likely to characterise the 21st century and shape how rural regions can succeed in a complex, dynamic and challenging environment. In rural regions, technological progress can mitigate some of the challenges caused by the structural changes discussed in previous chapters. These include demographic changes, shrinking local economies and a shortage of skilled labour and entrepreneurs. Digitalisation and the arrival of new technologies (e.g. 3D printers, delivery drones, autonomous vehicles and augmented reality) can reduce the cost of moving people and goods. They can also help regions to deliver quality services and transition to a low-carbon economy, These changes might lead to more evenly distributed production structures and working methods, making rural environments more attractive to people and firms. Likewise, reducing the transport and communication costs in low-density areas will propel rural economies forward, thus opening up wider possibilities to engage in regional, national and international markets.

Furthermore, the COVID-19 pandemic has highlighted the relevance of embracing technology for economic resilience and well-being. Confinement measures during the crisis fomented the use of teleworking, remote learning and e-services, which are particularly important for rural regions given their longer distances and commuting times. The aftermath of the COVID-19 crisis might further accelerate policy and society decisions to enhance digitalisation across all type of areas. The changes in working methods and ways to access services emerging from this crisis have ultimately the potential to boost the attractiveness of rural regions as places to work remotely while enjoying natural amenities.

Nevertheless, without this forward-looking approach, policy responses may not harness the potential benefits that digitalisation and new technologies can bring to rural communities, widening current inequalities and diluting growth opportunities for rural dwellers. An acceleration towards knowledge-based service economies might further challenge rural regions since most of today's knowledge-intensive services (e.g. tech start-ups, consulting firms) are predominantly located in urban areas. Likewise, rural communities face the highest risks of job automation, as their economies tend to have activities with a high share of repetitive tasks, low economic diversification and outmigration of high-skilled labour force.

Preparing rural economies to address the challenges and leverage the benefits of technological change is crucial to make the most of the digital age for people and businesses. Political will and forward-looking public policies that establish the necessary conditions at the local level (i.e. quality broadband and education) are instrumental to facilitate an effective uptake of the new technologies among rural dwellers and businesses.

This chapter outlines the digitalisation trend and its impact in rural regions as well as the policies needed to realise the promises of digital technologies for rural growth and well-being. The first section describes the effects of digitalisation in rural communities and examines the policies needed to harness the benefits generated by technological change. The second section maps a number of disruptive technologies and how governments may seize their benefits for rural communities. The last section outlines how the emerging opportunities for rural development can be used as a tool to reach countrywide and global SDGs in the rapidly approaching 2030 Agenda.

Making the most of digitalisation for rural regions

A growing number of people, services and products are going online. Digital transformation carries much the same weight as earlier industrial transformations propelled by general-purpose technologies like steam or electricity. Along with the spread of high-speed broadband, digital technologies can create new growth opportunities, enhance productivity (e.g. 3D printing), facilitate social connections (i.e. virtual reality) and change how economic activities impact the environment and services are delivered (e.g. automated mines and farms or e-Health and e-Education). Effective use of digitalisation in rural communities requires establishing the right conditions at the local level, including high-quality broadband and civil infrastructure, education/skills and future-proofed regulation and policies (OECD, 2019[1]).

Digitalisation will open new market opportunities for rural economies

Digitalisation can help rural regions to overcome some of their traditional challenges. Low density and shrinking local markets are two of the main bottlenecks for long-term sustainability in many rural economies (see Chapter 3). These characteristics tend to inhibit the formation of economies of scale, making it difficult for businesses to grow and for workers to find the right labour opportunities to apply their skills. Firms in small, local economies struggle when it comes to competing against firms in urban areas that can produce higher volumes at more strategic locations closer to customers (OECD, 2019[2]). Digitalisation can offer new growth possibilities and opportunities for better and more diversified jobs in rural regions. Some effects of the digital age that can provide a boost for rural regions include reduction of trade times and costs, the exchange of new types of products and services, and disruptive ways to work and join the labour market.

Technological change can reduce the costs of trade, opening up new market opportunities for rural regions. New technologies are likely to enable rural goods and services to reach more distant markets with a lower cost and greater speed than today. For example, driverless trucks can run 24 hours a day and cover much greater distances than traditional trucks, reducing transport costs and shipping time (OECD, 2019[2]). Likewise, drone-based deliveries are likely to be deployed first in rural regions since regulation is less strict and it is far more difficult for drones to navigate the infrastructure in densely populated cities (Xu, 2017[3]).

This type of delivery system can help rural regions to overcome challenges of geography and infrastructure. Many drone-based delivery projects have already been tested in different countries and companies like Amazon have projected that once the service is fully deployed they will be able to deliver more than 80% of their goods by air (Rao, Gopi and Maione, 2016[4]).

The digital age can modify how firms provide non-tradeable services. Traditionally, the exchange of non-tradeable services (e.g. law, health or hairdressers) occurs through face-to-face contact (e.g. getting a vaccine or a haircut). However, some researchers have claimed emerging technologies like virtual or augmented reality can make face-to-face contact less relevant for exchange of non-tradeable services (Baldwin, 2016[5]). The technology for administering a vaccine or providing a haircut through an automatised robot already exists (Anandan, 2018[6]; Decker, Fischer and Ott, 2017[7]). If a doctor can operate online with the assistance of a controlled robot, he/she might choose to live and practice in a rural area to benefit from better environmental quality, larger space and lower housing costs (see Chapter 3). Technological progress would thus enable rural economies to compete in the provision of non-tradeable services currently dominated by urban dwellers. Furthermore, the increased use of digital tools for service delivery can help firms (and governments) in rural regions deliver non-tradeable public services (e-Health, e-Education) during times of crisis, such as during the coronavirus pandemic.

New technologies can enhance the entrepreneurial business environment in rural economies. Technology is already making it easier for rural small- and medium-sized enterprises (SMEs) to trade. Commerce through digital platforms, or cross-border e-commerce, has become instrumental to lower entry barriers for firms and SMEs that aim to sell in global markets (OECD, 2019[1]). Likewise, new technologies like additive manufacturing (e.g. 3D printers) have the potential to reduce the need for economies of scale by making small-scale production more cost-effective (see next section for detailed explanation). 3D printers can also reduce the reliance on global value chains (GVCs) by allowing small firms to produce goods and standard parts tailored to local demand without the need for importing or warehousing large quantities of inputs from elsewhere. The opportunity to replace certain products from external markets can help develop local value chains for traditional rural sectors, including agriculture, mining and forestry.

Technological progress has the potential to spur innovation in rural communities. Emerging technologies have the scope to enhance the interaction of markets and ideas. Greater interaction among firms and people facilitate innovation processes. While agglomeration can facilitate this in urban areas, virtual and augmented reality can also make this possible in rural economies by simulating face-to-face collaboration among firms, academics and research institutions across rural regions and between rural and urban regions. Through cloud technology, workers or academics can work remotely or stationed in different offices, collaborating on the same projects and following up the evolution of creative processes.

Digital connectivity will help strengthen labour markets and improve skills to jobs matching. Online platforms and blockchain technologies directly link businesses to workers and customers, enabling the emergence of new forms of employment under labels such as "on-demand workers" or "crowd-workers" (OECD, 2016[8]). These workers supply various tasks ranging from low-skilled activities (Mechanical Turk) to higher-skilled ones (Freelancer, Upwork) (OECD, 2017[9]). The on-demand economy makes it easier for firms to outsource specific tasks and better match labour supply and demand. It could thus enable workers in rural regions to overcome a small labour market size and match their skills with firms outside of the local market. Furthermore, online learning platforms allow workers to gain additional skills adapted to new labour demand. For example, online companies like Coursera or Udacity offer Google designed IT certificate programmes or "nano degrees" in areas including data science and cloud computing (Mckinsey Global Institute, 2019[10]).

Technology is enabling wider use of remote working models, which contributes to job creation in rural regions. ICTs allow workers to be more mobile by working remotely from home, delocalised business centres, or satellite offices (Scaillerez and Tremblay, 2016[11]). In many OECD countries, workers and firms have increasingly adopted teleworking as a partial or full-time working practice that helps them cut costs of office space and catering as well as improve workers' quality of life by reducing commuting time and extending time with family. In the European Union (EU) for example, 12% of workers were working remotely every day or almost every day in 2018 (OECD, 2019[12]). The confinement measures during the coronavirus pandemic have accelerated remote working practices, leading many workers and firms to adapt themselves to new working methods and embrace digital solutions. For many businesses, teleworking has been a new experience that enables them to keep their economic activity. As a consequence of this crisis, firms and governments can shift towards flexible, partial or even permanent remote working in the long run.

Rural regions are well-positioned to benefit from the changes in working methods. They offer lower living cost and greater natural amenities than their urban peers (Clark, 2018[13]). In the United States (US), the areas with the greatest number of teleworkers before the COVID-19 crisis were medium and small towns rather than larger cities (Global Workplace Analytics, 2018[14]). Even before this crisis, some OECD countries had already explored teleworking as a policy strategy to boost rural economies. For example, Japan has used teleworking as a public policy to increase the participation of disabled populations in the labour force as well as contribute to regional revitalisation. Likewise, the US has promoted initiatives to build outposts/creative spaces where people can work remotely (Box 5.1). While the lockdown measures of 2020 revealed that capital regions had the highest rate of remote working due to the economic composition (OECD, 2020[15]), many urban dwellers during that period moved temporary to work from rural regions. Further analysis is required to measure the long-term effect of greater teleworking practices on the movement of new population to rural places.

Box 5.1. Teleworking initiative to revitalise rural economies

Teleworking policy in Japan

In Japan, teleworking is seen as an alternative policy to help boost rural economies. In 2017, about 13% of companies let their employees work remotely and the government has the goal to increase this figure to about 30% by 2020. It also contributes to efforts to reduce congestion and address the nation's chronically long working hours. In 2018, the Ministry of Economy, Trade and Industry (METI) launched the 2018 Telework Days campaign to encourage businesses to promote teleworking across Japan, declaring 24 July as National Teleworking Day. More than 950 organisations have joined the campaign with a big portion of businesses expanding their technological platforms.

Northern Japan uses the campaign to promote the adoption of flexible work styles by the nation's self-employed urban workers. Using a grant from the Ministry of Internal Affairs, Shari City has spent about JPY 4 million to transform its legal affairs office into a teleworking space with rooms for telecommuters.

In 2018, more than 20 companies sent employees to work in Shari. Teleworkers can use the facility's free Wi-Fi and teleconferencing system to link up with their corporate headquarters in Tokyo and elsewhere. They can also stay in guest rooms on the second floor, which have two bedrooms, a living room and a dining room with a kitchen.

Because Shari is just a 30-minute drive from the Utoro hot springs area, a popular tourism spot, visitors can easily explore the great outdoors by exploring the trails around Shiretoko's five lakes or taking cruises to watch dolphins and even bears on the wildlife-rich peninsula.

Rural Innovation Initiative in the United States

The Rural Innovation Initiative seeks to assist rural regions interested in building local workspaces, as well as creating digital skills training programmes to give residents the skills and workspace needed to take on remote jobs or to start their own companies.

The Center on Rural Innovation (CORI), a Vermont-based non-profit organisation, leads the technical assistance programme with support from the US Economic Development Administration (EDA). Rural Innovation Strategies Inc. launches the programme in an effort to bring prosperity and investment to rural regions in the digital age.

Interested communities applied at the beginning of 2019. CORI will first work with towns that have the most immediate potential for success, due to proximity to a higher education institution or a downtown district with under-utilised historic buildings ready for a new life. It will select the places that fit the US Census definition of a rural area and that have a combination of the following: existing high-speed broadband, real estate located in a New Market Tax Credit census tract and/or Opportunity Zone that make it possible for developers to obtain tax breaks. In addition, selected areas need to have a nearby university or community college and a non-profit willing to lead the initiative.

Then, CORI will assist communities in creating an economic development strategy to attract more digital and knowledge-economy jobs, as well as pointing them toward potential sources of funding from the EDA and other private groups.

The 2019 Regional Innovation Strategies programme awarded 44 grants to applicants from 28 states and 2 territories. The grants represent a combined USD 23 million in federal and USD 26 million in local investment.

Source: Ministry of Internal Affairs and Communications of Japan (2011[16]), "Efforts to Promote Telework in Japan", http://www.soumu.go.jp/main_sosiki/joho_tsusin/eng/presentation/pdf/110908_1.pdf; Rural Innovation Strategies Inc. (n.d.[17]), *Unlocking the Potential of Rural America*, https://ruralinnovationstrategies.com (accessed on March 2020).

Digitalisation will contribute to reduced costs of services provision

Structural characteristics of rural regions make the provision of services more challenging. The cost of public service provision tends to increase with the degree of remoteness and population sparsity due to transportation costs, loss of economies of scale and greater difficulty in attracting and retaining high-skilled workers (e.g. healthcare professionals) (OECD, 2010[18]). Furthermore, shrinking and ageing populations together with a lower tax base have pressed governments to adapt to new conditions amidst growing demand and higher costs. Providing access to public transportation, education and skills training as well as health services and care for the elderly population has become increasingly challenging in areas where the population is shrinking and geographically dispersed.

New technologies can contribute to improve the quality and reduce the costs of delivering services to rural communities. ICT solutions allow rural communities to access high-quality services by overcoming physical distances and road or rail infrastructure challenges. Virtual access to education (e-Learning) can help students participate in programmes without commuting, offering access to entire education programmes or courses from high-quality educational institutions. Some of the features of e-Learning are especially relevant to overcoming demographic challenges in rural regions (Box 5.2). Online health services, robotic surgeries and medical supplies delivered by drones are already complementing health services in some rural communities (OECD, 2019[1]). The e-Health trend has been accelerating since 2005 and now 58% of analysed countries (73) have developed a national e-Health strategy (WHO, 2016[19]). In the aftermath of the COVID-19 crisis, many governments can accelerate the deployment of e-Health and e-Learning services to increase the resilience of rural regions to external shocks. This shift can help rural communities retain young people and provide attractive public services to new residents.

Box 5.2. Digital learning tools for adults and lifelong learning

Digital technologies create new possibilities for education and training. Digital learning and open education come in many forms (e.g. post-secondary, undergraduate and graduate education, continuing education, short-term training and professional development). Formal educational institutions, industries and entrepreneurs in the education and training fields offer digital learning platforms. Digital learning can lower the cost of training, increase flexibility in training provision and better meet individual needs, among other benefits (OECD, 2019[20]). Digital learning and open education hold much promise to foster adult and lifelong learning.

One form of digital learning is online learning, which overcomes the challenges of distance and can be open to large numbers of students. Online learning includes tutorials, recorded lectures, online educational resources, as well as small, private online courses or massive open online courses (MOOCs). MOOCs have attracted much attention over recent years but their potential for education and training is still limited.

While formal post-secondary educational institutions offered the first popular MOOCs, focusing on traditional academic subject areas, more recent MOOCs aim to enhance skills and provide professional development. Traditional educational institutions have partnered with multinational corporations on many of these skills-oriented MOOCs in order to help set the curricula and assign certificates of completion that they accept in their hiring processes. For firms, MOOCs may provide a potentially cost-effective means of investing in their employees. Users of open education are largely employees that combine e-Learning with formal education.

One key challenge with many MOOCs is that completion rates are low, and patterns of participation and completion seem to replicate offline learning patterns, i.e. the highly educated and highly skilled are more likely to participate in and finalise courses than low-skilled ones. It is thus unclear whether MOOCs will reduce or actually reinforce inequalities in adult learning. For those who complete online courses, gaining recognition remains a challenge despite many innovative approaches to certification that have evolved with digital learning, e.g. digital badges, nano and micro degrees, and other alternative forms of credentials.

Source: Adapted from OECD (2019[1]), *Going Digital: Shaping Policies, Improving Lives*, https://dx.doi.org/10.1787/9789264312012-en; OECD (2016[21]), *Massive Open Online Courses (MOOCs): Trends and Future Perspectives*, OECD, Paris; OECD (2019[20]), *OECD Skills Outlook 2019: Thriving in a Digital World*, https://doi.org/10.1787/df80bc12-en.

Digitalisation enables better governance in rural communities and provides further opportunities for rural dwellers to participate in civic engagement (Chapter 5). The use of digital platforms is expected to improve the function of public administration and its relationship to the public. Most OECD countries have developed strategies of e-governance to involve greater numbers of citizens in the policy decision-making process (OECD, 2014[22]). Likewise, ICT provides an array of tools for people to share ideas and influence regional and national agendas. Countries like France have strategies to engage a broader population through ICT and offer proposals for policy reforms (*Grand débat national*).

Making automation a complement for rural economies

Automation brings positive and negative disruptive effects on local economies. Automation anxiety has been a recurrent theme ever since the first industrial revolution. Telegraph and telephone networks made many jobs obsolete, automated teller machines (ATMs) made some bank tellers redundant and industrial robots replaced plant workers. However, reduced costs as a result of technological progress have also increased wages and created new jobs. For example, the rise of ATMs increased demand for bank tellers as this labour-saving technology reduced the costs for banks to open new branches (Bessen, 2015[23]). Internationally, there is no clear consensus on the net effect of job automation (OECD, 2019[2]). On the upside, automation offers a path to revive productivity growth by creating new jobs and allocating low-skilled workers to new sectors (Autor and Dorn, 2013[24]). On the downside, automation can lead to large-scale job losses and high unemployment (Frod, 2015[25]).

Today, many rural communities are ill-prepared to face automation effects. Rural communities, especially remote rural economies, tend to experience low economic diversification, shrinking and relatively low-skilled labour force with lower levels of educational attainment (see Chapter 3). Regions highly concentrated in manufacturing with a lower share of service activities and those with low productivity face the highest risks of job automation (OECD, 2018[26]). Many rural economies fall into this group as they tend to have a high degree of specialisation in manufacturing and extractive industries whose production processes embed a high share of repetitive tasks (OECD, 2018[26]). For instance, operational tasks in mining such as drilling, blasting, and train and truck driving constitute over 70% of employment in mines (Cosbey et al., 2016[27]). In fact, all top five occupations with a higher risk of automation are extremely common in many rural communities (Table 5.1).

Table 5.1. Top 5 occupations in terms of jobs at risk of automation

Occupation (ISCO name)	Share of jobs at high risk of automation, average across TL2 regions (%)
Food preparation assistants	0.6
Drivers and mobile plant operators	3.5
Labourers in mining, construction, manufacturing and transport	2.2
Stationary plant and machine operators	2.6
Refuse workers and other elementary workers	0.8

Note: The table shows in the first column the five occupations that have the highest risk of automation (in descending order), and in the second column, their share of total employment, average across TL2 regions in the sample.
ISCO: International Standard Classification of Occupations.
Source: OECD (2018[26]), *Job Creation and Local Economic Development 2018: Preparing for the Future of Work*, https://doi.org/10.1787/9789 264305342-en.

Nevertheless, technological change can be an occasion to create more rewarding jobs and build better learning systems and career pathways. New technologies can complement high-skilled, non-routine cognitive tasks and replace mid-skilled routine tasks, while parts of the low-skilled workforce can shift to service and sales occupations (Autor and Dorn, 2013[24]). Policy makers must view technological change as substituting or complementing certain tasks rather than replacing occupations (Arntz, Gregory and Zierahn, 2016[28]). At the same time, technology is likely to create new jobs we cannot imagine today; academic research suggests that about 8% to 9% of jobs by 2030 will be ones that barely exist today (Mckinsey Global Institute, 2019[10]). Frey and Osborne (2017[29]) find that even occupations dominated by automatable tasks require other complementary tasks that are hard to automate.

Despite the uncertainty about the effects of automation, governments need to ensure that technological progress will enhance overall well-being and does not lead to rising inequality. Policy has a major role in shaping the consequences of automation in labour markets. Regulation and fiscal policies need to respond to the changes in the new digital era. For instance, different international actors have advocated for a tax system that takes into account a robot tax to compensate for the negative effects of automation (OECD, 2019[2]). The EU proposed but ultimately rejected, legislation to tax robots, citing concerns such a tax might stifle innovation (Reuters, 2017[30]).

Ensuring the enabling factors to mobilise digitalisation benefits

While future predictions on how technological progress and automation will affect rural economies are difficult to make, many rural regions still lack the adequate characteristics to face the forthcoming changes. Technological progress can reach everywhere and lead to negative or positives outcomes at the local level. To make the most of technological progress, rural regions need to invest in their local capacities by strengthening a number of factors including technological and civil infrastructure, quality education and skills training. These enabling factors need to be supported by sound institutional characteristics such as awareness, forward-looking regulations, administrative capacity and political will capable of triggering the needed long-term investments and policy foresight.

Ensuring high-quality broadband connectivity

Universal and high-quality broadband is the basis for creating new market opportunities for rural communities. As the Internet and ICT facilitate the transfer of information, they should be regarded as production factors (similar to electricity or labour) for productivity gains and economic growth either for places or individual businesses (Salemink, Strijker and Bosworth, 2017[31]; Tu and Sui, 2010[32]; Martínez and Rodríguez, 2008[33]).

Rural communities need sound communications networks to make the most of the new trends in technologies and digitalisation. Broadband access provides the physical means for using Internet-based digital services through a variety of technologies (e.g. Digital Subscriber Line (DSL), high-frequency 4G LTE, TV white spaces or satellite).[1] Access to broadband plays a key role in economic and social interaction and tends to have positive effects on firm productivity, the number of firms and local labour market outcomes (OECD, 2018[34]).

Differences in broadband access across geography persist within OECD countries. Rural communities face a comparatively larger lack of digital connectivity than urban areas, which is commonly known as the urban-rural digital divide (OECD, 2019[1]). In 31 out of 37 OECD countries, the share of rural households with Internet services is smaller than in urban areas (OECD, 2018[34]). Such divide also exists on devices and machine-to-machine connections, which is critical to embrace the whole functionality of new technologies (e.g. automotive cars).

Nevertheless, the gap in digital access among urban and rural communities is decreasing. The urban-rural digital divide in the OECD has halved since 2010 in almost all countries (OECD, 2019[1]). In some countries, like the Netherlands, the share of households in rural communities with broadband access is now similar to the share in urban areas (see Chapter 2). OECD countries have set the goal to provide universal broadband coverage high on their policy agenda. All OECD countries have specific national goals for broadband availability, where most goals are set in terms of speed of service offered and percentage of coverage (OECD, 2019[1]).

Despite the progress in access, the urban-rural gap on broadband quality remains significant. Rural regions are lagging behind cities in broadband access at sufficient speeds. During 2010 and 2018, OECD countries have increased, on average, the share of high-speed fibre in fixed broadband Internet (from a share of 12% in 2010 to 25% in 2018). Yet, most of that improvement has happened in urban areas. Across OECD countries, only 56% of rural households have access to fixed broadband with a speed of 30 megabytes per second (Mbps) or more, far below the 85% of urban households benefitting from such high-speed connections (OECD, 2019[1]).

The factors explaining the digital gap arise mainly from the geographic and demographic characteristics of rural regions. Geography (difficulty of terrain) and population distribution patterns, both in terms of density and dispersion, make it challenging to attract market players concerned about the profitability of such broadband investments. Yet, some OECD countries have proven that it is feasible to create the right market conditions to cover sparsely populated rural regions with high-speed broadband. Finland, Iceland and Sweden have some of the lowest population densities in OECD countries but rank among the top 10 OECD countries with the highest Internet coverage in rural regions (see Figure 2.28 in Chapter 2).

Quality broadband is fundamental to harness the benefits from new technologies. Quality broadband is a multi-dimensional concept that involves connection speed, the time taken to transfer data between users or devices and the number of errors arising in data transfer (OECD, 2019[12]). For example, low-speed networks (less than 20 Mbps) become a barrier in the adoption of many technologies, including advanced telemedicine and cloud computing (Box 5.3). There is a growing consensus that the minimum requirement to meet all digital demands and benefit from future technologies is a connection capacity of minimum 100 Mbps (Bain & Company, 2016[35]; Ministry of Enterprise and Innovation of Sweden, 2016[36]).

Box 5.3. The relevance of speed in broadband access

Some OECD countries measure broadband availability by collecting metrics on coverage. Most often, these access indicators are collected using a technology-based approach. It then takes into account a number of variables including the percentage of households/population, the share of xDSL, FTTx, cable TV networks, cable modem enabled networks as well as 3G and 4G mobile network coverage and the number of kilometres of fibre deployed. In addition to availability, speed and quality of service are also important for broadband access, as low speeds or poor quality may make it difficult or impossible to use certain Internet applications and services. Table 5.2 shows the type of services that different ranges of broadband download speeds can enable.

Table 5.2. Ranges of download speeds and services enabled

Average download bit rate	Description of service
>0.5 Mbps	0.5 Mbps web browsing, email, streaming audio, mobile-quality video streaming, voice and standard-definition (SD) video calling
0.5 – 2.0 Mbps	SD video streaming (360p), high-definition (HD) video calling
2.0 – 3.5 Mbps	Low bit rate HD streaming video (480p/720p)
3.5 – 5.0 Mbps	High bit rate HD streaming video (720p/1080p)
5.0 – 10.0 Mbps	Very high bit rate HD video streaming
10.0 – 20.0 Mbps	Ultra HD (UHD) video streaming
> 20.0 Mbps	High frame rate UHD video streaming, augmented reality, advanced telemedicine

Note: Mbps refers to megabytes per second.
Source: OECD (2018[34]), "Bridging the rural digital divide", https://doi.org/10.1787/852bd3b9-en.

Some countries have begun splitting the access indicators not by technology but by speeds of connections announced. Given the different capabilities within each speed threshold, this technology-neutral approach is desirable since it demonstrates the accessibility gaps in terms of quality of service offered for each area. Canada, Japan and the US are examples of countries using this speed threshold method. For example, the US measures access in terms of upload speeds, coupled with download speeds (25 Mbps for download and 3 Mbps for upload). For this threshold, 39% of the rural population in the US (23 million people) lack broadband access at these speeds, in contrast with only 4% of the urban population.

Source: OECD (2018[34]), "Bridging the rural digital divide", https://doi.org/10.1787/852bd3b9-en.

Governments need to avoid that the deployment of the new generation of access networks expands the quality broadband gap between rural and urban. The next generation of access networks such as the 5G network is required to meet the growing demand for high speeds and fast transfers. This network is essential to enabling machine-to-machine communication and make it possible for the functioning of autonomous technologies including self-driving cars and drones (Box 5.4). There is a growing concern that the gap between the most and least connected areas will further increase in the rollout of 5G. As this network requires high investments and thus a large demand, it is likely that market operators will opt to deploy it firstly in high-density areas. Policies should ensure high-speed connection networks are also deployed in rural regions. Incentivising innovation in broadband platforms such as high-powered fixed-wireless solutions or low Earth orbit (LEO) satellite systems can help to cover lower-density areas with higher speed access, where fixed solutions (cable, fibre) are not economical (Bain & Company, 2016[35]).

Box 5.4. Effects of 5G networks

5G networks are intended to support: enhanced mobile broadband; intelligent devices with fully automated data generation, exchange and processing; and critical communications and applications (ultra-reliable communications with very rapid upload and download of data).

While the international standard is not yet finalised, 5G will be the first generation of wireless networks conceived mainly for a future in which tens of billions of devices and sensors can connect to the Internet simultaneously. Major improvements upon previous network generations include higher speeds (i.e. 100 times faster than 4G), faster data transfer (i.e. 10 times less than 4G) and networks that better support diverse applications through the virtualisation of the physical layers (i.e. "network slicing"). Trials are underway in multiple countries, including through collaborations between network operators and vertical industries.

A major difference with 5G is that it can connect not just people but things, underpinning a world of machine-to-machine communication that takes place largely hidden from human eyes. For example, 5G networks will improve communication between self-driving vehicles, roads and traffic lights, making feasible – the automatic linking of vehicles on highways in a convoy so that they are much closer together than would be safe with human drivers. This could ease road congestion as well as improve safety and fuel efficiency. In addition, sensors embedded throughout farms will be able to communicate crops' water and fertilisation needs directly to agricultural machinery and systems.

Personal devices will download data at far higher speeds even in crowded areas, realising the potential coverage of on-demand media from almost any location reached by 5G networks.

Source: OECD (2019[1]), *Going Digital: Shaping Policies, Improving Lives*, https://dx.doi.org/10.1787/9789264312012-en.

Improving broadband access in rural regions

Active national policies along with private sector partnerships are instrumental to improve Internet quality in rural regions. A high-quality broadband provision in rural communities faces many challenges to attracting private investment. Low densities and geography often discourage commercial operators to invest, which in turn can make low-density areas more prone to natural monopolies. Thus, government involvement in broadband investments proves critical to promoting broadband investment in rural communities, either through direct investment with public-private partnerships or promotion of incentives for competitive tendering (e.g. tax exemption, changes to spectrum license arrangements, or loans) (OECD, 2019[1]). As Chapter 3 depicts, OECD countries have been active in addressing challenges in broadband access in rural regions (see Table 3.3).

Wider digital connectivity in rural regions will also benefit from clear regulations. Enhancing access to ICT for all individuals and businesses at an affordable price requires sound policy frameworks that reflect the need for a wider diffusion of digital networks. Ensuring competition in broadband provision, promoting private investments, setting minimum speeds and establishing an independent regulation are strategies that have been effective in extending broadband coverage across different OECD countries (OECD, 2018[34]).

No single high-speed transmission technology works for all types of rural regions. Instead, investment decisions should leverage the most cost-effective technology in each region. Some exercises have shown that providing rural regions with high-speed Internet requires a mix of technologies with a co-ordination of actors (telecom companies, broadcasters, technology firms and policy makers) (The Boston Consulting Group, 2018[37]). For instance, the Swedish broadband national programme underlines that different technologies are optimal for satisfying the need for broadband in different parts of the country (Figure 5.1).

Figure 5.1. The strategy of broadband connection by type of areas, Sweden

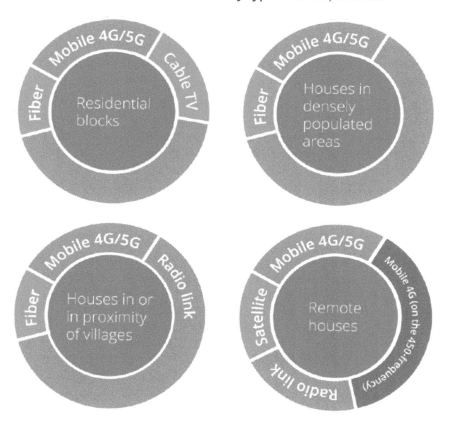

Note: Broadband via copper is not included in the illustration, neither has the extension of the individual technologies been taken into account.
Source: Ministry of Enterprise and Innovation of Sweden (2016[36]), *A Completely Connected Sweden by 2025 – A Broadband Strategy*, https://www.government.se/496173/contentassets/afe9f1cfeaac4e39abcdd3b82d9bee5d/sweden-completely-connected-by-2025-eng.pdf (accessed on 22 August 2019).

While market forces and national policies primarily drive broadband deployment, rural regions can also pursue their own initiatives to ensure high-quality Internet connection. A number of OECD municipalities and regions have been implementing bottom-up models to finance and deploy high-speed networks (OECD, 2018[34]). For example, municipal networks or high-speed networks, fully or partially facilitated or financed by local governments, have filled the gaps and provided substantial service to some regions. The "village fibre" in Sweden or Community Broadband Scotland in the UK are guiding examples of community-led schemes to provide and improve local broadband (Box 5.5).

Box 5.5. Community-led initiatives for broadband access

The village fibre approach in Sweden

In the 1990s, the liberalisation of the telecommunication market in Sweden not only encouraged the expansion of alternative operators and the creation of municipal networks but also the formation of local co-operatives for the rollout of fibre networks. This "village fibre" approach relies on community involvement to plan, build and operate local fibre networks in co-operation with municipalities and commercial operators. The Swedish Governmental Broadband Forum estimates that there are around 1 000 village fibre networks, which each connect 150 to 200 households on average.

Proponents say the village fibre approach facilitates fibre deployment at a considerably lower cost compared to that of commercial operators through a combination of three factors: handling of permissions; excavation work and trenching; and voluntary work with respect to aggregation of demand. Moreover, the deployment of fibre networks through village fibre as well as all other operators is facilitated by consumers' willingness to pay upfront fees of around USD 2 300 to connect single dwelling units as well as the possibility to apply for a subsidy from public funds.

A cornerstone of the village fibre approach is that members of local communities make a significant contribution through voluntary work by, for example, communicating with residents in order to raise interest and aggregate demand. On average, the penetration rate for village fibre projects is around 80% compared to roughly 50% in commercial fibre network projects. In addition to voluntary work, the individual households that participate in the construction of a village fibre network must pay a connection fee. Typically, the fee is around USD 2 300, roughly representing some 25% of the total cost of a rural broadband connection. Given that village networks develop in areas where no commercial operators are deploying fibre networks, they meet the key criteria for state aid.

Aside from public funding, Sweden's experience suggests that village networks require local initiatives and commitment as well as leadership through the development of local broadband plans and strategies. They also require co-ordination with authorities to handle a variety of regulatory and legal issues and demand competency on how to build and maintain broadband networks. The most decisive factor is the willingness of people in these areas of Sweden to use their resources and contribute with several thousand hours of work to make a village network a reality.

Community Broadband Scotland, United Kingdom

In the UK, Community Broadband Scotland is engaging with remote and rural communities in order to support residents in developing their own community-led broadband solutions. Examples of ongoing projects include those in Ewes Valley (Dumfries and Galloway) and Tomintoul and Glenlivet (Moray), which are inland mountain communities located within the Moray area of the Cairngorms National Park. Another example of a larger project can be found in Canada and the small Alberta town of Olds with a population of 8 500, which has built O-net, the town's own fibre network through the town's non-profit economic development network. The network will reach all households in the town with a number of positive effects reported for the community.

Source: OECD (2019[38]), *OECD Territorial Reviews: Småland-Blekinge 2019: Monitoring Progress and Special Focus on Migrant Integration*, https://doi.org/10.1787/9789264311640-en; OECD (2018[34]), "Bridging the rural digital divide", *OECD Digital Economy Papers*, No. 265, OECD Publishing, Paris, https://dx.doi.org/10.1787/852bd3b9-en

Providing quality infrastructure for business development

Many new technologies will require quality civil infrastructure. Even in the digital age, a strong infrastructure backbone is still required to provide quality ICT service. As more connections are made wirelessly, the speed and rate of download of these connections ultimately depend on the capacity of fixed networks (OECD, 2019[1]). Basic infrastructure can include workstations, high-speed network, projection/display technology, interactive devices and video conferencing equipment (Pramanik, Sarkar and Kandar, 2017[39]). Autonomous vehicles or trucks also need good quality roads to expand their service across the whole territory.

Quality infrastructure will continue playing an important role in providing opportunities for firms and people in rural regions. Despite the digital age promises of a lower necessity for physical movement, many reasons remain to promote well-connected rural communities. For example, the tourism sector is a relevant source for income and economic diversification for many rural communities. Good quality infrastructure can help spread the benefits from tourism across the whole territory. Well-maintained airports, roads and ports can unleash new economic opportunities for rural communities and allow greater exchange of products and movement of people.

Bridging education and skills gaps

Human capital is a critical factor influencing regional growth and development throughout all types of OECD regions. A skilled human capital base is at the essence of regional development and competitiveness. It contributes to the creation of a learning society that is able to absorb as well as create knowledge, drive innovation and facilitate local adaptability to changing labour demands and technology (OECD, 2019[40]).

Providing workers with the necessary education and skills to attain high-wage roles is instrumental to face automation. Workers with skills that complement technology and can perform non-routine tasks are the most likely to benefit from high-skilled/high-paid job opportunities in the digital age (OECD, 2019[1]). Likewise, lower average levels of education and skills in rural communities have a negative impact on adoption and use of ICT (Salemink, Strijker and Bosworth, 2017[31]). Investing in training for rural workers to acquire new skills can help them prepare for new jobs. Evidence shows that workers need more than digital skills to thrive in technology-rich work environments (OECD, 2019[20]). Workers require a mix of cognitive skills, such as literacy, numeracy and problem solving, along with analytical, ICT and behavioural skills.

Shaping career pathways focused on skills rather than jobs make it easier for occupational transition and enhances the life-long productive capacities of the rural labour force. Not all workers have to learn completely new skills during occupational transitions, as long as education and experience prepare all workers for less automatable occupations. In fact, many workers at high risk of job displacement have transferable skills that are compatible with occupations at lower risk of automation. For instance, accountants and auditing clerks have the skills to become insurance underwriters or credit analysts, which have higher median wages. To limit the cost of the education and training effort, governance can reduce occupational regulatory barriers (such as occupational quotas, high costs for certification) and promote future-looking skills-based educational policies that can facilitate transitions between occupations and harness the productive capacity of the rural labour force.

A mix of public and private training can provide the necessary skills and career path for workers. Most workers receive very short training focused on job-specific skills that are unlikely to facilitate occupation transitions (OECD, 2019[20]). Education and training providers, employers and labour unions can better co-ordinate their actions to provide training options that match workers' needs for career progressions and transitions. For example, industry-specific training programmes delivered through local educational institutions have proven effective in job placements (Mckinsey Global Institute, 2019[10]). For these training programmes to work, stronger co-ordination between regional programmes and local companies, fiscal incentives and enabling regulatory environments are required to increase workforce suitability with the current and future needs of the private sector.

Primary to tertiary education are essential to provide the skills needed for tomorrow's work. Governments need to work with education systems at the national and local levels to adapt the curriculum in rural schools along with promoting access to high-end devices. For example, student assessments rarely measure computer competencies, so there is little evidence on whether technology use in schools improves students' digital skills (OECD, 2019[20]). Encouraging schools to foster and measure general digital skills as well as creativity and computational and critical thinking can help prepare students for the new job scenarios of the future (OECD, 2019[20]).

Sound regulations, policies and information to benefit from new technologies

Adapting governance of regional development policy to account for technology is crucial to prepare rural regions for forthcoming changes. Long-term planning, projections and other foresight methods translated to policies can future-proof regional policy making (OECD, 2019[2]). OECD governments have conducted different methods of foresight planning to ensure policies are flexible and prepared to face rapid changes in the future (Box 5.6). Close work with communities and universities is important to ensure consensus on future scenarios and co-ordinated solutions.

Clear regulations will help rural regions face technological change. Apart from the regulations to enhance access to ICT mentioned above, regulatory changes need to happen to ensure this technology fits the needs of rural dwellers. For example, to harness the benefits from self-driving cars in rural regions, rural regions require regulations to address the low share of public transport in rural regions and promote usership rather than ownership in order to attain shared transport systems.

Box 5.6. Strategic foresight to better prepare for an uncertain future

Strategic foresight is a thought-driven, planning-oriented process for looking beyond the expected future to inform decision-making. It aims to redirect attention from knowing about the past to exercising prospective judgement about events that have not yet happened. For example, strategic foresight does not claim predictive power but maintains that the future is open to human influence and creativity, with an emphasis – during the thinking and preparation process – on the existence of different alternative possible futures (Wilkinson, 2017[41]). This generates an explicit, contestable and flexible sense of the future, where insight about different possible futures allows the identification of new policy challenges and opportunities and the development of strategies that are robust in face of change. Some governments have conducted such exercises to define possible future scenarios and adapt public policies.

Canada

A possible-scenarios assessment (MetaScan 3: Emerging Technologies) was used by the Canadian government in 2013 to explore how emerging technologies will shape the economy and society, and the challenges and opportunities they will create. The study involved research, consultations and interviews with more than 90 experts. The key findings include some of the following policy challenges:

- The next decade could be a period of jobless growth, as new technologies increase productivity with fewer workers.
- All economic sectors will be under pressure to adapt or exploit new technologies, in which case having workers with the right skills will be essential.

- New technologies are likely to significantly alter infrastructures, forcing governments to decide whether to maintain old infrastructures or switch and invest in new, more efficient ones.

United Kingdom: Megatrends analysis and scenario planning

In 2013, the UK Government Office for Science launched a plausible scenarios-led foresight assessment (Futures of Cities). The goal of the project was to develop an evidence base for the future of UK cities (challenges and opportunities towards 2065) and to inform national- and city-level policy makers. The office commissioned working papers and essays and conducted interactive workshops, with over 25 UK cities participating. By combining megatrends analysis and scenarios planning, the study imagined a plausible future consisting of considerable climate shocks presenting key urban challenges by 2065 – e.g. drier summers and heatwaves affecting the UK's southern cities and higher levels of precipitation affecting western cities during the winter.

Switzerland: Perspective 2030

The first step of the "Perspective 2030" report used online questionnaires submitted to experts and think tanks to identify influencing factors, changing trends and megatrends that will impact Switzerland in the next 15 years. During the second step, the surveyed experts assessed the influencing factors and trends by assigning them a value between 1 (low impact/low degree of uncertainty) and 10 (high impact/high degree of uncertainty). Third, the report integrated influencing factors and trends into four different plausible world scenarios that analysed the interaction between the Swiss and international influencing factors as well as the resulting potential "winners" and "losers" for each scenario.

Source: Adapted from OECD (2019[2]), *OECD Regional Outlook 2019: Leveraging Megatrends for Cities and Rural Areas*, https://dx.doi.org/10.1787/9789264312838-en; Wilkinson, A. (2017[41]), *Strategic Foresight Primer*, European Political Strategy Centre.

Paving the way for easy deployment of new technologies in rural regions also requires improving information systems. Tracking initiatives on work training or learning schemes as well as granular information of skills and demographics of workers will help make efficient policy decisions. Furthermore, promoting a comprehensive mapping of rural regions and enabling technological tests is instrumental to make the most of new technologies. For example, rural regions without a detailed and accurate online map can miss opportunities to expand the services from driverless cars or drones across the whole territory.

Furthermore, the political will to create awareness about the forthcoming changes and involve the community can lead to sustainability of policies. Preparing rural regions for coming technological changes also involves working and planning with communities to determine the solutions and strategies to face those changes. Many citizens are not aware of the benefits and challenges from the undergoing technologies on work and life. It involves the effect from automation or the possibilities to mitigate climate change by using new technologies. Therefore, broader information campaigns can provide space to answer and receive feedback from the community on the implementation of those new technologies as well as help rural dwellers make the most of the innovations.

Technologies impacting rural productivity and well-being

Technology is changing rapidly. Every year new types of devices are available and improved in the market. Many of these technologies have the potential to improve rural economies, their production processes and the traditional economic sectors as well as support the transition towards a low-carbon economy. New technologies are also able to modify how people access public services and interact with society.

This section maps a number of technologies and outlines the possible challenges and opportunities that can bring for rural regions. While many technologies are undergoing rapid transformation and promise disruptive effects, this section focuses on those technologies with the most rapid progress and greatest international recognition to modify life in rural communities (Table 5.3). The section will also outline those technological changes transforming traditional rural economic sectors: agriculture and mining. Other technologies such as deconcentrated energy systems (solar panels), blockchain or those associated with recycling will not be discussed in deep, but they also offer a great potential to reduce costs, expand the market and mitigate climate change in rural regions.

Table 5.3. Key technologies driving rural change

Technologies		Timeframe of technology availability	Opportunities for rural regions	Policies to harness the benefits for rural regions
	Self-driving cars	Next ten years	- Shared self-driving cars can improve public transport and reduce CO2 emissions from rural commuting - Increase attractiveness of living in rural regions. - Ease access to services and social networks.	- Ensure a quality broadband connection. - Define regulations for autonomous cars and the low modal share of public transport. - Promote usership rather than ownership. - Improve online-mapping and quality of rural roads.
	3D printers	Available	- Access mass-manufactured goods without waiting for delivery. - Produce goods to sell and adapt to rural industries. - Boost entrepreneurship. - Reduce the market dependence of rural regions on mass-manufactured goods (tools). - Increase the efficiency and autonomy of public services (healthcare inputs).	- Ensure a quality broadband connection. -Train professionals for maintenance and provision. - Disseminate information about technology.
	Drones	Next ten years	- Attract firms to test and conduct research projects with drones. - Improve access to goods (e.g. mass consumption goods, medicines). - Reduce productions and delivery costs.as well as CO2 emissions from transport. - Boost the productivity of rural businesses.	- Ensure a quality broadband connection. - Define regulation and privacy policies. - Incentivise testing and support pilot applications.
	Advanced communications techniques	Next ten years	- Attract and retain workers by improving the teleworking experience. - Enhance social and labour connections. - Allow for collaborative innovation systems among firms and research centres. - Increase the efficiency of rural business and training of workers.	- Ensure a quality broadband connection. - Support firms to invest in data and organisational change to improve teleworking. - Enhance knowledge and information about augmented reality (AR) and virtual reality (VR).
	e-Education	Available	- Enhance traditional learning experiences and make education more accessible and inclusive. - Retain the young population and attract families to settle in. - Support reskilling of the workforce to facilitate the shift of economic activity. - Improve teacher training.	- Ensure a quality broadband connection. - Awareness of the benefits of open education at the public and private levels. - Enhance teachers training and involvement of academic institutions with the technology. - Increase student support (either in person or virtually).

	Technologies	Timeframe of technology availability	Opportunities for rural regions	Policies to harness the benefits for rural regions
	e-Health	Available	- Increase healthcare coverage and quality in rural regions. - Enhance the skills of medical staff. - Improve information for patients and doctors. - Reduce transport cost in conducting a medical procedure.	- Ensure a quality broadband connection. - Train health professionals. - Conduct awareness campaigns. - Update ICT infrastructure and equipment in hospitals and medical centres.

The effect of technological progress on productivity

Self-driving cars can boost the vitality of rural communities

Car use is still a common mode of transport to reach the workplace and health and education centres in rural communities. While car use has decelerated in urban areas, it remains the prominent transport mode in rural communities (ITF, 2017[42]; Dender and Clever, 2013[43]). Public transport tends to be costly and inefficient in low-density areas, with long waiting times for passengers and underutilisation of systems. Autonomous or self-driving cars, vehicles connected to the Global Positioning System (GPS) and sensors capable of detecting the environment and navigating without human input, can become a solution to improve commuting for rural dwellers.

This technology is growing rapidly, and assisted driving (semi-autonomous cars that can complement human input, i.e. take over driving in heavy traffic) is already a reality (OECD, 2018[44]). Many cars sold today are capable of some level of automated operation and cars capable of driving autonomously have been tested on public roads in OECD countries (OECD/ITF, 2015[45]). However, fully autonomous vehicles are some time away and even optimistic projections foresee a gradual uptake since part of the existing stock of traditional cars will remain active despite the growing fleet with new technologies (OECD, 2018[44]). Most experts expect fully autonomous vehicles to be available on the market during the next decade. Studies have outlined that there will be a significant number of self-driving cars on the market by 2030, yet it is not clear to what extent these vehicles will be completely self-driving in all circumstances (OECD/ITF, 2015[45]).

Self-driving cars provide many benefits, including road safety, congestion reduction (as they make driving more efficient) and lower stress for drivers. They can support a more efficient use of time by freeing the driver from driving tasks in long commutes (providing extra time for work or leisure) and improve the mobility of people who cannot drive today.

Wider use of this technology can improve the traditional public transport system in rural regions. Shared self-driving cars can optimise routes and timetables (on-demand, small-scale bus systems), making the transport of passengers in rural regions more efficient and safer, especially in sparsely populated and less dense areas. Even in small- and medium-sized cities and towns, a shared fleet of self-driving vehicles could completely obviate the need for traditional public transport (OECD/ITF, 2015[45]). In rural regions, this technology would reduce the long waiting times for passengers or underutilisation of the system. On-demand transport can reach sparsely population with optimised routing, schedules adapted to local needs and pricing calculated on a per-hour or per-kilometre basis. A case study developed for Ann Arbor, Michigan, in the US, showed that for a population of 120 000 who travel less than 70 miles a day, the shared autonomous fleet could provide near-instantaneous access to a vehicle with only 15% of the current number of vehicles needed to carry out these trips (OECD/ITF, 2015[46]).

Self-driving cars can also increase the attractiveness of rural communities. As first porotypes are already able to overcome the threshold of a 60-minute commute autonomously (OECD/ITF, 2015[46]), self-driving cars can make rural regions close to cities more attractive for urban residents that seek bigger and cheaper spaces or more green areas with better environmental conditions. This technology can also improve accessibility and network capacity, especially in remote rural regions. They can ease access to services (e.g. banks, libraries or amenities) and social networks (e.g. bars or social events) in nearby areas.

Nevertheless, self-driving cars can bring some challenges to rural communities. Local amenities, i.e. shops and bars, can lose attractiveness, as people are able to more easily frequent other areas. Additionally, shared self-driving car systems will directly compete with the way in which taxi and public transport services are currently organised, reducing the demand for drivers or other workers in traditional public transport (e.g. bus fare collectors or inspectors). Furthermore, the engineering of self-driving cars using direct programming or artificial intelligence (AI) will have to incorporate the ethical decisions associated with accident aversion. It will be important for clear guidelines of the use of AI in situations that risk the welfare of individuals.

Policies and regulations need to ensure this technology fits the needs of rural dwellers. Defining regulations to address the low modal share of public transport in rural regions and promoting usership rather than ownership to aim for shared transport systems are instrumental. Ensuring and promoting a comprehensive mapping of rural regions is also needed to make the most of this technology. Self-driving cars are connected to GPS and satellite maps to trace the routes. Rural regions without a detailed online map can miss opportunities to expand the services across the whole territory. Finally, upskilling labour force and socialising the technology with workers in the traditional transport system will prepare the population to face this trend.

3D printing: Decreasing reliance on supply chains

3D printing or additive manufacturing is a process of making three-dimensional solid objects based on a digital file. It has the potential to transform the traditional manufacturing process of large centralised factories into decentralised workshops, allowing consumers to assemble the final products themselves, thereby integrating the whole value chain from idea and design to production and delivery. It is highly customisable and promotes the free design of complex products, as each design can be adapted to specific needs. It creates lightweight elements and can reduce production time by integrating assembly and production.

Deconcentrated manufacturing technologies can yield a disruptive change by making small-volume production much cheaper relative to mass production. It may, in turn, change the economic rationale for companies to locate in agglomeration economies in search of economies of scale by allowing firms to produce some goods in small volumes directly in the regions rather than shipping products from large factories to rural regions.

This technology is available today and the 3D printing market is growing rapidly. The number of 3D printers sold between 2005 and 2011 doubled and the market is projected to grow at around 20% per year from 2014 to 2020 (OECD, 2017[47]). 3D printers are already capable of printing in colour and some of the many final goods already on the market include aerospace products, jewellery and medical devices (Beyer, 2014[48]). While the commercialisation of fully 3D-printed products is still less common, various commercial products contain 3D printed parts. 3D printing is already significantly altering the market for machined plastic and metal parts. For instance, Boeing has replaced traditional manufacturing with 3D printing for over 20 000 units (OECD, 2017[49]). Mainstreaming 3D printing will largely depend on the cost of switching from mass-manufacturing methods to 3D printing, that will include adapting the local labour force to the skills demanded in the generation of 3D printing files, and supporting workers displaced due to the changing nature of the tasks required for working in the industry. The small size of current printers and requirement for quality input materials (plastics, resin, ceramic and metals) is still a barrier for wider production of some goods. However, with the advancement of other complements, this technology is likely to become more common for the production of different goods at competitive prices (OECD, 2017[47]).

With additive and distributive manufacturing, rural regions could access mass-manufactured consumer goods without waiting for delivery. Rural businesses or dwellers could themselves design, create or produce goods to sell and adapt to rural industries, opening up a market of mass-customisation (Conner et al., 2014[50]). Open source computer aided design (CAD) files for hand tools for agriculture (e.g. apple pickers), food industry (e.g. cassava press), animal management (e.g. ant trap; chicken feed holder) or machinery parts for water management (e.g. irrigation stake) already exist, ready to be printed (Pearce, 2015[51]). This can in turn boost entrepreneurship as prototyping of new products and tools becomes cheaper and faster. For example, the state of Hidalgo in Mexico has established a design lab where entrepreneurs can test their products by creating prototypes from a public 3D printer (OECD, 2019[40]).

Additionally, this technology can reduce the market dependence of rural economies on cities or market hubs. Using additive manufacturing can offer (short-term) solutions to bridge supply gaps for replacement or production of parts (e.g. auto-parts). 3D printing will allow printing replacement parts for legacy products that would otherwise be discarded (OECD, 2017[49]).

3D printers can also increase the efficiency and autonomy of public services in rural regions. For example, hospitals in rural regions can use 3D printing to prepare tailor-made casts or implants without the need to send specifications to specialised centres and wait for the final prosthesis to be delivered. In countries like South Sudan and Uganda, 3D printing technology is used to create prosthetic limbs (Ishengoma and Mtaho, 2014[52]).

Nevertheless, some challenges to the take-up of 3D printing technology exist for rural regions. So far, there is a lack of professionals for maintenance, provision and training for the technology. The high demand for professionals in this market could make it difficult for rural regions to attract and retain experienced workers (OECD, 2018[53]). Further, disseminating the information about the technology's possibilities should allow rural businesses to prepare and plan the production process.

Unmanned aerial vehicles: Improving productivity and well-being

Drones, or unmanned aerial vehicles, are aircraft that can fly autonomously or with user direction through software-controlled flight plans in their embedded systems, working in conjunction with onboard sensors, transmitters, imaging equipment and GPS.

Drones are already undertaking complex and even dangerous tasks in entertainment, agricultural, construction, retail and insurance industries. Firms are using drones to survey designated areas and remote infrastructure (e.g. oil pipelines and agricultural areas), count wildlife and monitor forest fires (Rao, Gopi and Maione, 2016[4]). Insurance companies are using this technology to survey crops before writing contracts, to determine the underwriting strategy and, after, to survey the damage. Industry experts predict the market size for drones to match that of hardware sales within the next few years. Yet, currently, short battery life and the lack of proper regulation (and enforcement) remain two major limitations for their rapid commercial adoption (Rao, Gopi and Maione, 2016[4]). A lack of harmonised regulation around the use of drones can also create delays. Currently, there are mostly national guidelines on the use of a drone, which leads to uncertainty on their deployment in rural regions (Levush, 2016[54]).

Rural communities can further benefit from conducting testing and research project in drones, activities generally prohibited in urban areas. As most regulatory frameworks in OECD countries prevent the use of drones in dense urban settings (OECD, 2018[53]), sparsely populated areas provide the best opportunity for firms to openly test and improve the technology. It makes rural communities attractive for technology and research and development (R&D) companies, which, if well managed, can generate knowledge spill-overs and new jobs in local communities.

As mentioned in the previous section, drones offer the opportunity to reduce production and delivery costs in rural communities. Drone-based delivery can open a new market for rural communities, especially remote areas that tend to face a higher cost of transport. This delivery method could also increase quality of life, as rural dwellers can access a variety of goods from elsewhere in an expeditious manner and without incurring major costs. Using drones in production processes boosts the productivity of rural firms. For instance, farms are using drones to monitor livestock and fields. These automated, intelligent systems do not require the farmer to monitor the video feeds but rather flag anomalies that need further investigation. Farmers can also undertake localised irrigation with drones, which contributes to saving resources and achieving greater agricultural outputs (OECD, 2018[53]).

However, drones can also create competition at the local level. Delivery of products via drones makes rural communities less dependent on their local shops, threatening the local retail infrastructure. Such risks might create further resistance within communities, which already view drones as a threat to privacy and information based on the ability of drones to take pictures and record videos. Defining regulation and privacy policies at the national level by involving regional authorities is needed to move forward with the benefits of this technology. Further, upskilling the labour force is crucial to making the most of drones in lifting the productivity of rural businesses (e.g. agriculture).

Box 5.7. Emerging technologies in rural regions

Drones offer the opportunity to make economies more productive and improve quality of life, particularly in rural regions. USA Drone Port selected Hazard, Kentucky, to build its new research and development centre for unmanned aerial vehicles (drones). The location provides assets found only in rural regions, such as uncontrolled airspace, a varied topography and low population density. With a 60-mile radius of Class G airspace surrounding the site, builders and pilots can fly without requesting permission from the Federal Aviation Administration (FAA).

From its unique location in an area best known for its coal mining past, the company is helping to address issues of both economic growth and well-being. The Drone Port is contributing to growth by helping to develop a high-tech workforce in the region and providing the opportunity to create jobs. Of the more than 70 pilots trained on site, many have started their own private companies in and out of the region. Already three firms involved in the drone industry have formed: a publishing company, a builder and a contractor, each working with USA Drone Port to advance the use of drone technology

Innovation in rural regions, often lacking the large R&D facilities found at universities in major urban areas, also takes a different form (Freshwater and Wojan, 2014[55]). Innovation is more likely to come from entrepreneurs who cannot find external solutions for inherently local problems. For example, USA Drone Port is now working with a hospital in rural North Dakota to improve access to medicine for its most remote residents. In this way, drone technology has created opportunities for rural entrepreneurs to increase both productivity and well-being in remote areas.

Source: USA Drone Port (n.d.[56]), *Our Vision*, https://www.usadroneport.com/our-vision.

Advanced communications techniques: Virtual and augmented reality

Rapid progress on communication techniques is modifying the way people interact at work and in private life. Remote working systems, including teleworking, co-working spaces or virtual teams are increasing rapidly. For instance, in the US, the share of workers who primarily work from home has more than tripled over the past 30 years, currently representing 2.4% of the workforce (OECD, 2019[2]). Remote work experience can be improved with augmented reality (AR) and virtual reality (VR). These technologies expand the possibilities of digital connectivity to conduct business meetings or conferences (Bastug et al., 2017[57]). They also provide the possibility for virtual meetings, conferences or networking cocktails where virtual models of people can talk and socialise while being connected remotely.

The market for AR and VR is growing quickly. Estimates show sales of this technology grew fourfold between 2015 and 2018 (Hall, Stefan; Takahashi, 2017[58]). Distinct corporate applications are emerging across a variety of tasks, tapping into more of the human senses. Entrepreneurs have used the technology in education, to simulate workplaces, for quality inspection, during driver training and for healthcare purposes (World Economic Forum, 2017[59]). VR could also improve online shopping experiences, help monitor the production process in agriculture or manufacturing and change how marketing is done (Glazer et al., 2017[60]). The expansion of digital technologies can bring dynamism to rural communities and create new business opportunities for local firms. Better ICT, VR and AR can improve the teleworking experience. The technology can also enable people to participate in meetings from distant locations with few differences in the quality of interaction. It will benefit rural regions by attracting people from urban areas and offering diverse income and job opportunities to rural workers, especially in the service sector (Stratigea, 2011[61]). It can further help retain talent in local communities and allow for collaborative innovation systems among firms (client-suppliers, urban-rural firms) and research centres as the technology simulating face-to-face meetings becomes widely available.

AR can help workers perform tasks more efficiently. It provides field workers with an in-depth view of the equipment and onsite conditions to make more accurate decisions and better allocate priority tasks (AgriFutures Australia, 2018[62]). This technology can also improve training for workers and simulate risk situations for some professions. For example, Castilla y León in Spain has developed a training centre with simulation technologies using VR to teach mining perforation and other techniques of mining extraction (Fundación Santa Barabara, 2019[63]).

However, wider use of communication technologies can pose some challenges for rural dwellers. VR and AR could threaten tourism in some areas if people were readily able to experience new and exotic locations without leaving the comfort of their own homes. For example, Australia and Canada have already developed immersive VR tours of some of their popular tourist destinations, and hotel chains have developed tours based on this technology for guests (OECD, 2018[64]). Some authors have argued that teleworking can enhance social isolation and weaken social networks, as teleworkers are mobile and able to change their location for work (Vassileios, Stratigea and Giaoutzi, 2012[65]).

To make the most of the benefits of communication technologies, policy should ensure that local communities have the capacities and skills to use and seize AR and VA. Further, governments should support firms to invest in other knowledge-based capital including data, organisational change and process innovation. It would complement the benefits of teleworking as well as maintain productivity in business. Enhancing access to quality broadband for all individuals and businesses is needed to allow a wider benefit of these technologies.

The effect of new technologies on public services

e-Education

Education can find support in technology to overcome some challenges in rural economies such as distance, small classroom size, limited curriculum options as well as teacher attraction/retention. The provision of education in rural areas is relatively more costly with a quality that in many cases is below urban areas. Students in large cities score 31 points higher on average science than their peers in small towns in OECD Programme for International Student Assessment (PISA) tests (OECD, 2017[66]).

ICT devices and the Internet hold the promise of enhancing traditional learning experiences and making education more accessible and inclusive. Long-distance education (or online courses), podcasting, interactive television teaching tablets, modular coursework and self-directed learning can enrich curriculum opportunities in remote schooling (OECD, 2017[66]). For example, online courses can be effective in terms of improved student-content, increased peer-to-peer interactions and greater use of teachers' limited time. Open online courses (MOOCs) have become extremely common, and large communities have formed around online courses (e.g. the online platform Coursera, for example, has more than 22 million course enrolments across 190 countries). Policies to foster online education are also more common. For example, in 2007, Italy launched the National Plan for Digital Schools, and the EU has undertaken a programme, Open Education Europe, to accelerate the digitalisation of education (Inamorato, 2017[67]).

Providing access to quality education in rural regions can help retain the young population and attract families to settle. Online models of education can also support the reskilling of adults to help them shift economic activity (e.g. from agriculture to ecotourism or marketing) (OECD, 2017[66]).

The government, as a service provider, can greatly benefit from technology to close existing gaps in education. By closing distances, policy can better involve local communities and take a place-based approach. Teacher training and ensuring their conformability with the technology as well as defining methods to increase student support (either in person or virtually) are important policies to support an efficient outcome from distance learning technologies (OECD, 2017[66]).

Wider use of online courses or other forms of education based on technology come also with some challenges for rural regions. Social interaction in a classroom experience is still important for the learning process. Commitment and progress in many online courses are also difficult to track (OECD, 2017[66]).

e-Health

Health relies on technology to improve the provision of healthcare and medical research. Social isolation, a lack of skilled medical staff along with an ageing population are pressing challenges for rural regions. Health technology and innovation are changing the way doctors and hospital staff address clinical and health problems. At the same time, these tools allow clinics to modify the procedures and practical styles for healthcare delivery through technologies like process innovations, e-Health and Big Data (OECD, 2017[68]). These transformations are changing the way individuals and communities engage with healthcare.

E-Health, or the use of ICT for health, is about improving the flow of information through electronic and digital means (WHO, 2016[19])). According to the World Health Organization, the e-Health trend has been accelerating since 2005 and now 58% of analysed countries (73) have developed a national e-Health strategy (WHO, 2016[19]). With the recent COVID-19 pandemic, e-Health services have been used as a solution to physical restrictions to traditional in-person meetings, clinic consultations and some forms of trial drug procedures. Mobile healthcare, for instance, is one of the ways in which this trend has progressed the most. Between 2013 and 2015, mobile health applications have doubled, reaching 165 000 available applications in 2015 (OECD, 2017[68]). Healthcare professionals are using technology: to perform various activities, such as continuous monitoring and timely response; for interactions between patients and health professionals beyond traditional settings; and communication with systems that can provide real-time feedback from prevention to diagnosis, treatment and monitoring (OECD, 2017[68]). In addition, healthcare provision is also evolving towards precision medicine, which entails tailoring treatments to individual patients.

Online communications and services provide a way to increase healthcare coverage and quality in rural regions. For example, the Swedish project My Healthcare Flows aims to provide holistic solutions based on the individual patient's needs, including innovative e-services and open data platforms. They have already deployed the e-service Patient Journey in at least seven county councils in Sweden, which is expected to increase quality of life and communication with patients (OECD, 2016[69]).

E-Health strategies are also improving the skills to manage the technology of medical staff in rural communities. In the rural region of Alentejo, Portugal, the telemedicine programme includes a tele-training initiative to address challenges faced in providing healthcare to a geographically large but sparsely populated area. The programme consisted of free tele-training sessions for nurses, doctors and diagnostic technicians in 52 locations (WHO, 2016[19]).

Policy making will play a key role in ensuring healthcare provision benefits from technology developments. Local governments should design policies for talent attraction, including affordable housing for health professionals or improving career development path. In terms of telemedicine, policy should work on mainstreaming mobile health applications and encourage the design of regional e-Health strategies aligned with the national level. Awareness campaigns in rural communities are needed to promote the benefits of using e-Health services. Finally, many e-Health procedures require advanced-technology equipment in hospitals including HD screens, sound ICT infrastructure and broadband quality.

Effect of technological changes in traditional sectors

The digital transformation of the economy can contribute to more resilient, productive and sustainable dynamics in traditional rural sectors, agriculture and mining. At the core of these technological innovations is the increasing capacity to capture and exchange data, automate repetitive tasks and create new market opportunities. Automation of farms and mines can create entirely new dynamics in the economies around these sectors and contribute to the transition to a low-carbon economy.

Automation of farms

The data-driven technologies that are enabling the surge of "smart farming" or "e-farming" leverage ICT, sensors, the Internet of Things (IoT), robots, drones big data, cloud computing, AI and blockchain technology (OECD, 2018[70]) (Box 5.8). The integrated use of these technologies is supporting farming innovations such as the use of satellite data to monitor crop growth and water resources or automated agricultural production and ICTs to connect farmers in new ways (OECD, 2018[70]).

Box 5.8. The digitalisation of agriculture

The digital transformation of the food and agricultural system has proved complex. The agricultural sector involves many stakeholders operating in a wide variety of contexts, including remote areas, which often face issues related to connectivity (see Chapter 3). Nevertheless, digital innovation in agriculture holds many promises, and advances in digital technologies could help boost productivity and potential savings in terms of seed, fertiliser, space, water and time.

Advances in remote sensing technologies have enabled increasingly granular data about soil, weather and environmental conditions. As the cost of digital technologies and the analysis of the data that they collect have fallen, farmers are now better able to draw insights about a range of aspects of agricultural production in a way that was not possible before.

Farms of the future could be autonomous, with machines tending livestock and harvesting food without much human intervention. In October 2017, a team of British researchers used commercially available agricultural machines and software to enable amateur drones and tractors to operate autonomously. The project culminated in the completely automated harvest of approximately 5 tonnes of spring barley, which had never been touched by human hands.

Source: OECD (2019[1]), *Going Digital: Shaping Policies, Improving Lives*, https://doi.org/10.1787/9789264312012-en.

Precision farming is a pioneering technique that provides farmers with near-real-time analysis of key data about their fields that is paving the way for fully automated farms (OECD, 2017[71]). This technique uses big data analytics to provide productivity gains through optimised use of agriculture-related resources, including savings on seed, fertiliser, irrigation and even farmers' time. Initially, it began with yield mapping and simple variable rate controls and, later on, integrated automated guidance technology (OECD, 2017[71]).

However, the biggest challenge rural agricultural communities will face is the changing role of the farmer and the local farming community in general. The *OECD Digital Economic Outlook* (2017[71]) has identified two scenarios regarding the role of farmers in relation to the automation of agriculture. In the first, farm enterprises become local caretakers of land, animals and data. They monitor operations centred at the lower end of the value chain. The job of the farmer would be to make sure that the interactions between the supply and demand sides of the agricultural systems work together properly. In an alternative scenario, the data and intelligence provided by analytics could help empower farmers, tailoring the processes to their knowledge of local and farm-specific idiosyncrasies.

Overall, automation of farms is an opportunity for rural and remote areas to make agricultural production more efficient and sustainable. In order to seize the benefits of the deployment of data collection technologies, policy makers should address persisting issues regarding connectivity, particularly in remote regions (OECD, 2018[70]).

Agricultural data governance and regulation will be central to ensuring that rural communities benefit from the automation of agriculture. The control of agricultural data by major agriculture technology providers has led to controversial discussions on the potential harm to farmers. The benefits of data-intensive equipment for farmers in the form of spill-overs can become uncertain when data ownership is in question (OECD, 2017[71]).

New ways to produce food

Synthetic meat is a niche technology that can attain the dual goal of coping with an increasing demand for food and protein while reducing the environmental impact of regular livestock (less land and water consumption) (Alexander et al., 2017[72]) (see more in Chapter 3). This technology, though recent, is already under production in firms, like Mosameat in the Netherlands. Research is still ongoing and it is expected that synthetic meat will be sold by retailers by 2021 (Alexander et al., 2017[72]).

Further technological developments in the field of aquaculture, more specifically land-based fish farming, is already changing aquaculture practices. Conventional aquaculture systems depend on flow-through of clean water from freshwater sources or coastal currents, thus depending on an ample supply of high-quality water. In recycling aquaculture systems, on the other hand, effluent water leaving the tanks is treated and refreshed before being returned, thereby reducing water consumption (Kvernevik, 2017[73]). Benefits include more flexibility for choosing location and species for farming as well as high yield potential. While research is still ongoing to implement the technologies at an industrial scale, some firms have already begun operations. In Norway, Niri is using advanced aquaculture systems for salmon farming and Maryland-based start-up Marvesta is doing the same to farm shrimp.

Automation in mining

Automation in mining is a trend with significant implications for local communities and economies. Technological change will make mines more autonomous, as currently, changes allow operators to work primarily from distant centralised control centres that rely on a geographic information system (GIS), GPS, equipment monitoring and programmable logic controllers. This automation will have an impact on local spending and employment, which ultimately can benefit local and Indigenous communities.

Data will determine the future of mining, as will the ability to organise, manage and process it. The transition to a future digital mine will change core mining processes and will encompass the automation of physical operations and digitalising assets. It includes the adoption of autonomous vehicles, drones, 3D printing and wearable technologies, all operated through a connected network that uses IoT sensors to capture data in real time. For example, at Rio Tinto's Yandicoogina mine in Western Australia, self-driving trucks work 24 hours a day hauling high-grade iron ore. This driverless technology can lead to a 15%-20% increase in output, a 10%-15% decrease in fuel consumption and an 8% decrease in maintenance costs (Cosbey et al., 2016[27]).

Automation is likely to reduce the number of operational jobs in areas such as drilling, blasting and train and truck driving. As outlined in the section above, repetitive tasks in mining constitute a large share of current employment in mines. Therefore, mining operations will require new roles to handle the development and monitoring of remotely controlled autonomous equipment and data processing.

Lastly, while there are many benefits to automation in the mining industry, it would be important to consider how automation in mining affects local communities and Indigenous populations. Advances in technology can be used to improve extraction processes improving work conditions and work-safety for miners and to increase productivity for mining firms. However, if local consultation processes do not simultaneously adapt to technological advances, local and Indigenous communities will be at a loss. The technological progress can be used to improve how benefit-sharing agreements are conceptualised and implemented with local and Indigenous communities. A more inclusive consultation process could be attained, for example, by using geographical scanning tools to overlay maps of mines and livelihood areas for local communities prior to the consultation process of extractive industry firms.

To fully embrace the transition and distribute the extractive industry's benefits to local communities, policy makers should seek to improve skills, re-train local workforce and ensure local and Indigenous communities can benefit from increased transparency associated with increases in technology in the extractive resources sector. Rural communities will need a strategy to identify and support one or more new and profitable regional activities to reduce regional dependence on extractive industries as well as create backward and forward productive linkages with existing industries.

Future-looking rural policies to address global agendas and climate change

In 2015, all UN member states adopted the 2030 Agenda, which established 17 Sustainable Development Goals (SDGs) to improve people's lives now and in the future. While the pattern is one of moderately positive overall changes, OECD countries are not universally on track or on pace to achieve targets by 2030 (OECD, 2019[74]). On average, OECD countries are closest to meeting their goals for Cities, Climate and Energy, but remain furthest away from targets on Gender Equality, Food, and Reducing Inequality. Achieving the SDGs will require participation at the local level, where governments are directly responsible for delivering on SDG targets. Policy makers predict that as much as 65% of the SDG agenda cannot be achieved without the involvement of local actors (UNSDSN, 2016[75]). As a result, rural policies are integral to the achievement of SDGs. As emphasised by the OECD's new programme, A Territorial Approach to SDGs, some of the SDGs that rural communities will specifically need to address include Good Health and Well-being, Quality Education, and Decent Work and Economic Growth.

The 2030 SDG Agenda includes health goals that particularly affect rural regions, even in OECD countries with universal health coverage. SDG Goal 3 strives to promote healthy lives and well-being at all ages. Regional differences in healthcare may stem from supply-side drivers of delivery, the booking system and waiting time, as well as the volume and distribution of resources (Brezzi and Luongo, 2016[76]). According to 2016 data, subnational governments in OECD countries commit 18% of their budgets to healthcare on average, demonstrating the significant stake local stakeholders have in achieving Good Health and Well-Being (OECD, Subnational Finance Statistics).

However, local governments in rural regions may not be able to meet the healthcare needs of its citizens due to higher service costs and lower tax revenues. Indeed, several EU member states have reported acute shortages of medical practitioners in rural regions. Access to health services was a particularly salient concern during the COVID-19 pandemic and was exacerbated by an unusual inflow of temporary urban migrants. Some countries, including Belgium, France, Lithuania and Portugal, have taken measures to incentivise physicians to work in rural regions (EC, 2018[77]). In spite of these efforts, regional disparities persist, particularly amongst females (Figure 5.2). Meeting SDG targets for health will therefore require local and national governments to work together in providing improved health outcomes for rural dwellers. Current technological advances in e-Health can help deliver services to rural regions that may be further away from high-density zones.

Figure 5.2. EU health disparities among individuals reporting "bad or very bad health"

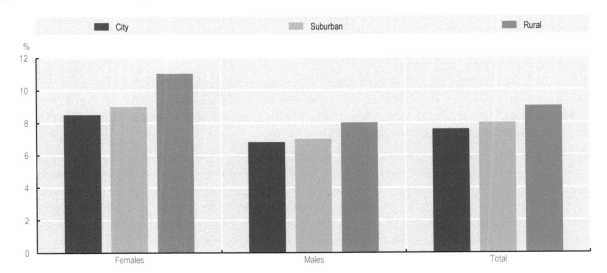

Note: Self-reported health.
Source: Eurostat (2018[78]), *Degree of Urbanisation (Health)*, https://ec.europa.eu/eurostat/web/degree-of-urbanisation/data/database.

SDG 4, which aims to ensure inclusive and equitable education for all, also faces regional disparities that governments must address. In OECD countries, the rural-urban gap in education is most significant in transitions to higher levels of education, where approximately half of urban students make the transition compared to only 30% of rural students (Echazarra and Radinger, 2019[79]). Access to quality education in rural regions is crucial to meet the needs of rural youth and to attract families to settle in these regions. Access to early childhood education, one of the SDG targets intended to ensure preparedness for primary education, is generally lower for students in rural regions. This disparity is particularly acute amongst Indigenous students in Australia, Canada and New Zealand (OECD, 2016[80]). If students in rural regions are going to develop the skills to meet the demand for regional labour markets in the future, an eye towards the SDGs will be necessary. While traditional education systems are key to developing the minds of the future, governments can encourage schools to use e-learning resources and update local schooling infrastructure and curricula to the changing education standards in urban areas.

Rural regions will be particularly important to achieving SDG 8, which promotes inclusive and sustainable economic growth, full and productive employment, and decent work for all. Achieving this goal requires intentional investment in rural economies, where diversification, technological change and innovation can help improve productivity. The rural economy has huge potential for economic growth and the creation of decent employment with the right policies. Knowing that agriculture is increasingly productive and not necessarily the predominant provider of income, policies that support local economies in developing higher value-added activities and preparing the local workforce for jobs in diverse types of employment will be necessary prerequisites to meet this goal. Furthermore, forward-looking skill anticipation strategies and regional employment councils that incorporate civil and business stakeholders can help future-proof the equilibrium between demand and supply of skilled workers in local rural economies.

Forward-looking policies for rural regions to support the transition to a low-carbon economy

Rural communities are key to attain environmentally related SDG objectives and move forward the transition to a low-carbon economy. These goals include enhancing the use and development of clean and affordable energy (SDG 7), responsible consumption and production (SDG 12) and climate actions for the environment (SDG 13). Rural economies tend to be focused on primary activities by relying on natural resource extraction and transformation. Agriculture and mining, for example, modify the land and consume important quantities of other natural resources (i.e. water) for the production. However, technological progress can optimise the consumption of resources and their impact on the environment (see more in chapter 3).

Increased awareness from society of an environmentally sustainable demand and the relevance of product traceability has driven change in the production of primary industries. For instance, some mining companies in OECD countries are embracing technology to achieve competitive advantages through responsible mining and metallurgic activities (Box 5.9). The transformation of traditionally extractive industries into environmentally friendly ones is a challenge for the industrial grid of a region. Taking an isolated view of industries neglects the great diversity of links between them. Therefore, the capacity of a primary sector to respond to this challenge is a great engine to drive further changes in the value chain.

Box 5.9. Towards environmentally sustainable mining

In an increasingly competitive market, consumers are demanding a greater environmental commitment from companies, with product traceability emerging as a guide for consumer choices. Industries such as mining, but also the textile and automotive industries, find in technological innovation a competitive advantage to embrace environmentally sustainable industrial process and materials.

The quest for a low-carbon mining value chain in Upper Norrland

The mining companies operating in Upper Norrland are at the forefront of technological development in the process of the carbon-free mining value chain (from mineral extraction to transformation). By 2030, mining companies in Upper Norrland have set themselves the goal of reducing their CO_2 intensity by 40%, in line with the Paris Agreement. Substantial investments are being made to achieve the target, striving to increase energy efficiency, mining recycling and decreasing the use of fossil fuels. It is in these regions of Norrbottenn, Upper Norrland and Vasterbotten that specific mining technology is increasingly being implemented to achieve CO_2-free minerals, and efforts are underway to enhance the traceability of their products.

Mining companies, in Upper Norrland as in the world, depend on access to land and water, and require important amounts of energy to operate. Due to their extractive nature, companies and governments are supporting a sustainable mining process to reduce the effects on the environment. The state-owned company LKAB is currently carrying out several key projects: use of energy-saving trolleys, production of fossil-free steel (CO_2-free pelletising process and fossil-free iron) and developing an autonomous mine, among others. In the case of Boliden, another active company in the region, projects and technologies are being embraced to produce minerals with low impact on nature and the climate. The large mining companies in the region (Boliden and LKAB) have carried out internal projects to achieve environmentally sustainable mining operations. Boliden carries out a series of projects for electrification, automation and deployment of 5G networks in the mines. Together, these innovation strategies may lead to the production of environmentally responsible minerals and materials, which can gain relevance in the demand from the market.

Technological innovation is in most cases not specific to one sector and can be transferred and scaled to other sectors. Reducing consumption, inputs and externalities are usually objectives shared by all sectors. The automotive sector for example, in the face of increasing constraints and growing market demand, is converting traditional fuel engines to electric-hybrid technologies, as well as investing in increased traceability of product manufacturing, automation, machine learning and 5G network deployment. There is a need for a shared technological effort among several sectors with overlapping necessities in addressing an increasingly demanding consumer.

Source: OECD (forthcoming[81]), *OECD Mining Regions and Cities Case Study of Västerbotten and Norrbotten*, OECD Publishing, Paris.

Supporting responsible consumption and production (SDG 12) in rural regions also requires close work with communities. As Chapter 3 argues, rural communities are key to help assess and manage the costs, risks and vulnerabilities from climate change on biodiversity, sustainable food production and ecosystem services. For this, governments need a closer working relationship with people and businesses in rural regions, prioritising and co-ordinating projects as well as funding and allocating resources to mitigate and prepare for forthcoming impacts.

The Rural Well-being Policy Framework acknowledges the importance of the multi-dimensional approach adopted by the SDGs. The framework provides the tools to prevent trade-offs between social, economic and environmental goals. By recognising the diversity of rural regions and the existence of urban-rural linkages, this output-oriented framework is ideal for achieving the 2030 Agenda by unleashing local development potential. As such, the OECD is contributing to efforts to merge SDGs with rural policy goals. Thematic works, such as projects on Indigenous communities and mining economies, together with the territorial reviews, play a key role in identifying best practices on a range of policy issues affecting rural communities. They inform policy makers on how to transform challenges into opportunities in the coming decades as we tackle structural changes such as climate change, digitalisation, ageing, services provision and inequality.

Turning the ambition of the SDGs into reality will require robust data to capture progress and evidence to inform decision-making. The OECD, by recently adopting an alternative typology on functional areas to classify regions, is helping in the analysis of trends and snapshots of the current socio-economic performance (Chapter 2). This regional classification is based on the level of access to cities and, in this way, takes into account regional diversity and regional linkages. This new classification is an approach that aims to avoid past barriers in geographical policy making by using real-time commuting and territorial distances to understand functional areas.

Concluding remarks

Technological change can benefit rural regions by unlocking new business opportunities and diversifying revenue sources for rural dwellers. New technologies can radically modify how people live and work for the better. The opportunity to reduce the cost of transport and in turn the relevance of location for workers and businesses can propel rural economies to compete effectively on national and international markets. The technology can also improve quality and access to services as well as political participation of rural populations. In all cases, to ensure rural communities can fully seize the benefits of the digital age and new technologies, policies need to:

- Ensure high-quality broadband in all types of rural regions.
- Strengthen infrastructure (e.g. telecommunications infrastructure and roads).
- Upskill the labour force.

- Develop forward-looking policies and regulations with greater involvement of rural communities.

Forward-looking rural policies also need to meet main global agendas and SDGs, including climate change, poverty reduction and gender equality. Achieving the SDGs will require participation at the local level, where governments are directly responsible for delivering on SDG targets. This includes leveraging on innovation and close work with local communities to support rural regions in their transition to a low-carbon economy.

References

AgriFutures Australia (2018), *Horizon Scan Final Report: Detecting Opportunities and Challenges for Australian Rural Industries*, https://www.agrifutures.com.au/wp-content/uploads/2018/04/18-009.pdf. [62]

Alexander, P. et al. (2017), "Could consumption of insects, cultured meat or imitation meat reduce global agricultural land use?", *Global Food Security*, Vol. 15, pp. 22-32, http://dx.doi.org/10.1016/j.gfs.2017.04.001. [72]

Anandan, T. (2018), "Robots and AI in the OR", *Robotics Industry Insights*, Robotic Industries Association, https://www.robotics.org/content-detail.cfm/Industrial-Robotics-Industry-Insights/Robots-and-AI-in-the-OR/content_id/7585 (accessed on 25 July 2019). [6]

Arntz, M., T. Gregory and U. Zierahn (2016), "The Risk of Automation for Jobs in OECD Countries: A Comparative Analysis", *OECD Social, Employment and Migration Working Papers*, No. 189, OECD Publishing, Paris, https://dx.doi.org/10.1787/5jlz9h56dvq7-en. [28]

Autor, D. and D. Dorn (2013), "The growth of low-skill service jobs and the polarization of the US labor market", *American Economic Review*, Vol. 103/5, pp. 1553-1597, http://dx.doi.org/10.1257/aer.103.5.1553. [24]

Bain & Company (2016), *Spatial Economics: The Declining Cost of Distance*. [35]

Baldwin, R. (2016), *The Great Convergence: Information Technology and the New Globalization*, The Belknap Press of Harvard University Press. [5]

Bastug, E. et al. (2017), "Towards interconnected virtual reality: Opportunities, challenges and enablers", *IEEE Communications Magazine*, Vol. 55/6, pp. 110-117, https://arxiv.org/pdf/1611.05356.pdf. [57]

Bessen, J. (2015), "Learning by doing: The real connection between innovation, wages, and wealth", https://www.researchgate.net/publication/303431417_Learning_by_Doing_The_Real_Connection_between_Innovation_Wages_and_Wealth (accessed on 6 August 2019). [23]

Beyer, C. (2014), "Strategic implications of current trends in additive manufacturing", *Journal of Manufacturing Science and Engineering*, Vol. 136/6, p. 064701, http://dx.doi.org/10.1115/1.4028599. [48]

Brezzi, M. and P. Luongo (2016), "Regional Disparities In Access To Health Care: A Multilevel Analysis In Selected OECD Countries", *OECD Regional Development Working Papers*, No. 2016/4, OECD Publishing, Paris, https://dx.doi.org/10.1787/5jm0tn1s035c-en. [76]

Clark, M. (2018), *Teleworking in the Countryside*, Routledge, http://dx.doi.org/10.4324/9781315189697. [13]

Conner, B. et al. (2014), "Making sense of 3-D printing: Creating a map of additive manufacturing products and services", *Additive Manufacturing*, Vol. 1-4, pp. 64-76, http://dx.doi.org/10.1016/j.addma.2014.08.005. [50]

Cosbey, A. et al. (2016), "Mining a mirage? Reassessing the shared-value paradigm in light of the technological advances in the mining sector", http://www.iisd.org (accessed on 24 September 2018). [27]

Decker, M., M. Fischer and I. Ott (2017), "Service robotics and human labor: A first technology assessment of substitution and cooperation", *Robotics and Autonomous Systems*, Vol. 87, pp. 348-354, http://dx.doi.org/10.1016/j.robot.2016.09.017. [7]

Dender, K. and M. Clever (2013), "Recent trends in car usage in advanced economies-slower growth ahead? Recent trends in car usage in advanced economies-slower growth ahead? Summary and conclusions", http://www.internationaltransportforum.org/jtrc/DiscussionPapers/DP201309.pdf (accessed on 23 July 2019). [43]

EC (2018), *Inequalities in Access to Healthcare: A Study of National Policies*, European Commission, https://ec.europa.eu/social/main.jsp?catId=738&langId=en&pubId=8152&furtherPubs=yes (accessed on 1 August 2019). [77]

Echazarra, A. and T. Radinger (2019), "Learning in rural schools: Insights from PISA, TALIS and the literature", *OECD Education Working Papers*, No. 196, OECD Publishing, Paris, https://doi.org/10.1787/8b1a5cb9-en (accessed on 3 July 2019). [79]

Eurostat (2018), *Degree of Urbanisation (Health)*, https://ec.europa.eu/eurostat/web/degree-of-urbanisation/data/database. [78]

Freshwater, D. and T. Wojan (2014), *User Entrepreneurship: Defining and Identifying an Explicit Type of Innovation*, https://tind-customer-agecon.s3.amazonaws.com/053e36e0-a9a7-494b-9ed0-f86a6fe83020?response-content-disposition=inline%3B%20filename%2A%3DUTF-8%27%27RuralInov.pdf&response-content-type=application%2Fpdf&AWSAccessKeyId=AKIAXL7W7Q3XHXDVDQYS&Expires=15603507 (accessed on 12 June 2019). [55]

Frey, C. and M. Osborne (2017), "The future of employment: How susceptible are jobs to computerisation?", *Technological Forecasting and Social Change*, Vol. 114, pp. 254-280, http://dx.doi.org/10.1016/j.techfore.2016.08.019. [29]

Frod, M. (2015), *Rise of the Robots: Technology and the Threat of a Jobless Future*, Perseus Books Group. [25]

Fundación Santa Barabara (2019), *Formación continua*, http://www.fsbarbara.com/home.html (accessed on 9 August 2019). [63]

Glazer, E. et al. (2017), *Virtual Reality Shopping Experience*, U.S. Patent and Trademark Office. [60]

Global Workplace Analytics (2018), *2017 State of Telecommuting in the U.S Employee Workforce*. [14]

Hall, Stefan; Takahashi, R. (2017), "Augmented and virtual reality: The promise and peril of immersive technologies", World Economic Forum, https://www.weforum.org/agenda/2017/09/augmented-and-virtual-reality-will-change-how-we-create-and-consume-and-bring-new-risks/ (accessed on 17 October 2018).　　[58]

Inamorato, A. (2017), *Going Open Policy Recommendations on Open Education in Europe (OpenEdu Policies)*, http://dx.doi.org/10.2760/111707.　　[67]

Ishengoma, F. and A. Mtaho (2014), "3D printing: Developing countries perspectives", *International Journal of Computer Applications*, Vol. 104/11, pp. 975-8887, https://arxiv.org/ftp/arxiv/papers/1410/1410.5349.pdf (accessed on 2 October 2018).　　[52]

ITF (2017), *ITF Transport Outlook 2017*, OECD Publishing, Paris, https://dx.doi.org/10.1787/9789282108000-en.　　[42]

Kvernevik, T. (2017), "Industrializing land-based fish farming for a protein-hungry future: An interdisciplinary approach to environmental and economic success", OECD, Paris, https://www.oecd.org/tad/crp/2.%20Trond-Inge_KVERNEVIK-Fish-farming.pdf.　　[73]

Levush, R. (2016), *Regulation of Drones*.　　[54]

Martínez, D. and J. Rodríguez (2008), "New technologies and regional growth: The case of Andalucía", *The Annals of Regional Science*, Vol. 43/4, pp. 963-987, http://dx.doi.org/10.1007/s00168-008-0231-1.　　[33]

Mckinsey Global Institute (2019), "The future of work in America People and places, today and tomorrow", http://www.mckinsey.com/mgi/publications/multimedia/ (accessed on 19 July 2019).　　[10]

Ministry of Enterprise and Innovation of Sweden (2016), *A Completely Connected Sweden by 2025 - A Broadband Strategy*, https://www.government.se/496173/contentassets/afe9f1cfeaac4e39abcdd3b82d9bee5d/sweden-completely-connected-by-2025-eng.pdf (accessed on 22 August 2019).　　[36]

Ministry of Internal Affairs and Communications of Japan (2011), "Efforts to promote telework in Japan", http://www.soumu.go.jp/main_sosiki/joho_tsusin/eng/presentation/pdf/110908_1.pdf.　　[16]

OECD (2020), *Capacity for remote working can affect lockdown costs differently across places*.　　[15]

OECD (2019), *Going Digital: Shaping Policies, Improving Lives*, OECD Publishing, Paris, https://dx.doi.org/10.1787/9789264312012-en.　　[1]

OECD (2019), *Measuring Distance to the SDG Targets 2019: An Assessment of Where OECD Countries Stand*, OECD Publishing, Paris, https://dx.doi.org/10.1787/a8caf3fa-en.　　[74]

OECD (2019), *Measuring the Digital Transformation: A Roadmap for the Future*, OECD Publishing, Paris, https://dx.doi.org/10.1787/9789264311992-en.　　[12]

OECD (2019), *OECD Regional Outlook 2019: Leveraging Megatrends for Cities and Rural Areas*, OECD Publishing, Paris, https://dx.doi.org/10.1787/9789264312838-en.　　[2]

OECD (2019), *OECD Skills Outlook 2019: Thriving in a Digital World*, OECD Publishing, Paris, https://dx.doi.org/10.1787/df80bc12-en.　　[20]

OECD (2019), *OECD Territorial Reviews: Hidalgo, Mexico*, OECD Territorial Reviews, OECD Publishing, Paris, https://dx.doi.org/10.1787/9789264310391-en. [40]

OECD (2019), *OECD Territorial Reviews: Småland-Blekinge 2019: Monitoring Progress and Special Focus on Migrant Integration*, OECD Territorial Reviews, OECD Publishing, Paris, https://doi.org/10.1787/9789264311640-en. [38]

OECD (2018), "Bridging the rural digital divide", *OECD Digital Economy Papers*, No. 265, OECD Publishing, Paris, https://dx.doi.org/10.1787/852bd3b9-en. [34]

OECD (2018), "Enhancing rural innovation", 11th OECD Rural Development Conference, OECD, Paris, https://www.oecd.org/rural/rural-development-conference/outcomes/Proceedings.pdf (accessed on 1 October 2018). [44]

OECD (2018), "How digital technologies are impacting the way we grow and distribute food", GFA 2018: "Digital technologies in food and agriculture: Reaping the benefits", 14-15 May 2018, OECD Conference Centre, Paris. [70]

OECD (2018), *Job Creation and Local Economic Development 2018: Preparing for the Future of Work*, OECD Publishing, Paris, https://dx.doi.org/10.1787/9789264305342-en. [26]

OECD (2018), *OECD Tourism Trends and Policies 2018*, OECD Publishing, Paris, https://dx.doi.org/10.1787/tour-2018-en. [64]

OECD (2018), "Proceedings 11th OECD Rural Development Conference: Enhancing Rural Innovation", OECD, Paris, http://www.oecd.org/rural/rural-development-conference/outcomes/Proceedings.pdf. [53]

OECD (2017), *New Health Technologies: Managing Access, Value and Sustainability*, OECD Publishing, Paris, http://dx.doi.org/10.1787/9789264266438-en. [68]

OECD (2017), *OECD Digital Economy Outlook 2017*, OECD Publishing, Paris, http://dx.doi.org/10.1787/9789264276284-en. [71]

OECD (2017), *OECD Economic Surveys: Austria 2017*, OECD Publishing, Paris, https://dx.doi.org/10.1787/eco_surveys-aut-2017-en. [9]

OECD (2017), *The Next Production Revolution: A Report for the G20*, OECD, Paris, https://www.oecd.org/g20/summits/hamburg/the-next-production-revolution-G20-report.pdf (accessed on 2 October 2018). [49]

OECD (2017), *The Next Production Revolution: Implications for Governments and Business*, OECD Publishing, Paris, http://dx.doi.org/10.1787/9789264271036-en. [47]

OECD (2017), *Trends Shaping Education 2017: Spotlight*, OECD, Paris. [66]

OECD (2016), *Digital Government Strategies for Transforming Public Services in the Welfare Areas*, OECD, Paris, http://www.oecd.org/gov/digital-government/Digital-Government-Strategies-Welfare-Service.pdf (accessed on 3 October 2018). [69]

OECD (2016), *Massive Open Online Courses (MOOCs): Trends and Future Perspectives*, OECD, Paris. [21]

OECD (2016), "New Forms of Work in the Digital Economy", *OECD Digital Economy Papers*, No. 260, OECD Publishing, Paris, https://dx.doi.org/10.1787/5jlwnklt820x-en. [8]

OECD (2016), *OECD Regions at a Glance 2016*, OECD Publishing, Paris, https://dx.doi.org/10.1787/reg_glance-2016-en. [80]

OECD (2014), "Recommendation of the Council on Digital Government Strategies", OECD, Paris, http://www.oecd.org/gov/digital-government/Recommendation-digital-government-strategies.pdf. [22]

OECD (2010), *Strategies to Improve Rural Service Delivery*, OECD Rural Policy Reviews, OECD Publishing, Paris, https://dx.doi.org/10.1787/9789264083967-en. [18]

OECD (forthcoming), *OECD Mining Regions and Cities Case Study of Upper Norrland*, OECD Publishing, Paris. [81]

OECD/ITF (2015), *Automated and Autonomous Driving Regulation Under Uncertainty*, http://www.internationaltransportforum.org (accessed on 1 October 2018). [45]

OECD/ITF (2015), *Urban Mobility System Upgrade - How Shared Self-driving Cars Could Change City Traffic*, OECD-ITF, https://www.itf-oecd.org/sites/default/files/docs/15cpb_self-drivingcars.pdf. [46]

Pearce, J. (2015), "Applications of open source 3-D printing on small farms", *Organic Farming*, Vol. 1/1, pp. 19-35, http://dx.doi.org/10.12924/of2015.01010019. [51]

Pramanik, J., B. Sarkar and S. Kandar (2017), "Impact of ICT in rural development: Perspective of developing countries", *American Journal of Rural Development*, Vol. 5/4, pp. 117-120, http://dx.doi.org/10.12691/AJRD-5-4-5. [39]

Rao, B., A. Gopi and R. Maione (2016), "The societal impact of commercial drones", *Technology in Society*, Vol. 45, pp. 83-90, http://dx.doi.org/10.1016/J.TECHSOC.2016.02.009. [4]

Reuters (2017), "European parliament calls for robot law, rejects robot tax", Reuters, https://www.reuters.com/article/us-europe-robots-lawmaking-idUSKBN15V2KM (accessed on 6 August 2019). [30]

Rural Innovation Strategies Inc. (n.d.), *Unlocking the Potential of Rural America*, Center on Rural Innovation, https://ruralinnovationstrategies.com. [17]

Salemink, K., D. Strijker and G. Bosworth (2017), "Rural development in the digital age: A systematic literature review on unequal ICT availability, adoption, and use in rural areas", *Journal of Rural Studies*, Vol. 54, pp. 360-371, http://dx.doi.org/10.1016/j.jrurstud.2015.09.001. [31]

Scaillerez, A. and D. Tremblay (2016), "Le télétravail, comme nouveau mode de régulation de la flexibilisation et de l'organisation du travail: Analyse et impact du cadre légal européen et nord-américain", *Revue de l'organisation responsable*, Vol. 11/1, p. 21, http://dx.doi.org/10.3917/ror.111.0021. [11]

Stratigea, A. (2011), "ICTs for rural development: Potential applications and barriers involved", *Netcom* 25-3/4, pp. 179-204, http://dx.doi.org/10.4000/netcom.144. [61]

The Boston Consulting Group (2018), *The Economic Case for Bringing Broadband to the Rural US*, http://image-src.bcg.com/Images/BCG-The-Economic-Case-for-Bringing-Broadband-to-the-Rural-US-June-2018_tcm9-193836.pdf (accessed on 22 July 2019). [37]

Tu, W. and D. Sui (2010), "A state transformed by information: Texas regional economy in the 1990s", *Regional Studies*, Vol. 45/4, pp. 525-543, http://dx.doi.org/10.1080/00343400903241568. [32]

UNSDSN (2016), *Getting Started with the SDGs in Cities*, http://unsdsn.org/wp-content/uploads/2016/07/9.1.8.-Cities-SDG-Guide.pdf (accessed on 26 July 2019). [75]

USA Drone Port (n.d.), *Our Vision*, https://www.usadroneport.com/our-vision. [56]

Vassileios, V., A. Stratigea and M. Giaoutzi (2012), "Teleworking: From a Technology Potential to a Social Evolution", School of Rural and Surveying Engineering, National Technical University Athens. [65]

WHO (2016), *Global Observatory for eHealth Global Diffusion of eHealth: Making Universal Health Coverage Achievable*, Report of the third global survey on eHealth, World Health Organization, http://apps.who.int/bookorders (accessed on 4 October 2018). [19]

Wilkinson, A. (2017), *Strategic Foresight Primer*, European Political Strategy Centre. [41]

World Economic Forum (2017), *Technology and Innovation for the Future of Production: Accelerating Value Creation*, http://www.weforum.org (accessed on 17 October 2018). [59]

Xu, J. (2017), *Design Perspectives on Delivery Drones*, Rand, http://www.rand.org/giving/contribute (accessed on 2 October 2018). [3]

Note

[1] The term broadband commonly refers to high-speed Internet access that is always on and faster than the traditional dial-up access. It includes several high-speed transmission technologies such as: Digital Subscriber Line (DSL), cable modem, fibre, wireless, satellite and broadband over powerlines (OECD, 2019[12]).

Lightning Source UK Ltd.
Milton Keynes UK
UKHW020209080222
398321UK00001B/3